CONVERSION
IN
LUKE-ACTS

CONVERSION IN LUKE-ACTS

Divine Action,
Human Cognition,
and the People of God

JOEL B. GREEN

Baker Academic

a division of Baker Publishing Group
Grand Rapids, Michigan

© 2015 by Joel B. Green

Published by Baker Academic
a division of Baker Publishing Group
P.O. Box 6287, Grand Rapids, MI 49516-6287
www.bakeracademic.com

Printed in the United States of America

Library of Congress Cataloging-in-Publication Data
Green, Joel B., 1956–
    Conversion in Luke-Acts : divine action, human cognition, and the people of God / Joel B. Green.
       pages cm
    Includes bibliographical references and index.
    ISBN 978-0-8010-9760-7 (pbk.)
    1. Conversion—Biblical teaching. 2. Bible—Psychology. 3. Bible. Luke—Criticism, interpretation, etc. 4. Bible. Acts—Criticism, interpretation, etc. I. Title.
BS2589.6.C59G74 2015
226.6'06—dc23   2015020880

In keeping with biblical principles of creation stewardship, Baker Publishing Group advocates the responsible use of our natural resources. As a member of the Green Press Initiative, our company uses recycled paper when possible. The text paper of this book is composed in part of post-consumer waste.

15   16   17   18   19   20   21   7   6   5   4   3   2   1

Contents

Acknowledgments

This work represents the confluence of two streams of research that have long captured my attention, the study of Luke-Acts and the potential of the neurosciences for theological study. The former stems above all from an invitation from F. F. Bruce to write on Luke's Gospel for the New International Commentary on the New Testament, followed by an invitation from Gordon Fee to continue my work on Luke's narrative by contributing a volume on the Acts of the Apostles to the same series. I trace the latter interest to what seemed at the time an innocuous invitation from Nancey Murphy to join a small research group related to the Travis Research Institute at Fuller Theological Seminary, which included Warren Brown and Malcolm Jeeves, concerned with "portraits of human nature." Who would have imagined that this opportunity would lead to others and eventually to further graduate work in the neurosciences and ongoing reflection on the importance of the natural sciences for a wide range of concerns in theological and biblical studies? (And who would have imagined that, in time, I would find myself on the faculty of Fuller Theological Seminary?) I am grateful to these friends for their encouragement along the way.

Some of the material in this volume incubated in other contexts, including presentations and lectures in the following formal venues: Consultation on the Use of Cognitive Linguistics in Biblical Interpretation, Society of Biblical Literature Annual Meeting; the Institute for Biblical Research Annual Lecture; the Deere Lectures at Golden Gate Seminary; the McCown Symposium Lectures at Northeastern Seminary and Roberts Wesleyan College; the Dean's Lecture at Candler School of Theology; and graduate seminars at Pepperdine University, Trinity Western University, and Logos Evangelical Seminary. I am grateful for these opportunities and the interaction they afforded. The book itself is an expansion on ideas first published as "Being Human, Being Saved," in *Body, Soul, and Human Life: The Nature of Humanity in the Bible*, Studies in Theological Interpretation (Grand Rapids: Baker Academic, 2008), 106–39. Portions of chapter 3 are adapted from my essay, "Conversion in Luke-Acts: God's Prevenience, Human Embodiment," in *The Unrelenting God: Essays on God's Action in Scripture in Honor of Beverly Roberts Gaventa*, ed. David J. Downs and Matthew L. Skinner (Grand Rapids: Eerdmans, 2013), 15–41 (reprinted by permission of the publisher; all rights reserved).

Abbreviations

General

cf.	*confer*, compare	MT	Masoretic Text
chap(s).	chapter(s)	n.s.	new series
ed.	edition; edited by	NT	New Testament
e.g.	*exempli gratia*, for example	OT	Old Testament
esp.	especially	p(p).	page(s)
ET	English translation	v(v).	verse(s)
i.e.	*id est*, that is	viz.	*videlicet*, that is, namely
LXX	Septuagint		

Ancient Texts

1QM	*War Scroll* (from Qumran Cave 1)
1QS	*Rule of the Community* (from Qumran Cave 1)
Ant.	Josephus, *Jewish Antiquities*
Decalogue	Philo, *On the Decalogue*
Eth. nic.	Aristotle, *Nicomachean Ethics*
Jos. Asen.	*Joseph and Aseneth*
J.W.	Josephus, *Jewish War*
Polybius	Polybius, *The Histories*
T. Ab.	*Testament of Abraham*
Thucydides	Thucydides, *History of the Peloponnesian War*

Contemporary Literature

AB	Anchor Bible
ABRL	Anchor Bible Reference Library
AcBib	Academia Biblica

ACCS	Ancient Christian Commentary on Scripture
AGJU	Arbeiten zur Geschichte des antiken Judentums und des Urchristentums
AnBib	Analecta Biblica
ANRW	*Aufstieg und Niedergang der römischen Welt: Geschichte und Kultur Roms im Spiegel der neueren Forschung.* Edited by Hildegard Temporini and Wolfgang Haase. Berlin: de Gruyter, 1972–.
BAFCS	The Book of Acts in Its First Century Setting
BBR	*Bulletin for Biblical Research*
BC	Beginnings of Christianity
BDAG	Bauer, Walter, et al. *A Greek-English Lexicon of the New Testament and Other Early Christian Literature.* 3rd ed. Revised and edited by Frederick William Danker. Chicago: University of Chicago Press, 2000.
BDF	Blass, Friedrich, and Albert Debrunner. *A Greek Grammar of the New Testament and Other Early Christian Literature.* Revised and edited by Robert W. Funk. Chicago: University of Chicago Press, 1961.
Bib	*Biblica*
BibIntS	Biblical Interpretation Series
BThSt	Biblisch theologische Studien
BZNW	Beihefte zur Zeitschrift für die neutestamentliche Wissenschaft
CBQ	*Catholic Biblical Quarterly*
CBR	*Currents in Biblical Research*
CEB	Common English Bible
CIT	Current Issues in Theology
CTL	Cambridge Textbooks in Linguistics
CTM	*Currents in Theology and Mission*
CTR	*Criswell Theological Review*
DJG	*Dictionary of Jesus and the Gospels.* Edited by Joel B. Green and Scot McKnight. Downers Grove, IL: InterVarsity, 1992.
DJG²	*Dictionary of Jesus and the Gospels.* 2nd ed. Edited by Joel B. Green. Downers Grove, IL: IVP Academic, 2013.
DSD	*Dead Sea Discoveries*
EDEJ	*The Eerdmans Dictionary of Early Judaism.* Edited by John J. Collins and Daniel C. Harlow. Grand Rapids: Eerdmans, 2010.
EDNT	*Exegetical Dictionary of the New Testament.* Edited by Horst Balz and Gerhard Schneider. 3 vols. Grand Rapids: Eerdmans, 1993.
EKKNT	Evangelisch-katholischer Kommentar zum Neuen Testament
ETL	*Ephemerides theologicae lovanienses*
ETSMS	Evangelical Theological Society Monograph Series
EvQ	*Evangelical Quarterly*
ExAud	*Ex Auditu*
ExpTim	*Expository Times*
FAT	Forschungen zum Alten Testament
FRLANT	Forschungen zur Religion und Literatur des Alten und Neuen Testaments
GNS	Good News Studies
GTA	Göttinger theologischer Arbeiten
HBT	*Horizons in Biblical Theology*
HNT	Handbuch zum Neuen Testament

HTKNT	Herders theologischer Kommentar zum Neuen Testament
HTR	*Harvard Theological Review*
IBMR	*International Bulletin of Missionary Research*
ICC	International Critical Commentary
JAAR	*Journal of the American Academy of Religion*
JBL	*Journal of Biblical Literature*
JPT	*Journal of Pentecostal Theology*
JPTSup	Journal of Pentecostal Theology Supplement Series
JSNT	*Journal for the Study of the New Testament*
JSNTSup	Journal for the Study of the New Testament Supplement Series
JTI	*Journal of Theological Interpretation*
JTISup	Journal of Theological Interpretation Supplement Series
JTS	*Journal of Theological Studies*
KEK	Kritisch-exegetischer Kommentar über das Neue Testament
KEKS	Kritisch-exegetischer Kommentar über das Neue Testament: Sonderband
KJV	King James Version of the Bible
LCL	Loeb Classical Library
LNTS	Library of New Testament Studies
LSJ	Liddell, Henry George, Robert Scott, and Henry Stuart Jones. *A Greek-English Lexicon*. 9th ed. with revised supplement. Oxford: Clarendon, 1996.
LumVie	*Lumière et vie*
MHT	Moulton, James Hope, Wilbur Francis Howard, and Nigel Turner. *A Grammar of New Testament Greek*. 4 vols. Edinburgh: T&T Clark, 1906–76.
MNTS	McMaster New Testament Studies
ModT	*Modern Theology*
NAB	New American Bible
NDBT	*New Dictionary of Biblical Theology*. Edited by T. D. Alexander and Brian S. Rosner. Downers Grove, IL: InterVarsity, 2000.
NETS	*A New English Translation of the Septuagint*. Oxford: Oxford University Press, 2007.
NIB	*The New Interpreter's Bible*. Edited by Leander E. Keck. 12 vols. Nashville: Abingdon, 1994–2002.
NICNT	New International Commentary on the New Testament
NIDB	*New Interpreter's Dictionary of the Bible*. Edited by Katharine Doob Sakenfeld. 5 vols. Nashville: Abingdon, 2006–9.
NIDOTTE	*New International Dictionary of Old Testament Theology and Exegesis*. Edited by Willem A. VanGemeren. 5 vols. Grand Rapids: Zondervan, 1997.
NIGTC	New International Greek Testament Commentary
NIV	New International Version (2011)
NLT	New Living Translation
NovT	*Novum Testamentum*
NovTSup	Supplements to Novum Testamentum
NRSV	New Revised Standard Version of the Bible
NTD	Das Neue Testament Deutsch
NTS	*New Testament Studies*
OBT	Overtures to Biblical Theology

OCD	*Oxford Classical Dictionary*. Edited by Simon Hornblower and Antony Spawforth. 3rd ed. Oxford: Oxford University Press, 1996.
OTL	Old Testament Library
OTM	Oxford Theological Monographs
OTP	*Old Testament Pseudepigrapha*. Edited by James H. Charlesworth. 2 vols. New York: Doubleday, 1983–85.
PBM	Paternoster Biblical Monographs
RBL	*Review of Biblical Literature*
RCS	Reformation Commentary on Scripture
ResQ	*Restoration Quarterly*
RevExp	*Review and Expositor*
RevRel	*Review for Religious*
RSR	*Religious Studies Review*
S&CB	*Science & Christian Belief*
SANT	Studien zum Alten und Neuen Testaments
SBLDS	Society of Biblical Literature Dissertation Series
SBLSP	*Society of Biblical Literature Seminar Papers*
SBLSymS	Society of Biblical Literature Symposium Series
SBT	Studies in Biblical Theology
SJT	*Scottish Journal of Theology*
SNT	Studien zum Neuen Testament
SNTSMS	Society for New Testament Studies Monograph Series
SNTW	Studies of the New Testament and Its World
SP	Sacra Pagina
STI	Studies in Theological Interpretation
TDNT	*Theological Dictionary of the New Testament*. Edited by Gerhard Kittel and Gerhard Friedrich. 10 vols. Grand Rapids: Eerdmans, 1964–76.
TDOT	*Theological Dictionary of the Old Testament*. Edited by G. Johannes Botterweck and Helmer Ringgren. Translated by John T. Willis et al. 15 vols. Grand Rapids: Eerdmans, 1974–2006.
TLNT	*Theological Lexicon of the New Testament*. By Ceslas Spicq. Translated and edited by James D. Ernest. 3 vols. Peabody, MA: Hendrickson, 1994.
TNIV	Today's New International Version
TOTC	Tyndale Old Testament Commentary
TSc	Theology and the Sciences
TSS	Themes in the Social Sciences
TynBul	*Tyndale Bulletin*
TZ	*Theologische Zeitschrift*
UCPNES	University of California Publications, Near Eastern Studies
VCSup	Supplements to Vigiliae Christianae
WBC	Word Biblical Commentary
WMANT	Wissenschaftliche Monographien zum Alten und Neuen Testament
WUNT	Wissenschaftliche Untersuchungen zum Neuen Testament
ZNW	*Zeitschrift für die neutestamentliche Wissenschaft*
ZS: NT	Zacchaeus Studies: New Testament

1

Questioning Conversion in Luke-Acts

As motifs in the narrative of Luke-Acts,[1] conversion and repentance are ubiquitous. Their importance is signaled immediately in the opening chapter of the Gospel,[2] in the angel Gabriel's summary of the anticipated consequences of John the Baptist's ministry:

> *He will turn* many of the people of Israel to the Lord their God . . . he
> will go before him,
> *to turn* the hearts of fathers to their children, and
> *[to turn]* the disobedient to the wisdom of the righteous,
> to make ready a people prepared for the Lord. (Luke 1:16–17)[3]

1. I take it as axiomatic that the Gospel of Luke and the Acts of the Apostles constitute a single narrative in two parts, and therefore I use the nomenclature "Luke-Acts." Mikeal C. Parsons and Richard I. Pervo (*Rethinking the Unity of Luke and Acts*) appropriately called for critical attention to fuzzy, but pervasive, assumptions about the relationship between Luke and Acts held since Henry J. Cadbury had affixed that hyphen early in the twentieth century (*Making of Luke-Acts*, first published in 1927). Responses to Parsons and Pervo have been legion (for surveys, see Spencer, "Unity of Luke-Acts"; Bird, "Unity of Luke-Acts"), with the result that our understanding of what "unity" entails is now clearer and the basis for asserting the unity of Luke-Acts more secure. I have addressed recent challenges to the unity of Luke-Acts in Green, "Luke-Acts, or Luke and Acts?"—focusing my attention particularly on "narrative unity"; see also Marguerat, *First Christian Historian*, 43–64.

2. This is emphasized by Witherup, *Conversion in the New Testament*, 44–47.

3. Translations of texts in Luke and Acts are my own. Apart from Luke-Acts, unless otherwise noted, I follow the NRSV.

1

This opening reference to repentance (ἐπιστρέφω, *epistrephō*, "to turn") signals, first, the degree to which this is God's story. Repentance in Luke-Acts is centered on God. Gabriel's sketch of John's vocation is profoundly theocentric. He will turn people to *the Lord*, go before *the Lord*, and prepare people for the advent of *the Lord*. God is at work, the angel announces, and this invites response: repentance, obedience, and readiness. If the third evangelist proceeds to identify Jesus as the "Lord" before whom John will go (3:4–6), this is because, for Luke, Jesus shares in God's own identity.[4] This theocentrism is carried forward into the Acts of the Apostles, as in Peter's directive to his Jerusalem audience, "Repent, therefore, and turn [to God]!" (Acts 3:19), for example, or Paul's proclamation in Lystra, "Turn to the living God!" (Acts 14:15; cf. 26:20).

Gabriel's Speech	Israel's Scriptures
He will turn many of the people of Israel to the Lord their God . . . he will go before him, to turn the hearts of fathers to their children, and the disobedient to the wisdom of the righteous, to make ready a people prepared for the Lord. (Luke 1:16–17)	"return to the Lord your God" (Deut. 30:2) "he turned many from iniquity" (Mal. 2:6) ". . . who will restore the heart of the father to the son" (Mal. 4:6 NETS) "to turn the heart of a father to a son" (Sir. 48:10 NETS) "I am sending my messenger to prepare the way before me" (Mal. 3:1) "Prepare the way of the Lord . . ." (Isa. 40:3 NETS)

Second, those with ears to hear will recognize how Israel's Scriptures have influenced Gabriel's speech (see table for comparison). These scriptural resonances embed John's ministry of calling Israel to repentance deeply within Israel's story and, especially, locate John squarely within the story line of Israel's anticipation of God's eschatological restoration of God's people. Indeed, this is the first of two clear allusions in Luke's birth narrative to Isa. 40:3, the second appearing in Zechariah's song (1:76)—both of which anticipate the citation of Isa. 40:3–5 in Luke 3:4–6.[5]

Third, from the beginning of the Gospel narrative, we learn that repentance is for Luke no theological abstraction. Rather, "turning" is aimed at

4. According to C. Kavin Rowe, "The strong repetition within the passages 1:16–17, 1:76 and 3:4–6 in connection with the structure of the beginning of the Gospel is simply too significant to be coincidental. Rather, we should take it as part of Luke's carefully crafted point, or narrative theological program. In this light the ambiguity in the referent [of κύριος, *kyrios*, "Lord"] expresses the fundamental correlation and continuity between the God of Israel and Jesus" (*Early Narrative Christology*, 76).
5. See Böhlemann, *Jesus und der Täufer*, 100; Pao, *Isaianic New Exodus*, 40–45.

a transformation of day-to-day patterns of thinking, feeling, believing, and behaving. This is decisively emphasized in Luke 3:7–14, where John identifies the markers of repentance in especially socioeconomic terms for the crowds, tax collectors, and soldiers. In the Acts of the Apostles, too, economic *koinōnia* and hospitality are typical correlates of conversion (e.g., 2:42–47; 16:13–15, 30–34).

What begins with the angelic message in Luke 1 continues throughout the Lukan narrative. John proclaims a "baptism of repentance" and urges the crowds that come out to him "to produce fruits in keeping with repentance" (Luke 3:3, 8; cf. Acts 13:24; 19:4). Jesus summarizes his mission as calling sinners to repentance (Luke 5:32), reports rejoicing at the repentance of even one sinner (15:7, 10), and informs his followers that the Scriptures themselves have it that repentance must be proclaimed to all nations (24:47). Early on in Luke's second volume, at the close of the Pentecost address, Peter sketches the appropriate response to the good news: "Repent, and be baptized" (Acts 2:38). At Athens, Paul announces that "[God] now directs all people everywhere to repent" (17:30). Toward the end of Acts, Paul retrospectively summarizes his entire ministry as declaring "first to those in Damascus, in Jerusalem, and in every region of Judea, and also to the gentiles . . . that they should repent and turn to God, producing deeds in keeping with conversion" (26:20).

This judgment regarding the centrality of repentance and conversion to Luke-Acts finds easy support in recent scholarship. Thomas Finn detects twenty-one conversion accounts in the Acts of the Apostles and claims that "conversion is the major theme in Luke's second volume."[6] Charles Talbert finds only ten such accounts in Acts, but refines Finn's overarching judgment only slightly: "Conversion is a central focus of Acts, maybe *the* central focus."[7] Beverly Gaventa eschews any conversion "pattern" in Luke-Acts but, importantly for our purposes, devotes just over half of her important study of "aspects of conversion in the New Testament" to the Lukan narrative.[8] For Guy Nave, repentance is "a keynote of the message in Luke-Acts," and the book of Acts is "full of conversion stories."[9]

Heightened emphasis on Luke's part has not led to a long history of study of repentance and conversion in Luke-Acts, however, or to general agreement around what conversion entails for Luke. Until recently, conversion attracted little attention in Lukan studies. When scholars studied this motif, they tended to refer only to the second half of Luke's two-part narrative, engaging little

6. Finn, *From Death to Rebirth*, 27.
7. Talbert, "Conversion in the Acts of the Apostles," 135.
8. Gaventa, *From Darkness to Light*, 52–129.
9. Nave, *Repentance in Luke-Acts*, 3; Nave, "Conversion," 729.

or not at all with the Gospel of Luke. This is true of Finn and Talbert, for example, and the same can be said of the important article by Jacques Dupont, which Talbert takes as the point of departure for his own study.[10] Studying the "paradigmatic experiences [of conversion] found in the New Testament," Richard Peace declares his interest in the Gospel of Mark and Paul, which leads him to consider the Lukan narrative only for its accounts of Paul's experience on the way to Damascus.[11] Of the five dissertations published in recent years on our motif, one concerns itself with the book of Acts but not with Luke's Gospel (Babu Immanuel), and one is focused on the Gospel but not Acts (Fernando Méndez-Moratalla).[12] Although the others examine conversion in the narrative of Luke-Acts, Mihamm Kim-Rauchholz deals with only two conversion accounts in Acts, Nave devotes a mere twenty pages to conversion in Acts, and David Morlan focuses on only three texts as he paves the way for a comparison of conversion in Luke and Paul.[13] The earlier dissertation by Robert Allen Black, completed in 1985, concerns itself, too, with conversion in the Acts of the Apostles.[14] If study of this important Lukan motif has suffered neglect since the onset of scholarly interest in Luke-Acts in the mid-twentieth century, the renaissance of interest in more recent years has not yet exhausted the witness of Luke's two volumes.

What Is Conversion?

Before surfacing key issues and unanswered questions from recent contributions to the study of Luke-Acts, I should first register the surprising, general lack of explicit, critical reflection concerning how the biblical writers seem to have defined conversion. That is, recent study of the motif in Luke-Acts has focused on an array of significant and relevant issues—for example, whether conversion is a moral or a cognitive category, what conversion is from and/or to, or whether conversion and repentance are discrete categories. What conversion entails, however—how best to define conversion for Luke-Acts—seems largely to have been assumed.

The importance of *definition* can hardly be exaggerated. After all, what one assumes conversion to be will determine what one looks for in the Lukan narrative and how one knows when one has found it. With the rise of conversion

10. Dupont, "Conversion in the Acts of the Apostles."
11. Peace, *Conversion in the New Testament*, 8.
12. Immanuel, *Repent and Turn to God*; Méndez-Moratalla, *Paradigm of Conversion*.
13. Kim-Rauchholz, *Umkehr bei Lukas*; Nave, *Repentance in Luke-Acts*; Morlan, *Conversion in Luke and Paul*.
14. Black, "Conversion Stories."

studies in the past few decades, though, how best to understand conversion has become a topic of some controversy. In fact, in their introduction to *The Oxford Handbook of Religious Conversion*, Lewis Rambo and Charles Far-hadian begin their discussion of contemporary problems in conversion studies with this claim: "One of the most important and also most contentious issues in conversion studies is defining the term 'conversion' itself." They go on to adopt a minimalist starting point, using the terms "change" and "transformation," noting that the converting process is itself "dynamic and malleable."[15]

A Question of "Frame"

Today, someone asking "Have you been converted?" could be heard in a variety of ways, depending on the context within which the question is asked. In an electronics store, the question might relate to one's finally "seeing the light" and adopting one computer brand over another. Those witnessing a street-corner evangelist are likely to conjure images of an altogether different sort. In the field of cognitive linguistics, questions of context like this are understood in terms of "framing," the larger patterns within which we locate, experience, and make sense of terms, concepts, and experiences. Thus, those of us who are interested in how institutions "think" can *frame* those institutions—like a university, a church, or a dot-com—so as to draw attention to their organizational charts, the giftedness of their people, the distribution and exercise of power, or the values they want to inculcate. An organization is all of these things and more, but different people visualize them through different frames, so they see different things.

For Vyvyan Evans and Melanie Green, "frame" refers to "a schematisation of experience (a knowledge structure) . . . represented at the conceptual level and held in long-term memory. The frame relates the elements and entities associated with a particular culturally embedded scene from human experience."[16] We associate terms and experiences with whole patterns of thought and belief. "Student" is thus automatically associated with "teacher," and a host of related terms—aspects and types related to the student experience—are signaled: syllabi, textbooks, exams, papers, online discussion groups, and library hours. The experience of being a student extends into other realms as well: increased coffee consumption, concerns about future repayment of student debt, balancing time, and so on. Like knocking over a single domino, thinking of a single concept sets in motion an entire experience structure.

15. Rambo and Farhadian, "Introduction," 9.
16. Evans and Green, *Cognitive Linguistics*, 222.

The question then is what experience schema or knowledge structure is signaled by the term "conversion"? The way questions about conversion are typically framed—for example, "change of mind versus change of behavior" or even "moral versus cognitive"—reflects the enduring and pervasive status of a particular definition of "conversion": *the resolution of a subjective, inner crisis of an autonomous individual.* Accordingly, the conversion frame would entail an interest in crisis events, interior change, and an individual converting or being converted in his or her relative solitude. If these are the typical entailments of conversion, then it is not difficult to conclude that modern-day thinking about conversion—in the study of Luke-Acts as well as more generally—is deeply indebted to the century-old perspectives of William James. Not only because of its extraordinary influence, but also because my focus in the present study is guided by an interest in the potential contribution of the cognitive sciences to the question of conversion in Luke-Acts, James's work merits brief attention.

William James's Influence

William James (1842–1910) was a polymath whose interests occupied the interstices of numerous disciplines, especially psychology, physiology, and philosophy. He received an MD from Harvard Medical School, established the first laboratory for psychological research in the United States, and was appointed to a professorship at Harvard to teach both psychology and philosophy. Our particular interest lies in his 1901–2 Gifford Lectures at Edinburgh University, published in 1902.[17] Here, James articulates his view that religious experience is primary for human nature and gives rise to myriad theologies, philosophies, and religious institutions. Primary, then, are *"the feelings, acts, and experiences of individual men* [sic] *in their solitude, so far as they apprehend themselves to stand in relation to whatever they may consider the divine."*[18] Given this dual emphasis on individuality and interiority, James's definition of "conversion" is as unsurprising as it may be familiar, at least in its broad strokes:

> To be converted, to be regenerated, to receive grace, to experience religion, to gain an assurance, are so many phrases which denote the process, gradual or sudden, by which a self hitherto divided, and consciously wrong inferior and unhappy, becomes unified and consciously right superior and happy, in consequence of its firmer hold upon religious realities. This at least is what

17. James, *Varieties of Religious Experience.*
18. Ibid., 31, emphasis original.

conversion signifies in general terms, whether or not we believe that a direct divine operation is needed to bring such a moral change about.[19]

Following the lead of the American psychologist Edwin Diller Starbuck (1866–1947), James differentiates between two types of conversion: the "volitional type," in which "the regenerative change is usually gradual, and consists in the building up, piece by piece, of a new set of moral and spiritual habits," and the "type of self-surrender," marked by a crisis generated by "first, the present incompleteness or wrongness, the 'sin' which he [sic] is eager to escape from; and, second, the positive ideal which he longs to compass."[20] His parade example of conversion-as-self-surrender is Paul, whose conversion, he avers, represents "those striking instantaneous instances . . . in which, often amid tremendous emotional excitement or perturbation of the senses, a complete division is established in the twinkling of an eye between the old life and the new."[21] We might be tempted to celebrate James's use of the language of old and new life in his characterization of Paul's conversion (cf. 2 Cor. 5:14–17), but the wider context of his extended discussion of the need for and experience of conversion makes clear that, by "life," James refers more narrowly to nothing other than the inner self—that is, the movement from self-estrangement to that place where the "spiritual emotions are the habitual centre of the personal energy."[22]

For James, then, conversion follows a pattern grounded centrally in the experience of "the sick soul" and "divided self," which he describes in terms approaching the psychopathological: "Not the conception or intellectual perception of evil, but the grisly blood-freezing heart-palsying sensation of it close upon one." From here, he is able to identify "the real core of the religious problem: Help! Help!"[23] Framed in this way, conversion is the resolution of the individual's inner, subjective crisis.

19. Ibid., 189.
20. Ibid., 206, 209; he is dependent here on Starbuck, *Psychology of Religion*, for which James wrote a preface.
21. James, *Varieties of Religious Experience*, 217. James is able to achieve this reading of Paul by conflating Luke's accounts of Paul's Damascus Road "conversion" with Paul's presumed preconversion turmoil, his "divided self," as witnessed in Rom. 7:15: "Wrong living, impotent aspirations; 'What I would, that do I not; but what I hate, that do I,' as Saint Paul says; self-loathing, self-despair; an unintelligible and intolerable burden to which one is mysteriously the heir" (171, citing the KJV). It was against reading "a trembling and introspective conscience" into Rom. 7 that Krister Stendahl directed his landmark essay, "Paul and the Introspective Conscience of the West"; he did so, however, without touching on questions related to the experience of conversion.
22. James, *Varieties of Religious Experience*, 271.
23. Ibid., 162.

As Charles Taylor (1931–) recognizes, James thus participates in ways of understanding human experience that continue to pervade the modern world.[24] These perspectives include James's emphasis on individual experience rather than corporate life and his notion that the real locus of religion lies in experience, that is, in feeling. Of course, Taylor is quick to recognize that James distills in his understanding of religious experience a lengthy history of influences, some of which we find in Scripture itself (e.g., Ps. 51, with its interest in a contrite heart over against ritual offerings of bulls and sheep). Nevertheless, James articulates well what is axiomatic for many, namely, this stress on individual-oriented, feeling-based, interior religion.

References to James do not pervade contemporary study of the NT, but this is hardly relevant. In fact, the lack of explicit engagement with James is something of a barometer of his influence. James's work has come to us indirectly, as though it were in the air we breathe. On the one hand, he has bequeathed to us a conversionary frame, a way of ordering our experience, a taxonomy with which to categorize religious life, a kind of pen for drawing lines separating one period of life from another or one class of people from another. On the other hand, James's thought was mediated to a generation of NT scholars by the British classicist Arthur Darby Nock (1902–63), who taught at Harvard from 1929 to 1963. He writes in his landmark study, "By conversion we mean the reorientation of the soul of an individual, his [*sic*] deliberate turning from indifferent or from an earlier form of piety to another, a turning which involves a consciousness that a great change is involved, that the old was wrong and the new is right." Explicitly referring to the work of William James, Nock goes on to write of "a passion of willingness and acquiescence, which removes the feeling of anxiety, a sense of perceiving truths not known before, a sense of clean and beautiful newness within and without and an ecstasy of happiness."[25] Here are reverberations of James's interest in individuality and interiority, with affective turmoil playing a pivotal role.

Questioning James

For many of us, James's understanding of conversion seems right at an intuitive level. It just seems right. This could be because, at key points, his conversionary frame shares central ingredients of the "modern self" as these are sketched in another work by Charles Taylor.[26] Taylor's work is a compelling

---

24. James's "blind spots . . . are just as operative in our age as in his" (Taylor, *Varieties of Religion Today*, 4).

25. Nock, *Conversion*, 7–8.

26. Taylor, *Sources of the Self*.

historical reconstruction of the making of modern identity aimed at articulating what many of us take for granted as factors composing human selfhood in the modern West. Among Taylor's overarching theses is the claim that a certain inwardness is central to "modern identity." We construct ourselves not so much in external terms—for example, in our relation to the cosmos or with regard to how we measure up (or fail to measure up) in our networks of social relations—as by turning inward. Taylor finds that personal identity has come to be shaped by such assumptions as these: human dignity lies in self-sufficiency and self-determination; identity is grasped in self-referential terms; persons have an inner self, which is the authentic self; and basic to authentic personhood are self-autonomy and self-legislation. The resultant portrait is represented well in that thoroughly modern cartoon figure, Popeye the Sailorman: "I yam what I yam, and I tha's all that I yam." Although Taylor does not focus on the notion of a metaphysical entity commonly referred to as the "soul," it is nonetheless clear from his analysis that this view of personal identity has been cultivated in the garden of anthropological dualism. Indeed, he (as others before him) identifies the precondition for the modern emphasis on the human sense of the "authentic, inner person" in the Platonic concept of the "soul" (ψυχή, *psychē*).

James's psychological description of conversion finds a ready home in this understanding of the human person, so it is critical that we recognize that this "modern self" is not only modern but non-Eastern—or, to put it more succinctly, this description of the "self" is neither transhistorical nor transcultural. Nor is it particularly biblical. For example, in an important essay Robert Di Vito locates OT anthropology in relation to Taylor's sketch of the modern self, urging in the case of the OT a very different portrait. For Di Vito, the OT presents a human who

> (1) is deeply embedded, or engaged, in its social identity, (2) is comparatively decentered and undefined with respect to personal boundaries, (3) is relatively transparent, socialized, and embodied (in other words, is altogether lacking in a sense of "inner depths"), and (4) is "authentic" precisely in its heteronomy, in its obedience to another and dependence upon another.[27]

Similarly, in his "biblical psychology," Klaus Berger concerns himself with the NT's portrait of several related motifs: personal identity, the nature of embodied existence, and the notion of an "inner" and "outer" person. In the NT world, he urges, the elements of such polarities as visible and invisible,

27. Di Vito, "Old Testament Anthropology," 221. See also his essay, "Here One Need Not Be One's Self."

knowledge and behavior, and faith and works resist unambiguous differentiation; moreover, the self is experienced as outer directed, in terms of one's community.[28] With such emphases as these, we have moved a country mile away from the mainstay of James's definition of conversion: a "self" experiencing subjective crisis and inner resolution.

Psychology, Sociology, Cognitive Science

Psychological study of conversion did not end with James, of course. Lewis Rambo, for example, urges that, since human beings are socially embedded in local contexts as well as participants in larger cultural and religious patterns, any attempt to explain conversion must go beyond the parameters of psychology. An interdisciplinary study of conversion would include psychology but also sociology, anthropology, theology, history, and religious studies.[29] Rambo's work has done little to influence biblical studies directly, but some scholars have begun to create separation, with varying degrees of distance, between the seminal work of James (and Nock) and the witness of the NT materials. Gaventa herself criticizes prevailing notions of conversion for their monochromatic approach to this religious phenomenon and finds in the NT evidence of three types of conversion: the pendulum-swing *conversion*, the *alternation* from one religious affiliation to another, and the *transformation* found in one's reinterpretation (but not rejection) of one's past.[30] Immanuel goes further. Warning against transposing modern categories of conversion onto the pages of the Acts of the Apostles, he draws a sharp line between psychological approaches that construe conversion as a mental process and Luke's interpretation of conversion as an actual turning to God.[31] Although Immanuel's concern with the potential reductionism of psychological approaches is well grounded, the distinction he wants to draw makes little sense. This is because there is no actual turning to God that does not involve human psychological processes.

Other NT scholars have attempted to sidestep psychological approaches to conversion in favor of sociological analysis. Setting aside the cerebral aspects of conversion in favor of the social, for example, Nicholas Taylor attempts to sketch a model for further study of conversion in the early Christian world

28. K. Berger, *Identity and Experience*.
29. See Rambo, "Current Research on Religious Conversion"; and, especially, Rambo's own interdisciplinary study, *Understanding Religious Conversion*.
30. Gaventa, *From Darkness to Light*. See also Morlan, *Conversion in Luke and Paul*, 11–15.
31. Immanuel, *Repent and Turn to God*.

involving conviction, conformity, and community socialization.[32] Zeba Crook offers a wholesale rejection of approaches to conversion indebted to Western psychology, favoring instead an understanding of conversion determined by the reciprocal nature of ancient social interaction. "The ancient conversion experience would have been framed not within the religious experience of the idiocentric psychological self, but the dyadic (sociocentric, allocentric, collectivistic) experience of an unbounded self."[33]

I take it as axiomatic that sociological work has much to offer our understanding of conversion in the NT materials, and that the work of Peter Berger (which synthesizes earlier work in the sociology of religion) in particular has much to offer, with its emphasis on the religious ordering and reordering of reality.[34] It almost goes without saying, though, that these attempts to reconsider the NT materials on conversion from social-scientific perspectives are themselves subject to the now-familiar criticisms of anachronism and reductionism. Even Peter Berger develops his understanding of coming to and having faith (we might say, "conversion") in terms inimical to the narrative of Luke-Acts, for example, finding in Luke's portrait of Paul's encounter with the risen Christ on the road to Damascus a prototype of modern individualism in the West. As we will see, such a reading is possible only when one brings to the Lukan narrative a preunderstanding of the nature of conversion that is alien to that narrative.[35] Moreover, however fully human beings can be understood in sociological terms, there is always more to the human story than sociology can recount, not least when the materials before us compose the NT, those manifestly theological documents that can hardly be mistaken for raw materials awaiting social-scientific analysis.

Nor can psychology be so easily set aside, even if one might wish to set aside the particular psychological approach to conversion articulated by William James. Instead, one must account for how psychology has been transforming itself both in its intercultural sensitivities and in relation to the cognitive

32. N. H. Taylor, "Social Nature of Conversion"; cf. Meeks, *Origins of Christian Morality*, 18–36.

33. Crook, *Reconceptualising Conversion*, 253. Crook's pessimism regarding the potential contribution of psychology to NT studies is not complete (51), but it is unclear what shape that contribution might take.

34. E.g., Berger and Luckmann, *Social Construction of Reality*; Berger, *Sacred Canopy*.

35. Berger claims that the immediate consequence of Paul's encounter with the risen Christ on the road to Damascus "was to tear him, radically and painfully, out of the community in which he had previously invested his entire being" (*Far Glory*, 88). It is hard to reconcile this with Luke's representation of Paul's apologetic speeches in Acts—e.g., his claim before the Jerusalem Council, "Brothers, I am a Pharisee, a son of Pharisees. I am on trial concerning the hope of the resurrection of the dead" (23:6).

sciences. In fact, in an admirable soft apology for anthropological study of the biblical materials, Louise Lawrence seeks to overcome the reductionism of social-scientific analysis in part by underscoring the importance of our recognition of the embodiment of human behavior;[36] although this is not Lawrence's point, it remains the case that this recognition arises from and is central to the cognitive sciences. Hence, even if we may appreciate the direction Nicholas Taylor has taken our understanding of conversion in the NT, the bottom line is that the cerebral aspects of conversion simply cannot be set aside in favor of the social. Psychology will not go away. Human beings and their experiences in the world, even their religious experiences in the world, are not part cerebral and part social but fully integrated in their embodiment.

I have permitted myself this introductory foray into how conversion has been defined, and particularly the influence of psychology on our understanding of conversion, because of my own methodological interests. I have become increasingly convinced that those who practice NT study have never been hermetically sealed off from other disciplinary influences, despite the typical aspirations and claims of NT scholars to their relative objectivity. New Testament exegesis has never existed and cannot exist in such a vacuum. Although many would agree with this last observation, its sequelae are less immediately recognized. More often than not, perhaps, the influence of other disciplines, especially the sciences, has been unacknowledged because of their taken-for-granted status. Conversion, for example, *simply is* such-and-such a phenomenon, or so it was thought until the prevailing Jamesian psychological model itself began to come under critical scrutiny. Being explicit about one's perspective within the sciences, then, is simply a means of engaging more fully in the critical task of NT scholarship, that is, of pulling back the curtain to reveal more fully one's own interpretive horizons.

My attempt in what follows to explore the contribution of the cognitive sciences to the question of conversion in Luke-Acts should not be read as an attempt to allow contemporary science to determine the results of NT exegesis. There is a dialectical relationship between the presumptions brought by the interpreter and the enterprise of interpreting these texts. As a result, the question is not *whether* scientific preunderstandings will be allowed a voice in the conversation, but rather, *which* science(s) will be allowed to speak. Doing exegesis in an age of science increases our awareness of the scientific assumptions at work in the history of interpretation—indeed, that have shaped the history of interpretation itself—and that have the potential to set artificially the parameters for our own understanding of biblical texts. Situating

36. Lawrence, *Reading with Anthropology*.

our exegetical work in relation to the cognitive sciences has the potential to liberate us from certain predilections that might guide our work unawares and to allow questions to surface that might otherwise have remained buried. Reading biblical texts in the light passing through this prism, what do we find in these texts that would otherwise have remained in the shadows?

My agenda, then, is to join a small number of recent students of Luke in addressing the neglected topic of conversion in the Lukan narrative. My interests will be guided by the potential contribution of the cognitive sciences to this inquiry. Having first surfaced some of the controverted issues, I will demonstrate that the cognitive sciences both provide a prophylactic against the shallow dualisms or polarities (e.g., repentance versus conversion, intellectual versus moral, internal versus external, event versus process) that have plagued much of the discussion heretofore, and help to map a more textured terrain for understanding conversion in the Lukan narrative.

Controverted Questions

Before sketching the potential of a cognitive approach to our study and turning more pointedly to the narrative of Luke-Acts to see how perspectives from cognitive science might move us forward in an exploration of conversion, some stage setting is necessary. A brief sketch of recent issues in the study of Luke's theology of conversion will provide us with the lay of the land.

Even though the concept of conversion has become associated especially with the Christian faith, it is not a particularly biblical term, nor is this concept peculiar to early Christian proclamation and literature in the ancient world.[37] As in Greek literature more widely, so in the NT, the concept is typically lexicalized with the noun μετάνοια (*metanoia*, "repentance") and its verbal form, μετανοέω (*metanoeō*, "to change one's course"), or the noun ἐπιστροφή (*epistrophē*, "a turning [toward]") and its verbal form, ἐπιστρέφω (*epistrephō*, "to turn around"). On the basis of word usage alone, however, many issues important to the interpreter remain ambiguous. Is conversion an event, a process, or both? Is conversion a cognitive or a moral category, or both? What is the relationship between "rejection of one way of life for another" and "embracing more fully the life one has chosen"? Is conversion a crossing of religious boundaries? If we move beyond lexical explanation to pragmatics—that is, to an analysis of the assumptions in place and the contextual implications of the use of this terminology, and not simply to the

37. See, e.g., Finn, *From Death to Rebirth*; Rousseau, "Conversion"; Nave, *Repentance in Luke-Acts*, 39–144.

terms themselves—what might we say about conversion? And what are we to make of those potential appearances of the concept of conversion in those cases where the usual terminology is lacking?

Collating the issues raised by recent scholarship on the motif of conversion within the Lukan narrative brings to the surface a number of controverted issues, including the following.

1. *Is conversion a cognitive category, a moral category, or both?* Originally published in 1960, Dupont's essay on conversion in Acts set the stage for subsequent discussion of the human situation that makes conversion necessary in Luke's theology.[38] Dupont's interest is captured by Luke's emphasis on salvation as forgiveness of sins and, thus, on the person's consciousness of his or her own sinfulness and need for pardon. This leads Dupont to articulate the nature of conversion in moral terms, concluding that "we remain faithful to the spirit of the early preaching when we contemplate the details of Jesus's passion in such a way as to grow increasingly aware of the ugliness of sin and arouse in ourselves that sincere repentance to which the promise of forgiveness is tied."[39] The next major voice in the discussion reaches the opposite conclusion. Jens-W. Taeger finds that the human condition in Lukan thought is characterized by ignorance needing correction, not sin needing forgiveness; hence, he concludes his monograph in a single sentence: "People do not need salvation, but correction."[40] Responding to Taeger, Christoph Stenschke seeks to provide balance by insisting that the choice between salvation and correction is for Luke a false one. For Luke, Stenschke writes, gentiles have misconceptions that need to be exposed, corrected, and replaced, but Luke's portrait also embraces God's work of removing sin, purchasing a people, and releasing people from Satan's power.[41] Reflecting narrowly on Dupont's work, Talbert reaches what appears to be a similar conclusion, namely, that conversion is for Luke both a cognitive and a moral category. This similarity may be fleeting, though, since Talbert infers that conversion is sometimes cognitive and sometimes moral (rather than saying that conversion is both cognitive and moral). Thus, he writes, "In Acts, Jews and God-fearers are offered forgiveness for sins through Jesus (a moral type of conversion) while pagans are called upon to experience a shift from polytheism to monotheism (a cognitive type of conversion)."[42] Can this distinction be sustained?

38. Dupont, "Conversion in the Acts of the Apostles."
39. Ibid., 69.
40. "Der Mensch ist kein salvandus, sondern ein corrigendus" (Taeger, *Der Mensch und sein Heil*, 225).
41. Stenschke, *Luke's Portrait of Gentiles*.
42. Talbert, "Conversion in the Acts of the Apostles," 135–36n4; at this point, Talbert is dependent on the analysis of Shumate, *Crisis and Conversion in Apuleius' Metamorphoses*.

2. *Are repentance and conversion discrete or convergent categories?* Talbert distinguishes between two categories of conversion, one for Jews and God-fearers and the other for pagans, thus preparing us for Nave's distinction between repentance and conversion. Repentance, Nave argues, has to do with a change of thinking with regard to Jesus, so this is the appropriate response category for the Jewish people in Acts. Conversion, on the other hand, refers to a change of religion, so it is descriptive of the gentile response. Is this an accurate assessment of Luke's theology?

Corollaries of these two points of discussion are easy to identify. For example: (3) *Is conversion a crossing of religious boundaries and rejection of one manner of life, an embracing more fully the life one has chosen, or both?* This potential distinction is important for identifying how best to represent Paul's experience on the Damascus Road: Was Paul "converted"? If so, in what sense? This distinction also bears on the more general question of whether Jews, like gentiles, "convert." (4) *What is the relationship between conversion as a "change of mind" and behavioral transformation?* (5) *Is conversion an event or a process?* In recent discussion, the nexus between "change of mind" and "transformation of behavior" is tightly drawn, with the result that conversion, it would seem, would need to be understood especially in terms of an ongoing process. Nevertheless, scholars tend to portray conversion in event-oriented, static terms, even when developing its logical consequences in terms of behavioral change.

6. *Is conversion a matter of human self-correction, or is it the consequence of divine initiative?* Taeger's work, mentioned earlier, raises this question in a pointed way. This is because, for his reading of Luke-Acts, the problem of human understanding can and must be addressed by self-correction. Other studies have championed the priority of divine initiative.[43] Here is a central question in conversion studies today, namely, the question of *agency*: Are converts portrayed as seekers who make plans and decisions, or as recipients of life changes?

7. *Does Luke's narrative support a "pattern" of conversion?* Some recent studies suggest that Luke follows an orderly form in his conversion accounts. Méndez-Moratalla claims to have identified a consistent paradigm of conversion in the Gospel of Luke: divine initiative especially among the marginal, conflict or polarized responses to God's plan, the universal need for a response of repentance, the expression of repentance in the proper use of possessions, the offer of forgiveness (sometimes expressed in joy and

---

43. Bovon, *L'œuvre de Luc*, 165–79; Kim-Rauchholz, *Umkehr bei Lukas*; Stenschke, *Luke's Portrait of Gentiles*; Wenk, "Conversion and Initiation."

table fellowship), and a climactic statement regarding the nature of Jesus's ministry.[44] Talbert identifies five stable components in ancient conversion accounts (context, catalyst leading to conversion, obstacles to conversion, the conversion itself, and postconversion confirmation of the authenticity of the conversion), allowing him to identify ten such accounts in Acts.[45] Neither Méndez-Moratalla nor Talbert extends the inquiry into the other volume of Luke's two-part narrative, however, so neither resolves the question whether Luke has plotted throughout his narrative a consistent pattern for portraying conversion.

Apart from such form-critical interests, what of conversion itself? Does Luke narrate a step-by-step sequence of actions or process of conversion? Two texts might urge that he has identified a paradigm of response, following as they do the direct questions, "What shall we do?" (Acts 2:37–38) and "What must I do to be saved?" (16:30–34).[46] In the first case, though, Peter counsels his audience to repent and be baptized. In the second the jailer is told (simply) to believe, though he and his household respond also with hospitality and baptism. If these texts were to be understood as establishing a pattern of response, then, they do so poorly. After all, the instructions given in the one case may complement but certainly do not mimic the other. If one were able to discern an "order of salvation" in these accounts, it might appear on a much grander scale—for example, God initiates → people hear the message of salvation → people respond. In fact, this is the heart of Peter's defense of the inclusion of gentiles in the community of God's people in 15:7–11: "God made a choice" → "gentiles hear the message of the good news" → they become "believers." Since Gaventa's important study of conversion, we find little support for the view that the Lukan narrative has identified a technique or pattern of conversion.[47]

8. *What catalyzes conversion in Luke-Acts?* The importance of miracles and preaching as catalysts for conversion has long been observed.[48] What is less clear is why or how miracles and preaching might function in this way.

This is not an exhaustive list, but it does provide us with something of the horizons within which contemporary issues related to conversion in the Lukan narrative have been discussed.

44. Méndez-Moratalla, *Paradigm of Conversion.*

45. Acts 2:1–47; 3:1–4:37; 8:4–25, 26–40; 9:1–22; 10:1–48; 13:6–12, 13–52; 16:11–15, 25–34 (Talbert, "Conversion in the Acts of the Apostles," 135n2).

46. See also Luke 3:10–14.

47. Gaventa, *From Darkness to Light,* 52–129. See also O'Toole, *Unity of Luke's Theology,* 191–224.

48. E.g., Dupont, "Conversion in the Acts of the Apostles"; Black, "Conversion Stories"; Immanuel, *Repent and Turn to God.* See also Talbert, "Conversion in the Acts of the Apostles."

The Road Ahead

In the pages that follow, I will begin to craft a different set of lenses by which to appreciate the Lukan material on conversion, then take up a series of questions, issues, and texts that together allow for a representative—though not exhaustive—exploration of Luke's narrative theology of conversion. Chapter 2 asks what the cognitive sciences bring to our discussion, then sketches some of the relevant research in the cognitive sciences and considers the ramifications of that research for Luke's portrayal of conversion. I urge that we cannot think about conversion in narrowly religious and/or spiritual terms, since there can be no transformation that is not transformation of the self, understood in embodied, holistic terms and set within a web of relationships. Chapter 3 begins with the problem of trying to identify a conversionary pattern or schema within the Lukan narrative before arguing against attempts to find a meaningful distinction in Lukan usage between the two terms "repentance" and "conversion." Most of the chapter is given over to further orientation to Luke's theology of conversion, framed as an analysis of Luke 3:1–14. We see that Luke's introduction of John the Baptist and his ministry is pivotal for understanding the larger Lukan themes of restoration and repentance, and particularly the primary contours of Luke's theology of conversion. With an emerging, working definition of conversion in hand, our interpretive work in chapters 4 and 5 allows us to expand on and clarify further Luke's presentation by taking up a series of representative texts—including some of the usual suspects that are obviously concerned with conversion, as well as others that are not so obvious. Along the way, we explore a number of important motifs, such as conversionary practices, the nature of conversion as movement from one sphere of influence to another, the question of divine versus human agency in conversion, and the possibility of deconversion. Again and again, we will find ourselves pressed to conceptualize conversion as a journey, including emphases on the trajectory of one's life path, the practices that are integral to this journey, and the quality of one's traveling companions along the way.

2

☼

Conversion and Cognition

What does cognitive science bring to the discussion of conversion? The essential characteristic of a cognitive approach is its nonnegotiable emphasis on embodiment—that is, "the role of an agent's own body in its everyday, situated cognition,"[1] its irreducible emphasis on somatic existence as the basis and means of human existence, including religious experience and the exercise of the mind. This essential interest in embodiment extends even to human language, as we will see. Embodiment refers to the human body (and not only the brain[2]) as the site of cognitive processes, to the individuated body as a lived, experiential structure, to the expression of human capacities in mutual interaction with other humans, and to the nesting of the human within the cosmos. Embodiment extends also to human experience of God—or, more generally, to religious experience or experience of the divine. This is not because God can be reductively explained as an expression of embodied cognitive functions, but because the capacities that allow humans to experience God are themselves embodied and subject to study by means of the cognitive sciences.[3] Even the language we use to describe experiences of human transformation is shaped by lived, embodied experience.

1. Gibbs, *Embodiment*, 1.
2. See the summary report by Ananthaswamy, "Bodily Minds"; cf. Loetscher et al., "Eye Position." For fuller discussion, see Lakoff and Johnson, *Philosophy in the Flesh*; Feldman, *Molecule to Metaphor*.
3. That is, the competence of the cognitive sciences does not extend to claims regarding the existence or character of God (or the gods).

19

A Cognitive Perspective?

How does cognitive science impinge on a discussion of conversion in the narrative of Luke-Acts? Before supporting these claims about embodiment and pressing forward with a consideration of their significance for studying Luke's portrayal of conversion, let me anticipate a possible concern. Some might worry that the use of cognitive categories in this study will intrude into Lukan theology as alien thought forms, concepts from another world read back into these first-century documents. The situation is neither so simple nor so ominous. It is always the case that what we perceive is both enabled and to some degree constrained by our prior conceptions.[4] Our hermeneutical biases are well formed, like deep grooves or ruts that lead us to our interpretive destination with little effort at navigation. Were we, under the influence of William James, to study conversion in an ancient narrative such as Luke has penned, we should not be surprised to find ourselves reflecting on moments of crisis, struggling with what to make of "household conversions," segregating moral and cognitive categories, distinguishing between changes of mind and changes of behavior, and the like. This is true even, or perhaps especially, if that Jamesian influence on us were unacknowledged. This is not so much because we have read Jamesian categories into the Lukan narrative, but rather because our reading of the Lukan narrative was itself enabled and constrained by such categories. We are reading not so much "into" the Lukan text as we are reading "from" a committed position that predetermines what we allow ourselves to see.

An advertisement prepared by Transport for London that has now gone viral on YouTube illustrates the point. Having been invited into an "awareness test," we are asked to observe the number of times a team of players dressed in white clothing passes a basketball among themselves. So focused are we on completing the assignment, we easily neglect even to notice that, amidst the seemingly random choreography of the teams and the jumbled tossing of the balls, a bear dances across the screen. The moral: "It's easy to miss something you're not looking for."[5] The advertisement was designed to encourage motorists to look out for cyclists, but it is equally effective for readers of Luke's narrative.

Mark Allan Powell has provided an illustration more at home in biblical studies.[6] He asked three different sets of students—one made up of Americans; another made up of residents of St. Petersburg, Russia; and the third a

---

4. Babuts, *Memory, Metaphors, and Meaning.*
5. Transport for London, "Test Your Awareness."
6. Powell, *What Do They Hear?*, 11–27.

group of Tanzanians—to listen to Luke's parable of the lost son (also known as the parable of the prodigal son; Luke 15:11–32). In different ways, then, he solicited answers to the question: Why does the younger son end up starving in a pigpen? To his astonishment, and perhaps ours as well, he received three disparate answers. The Americans attributed the younger son's situation to his wasting his money on immoral living. Those in St. Petersburg traced the cause of his starvation to the famine. And the Tanzanians drew attention to the fact that no one gave the younger son anything to eat. On reflection, Powell was able to comment on how, in each case, contemporary social locations and cultural conventions were determinative factors in what each group heard in the parable. What should not escape our attention, though, is that all three of these answers have good bases in the Lukan text: the younger son's "wasteful lifestyle" (15:13) is represented by his older brother as "gobbling up" their father's "estate on prostitutes" (15:30 CEB), the parable turns on a severe famine (15:14), and Jesus reports of the younger son that "no one gave him anything" (15:16). Different readers were drawn to different aspects of the same text on account of the different patterns by which they had been shaped to see and experience the world.

Our agenda, then, is not to transform the narrator of Luke-Acts into a cognitive scientist. Nor do we assume that Luke was an "anonymous cognitive scientist," as though he were working with cognitive categories unknowingly. Instead, a cognitive approach functions as a place to stand in order to survey the landscape of the Lukan narrative, a viewing point that allows vistas unavailable to those whose starting point has been determined by William James. Does a cognitive approach in fact shed new light on conversion in Luke-Acts?

The Embodied Self

Challenges to Studying Religious Experience

Three immediate challenges face anyone interested in studying religious experience from a cognitive perspective.[7] The first is an issue of definition: What constitutes religious experience? Or, perhaps better: What makes an experience "religious"? Because any given experience can be interpreted in various ways, the only way to determine that an experience is religious is to interpret it as such. The necessary circularity of this claim resides in the fact that an experience will be cataloged as "religious" only within and by those

---

7. See the useful methodological comments in Werline, "Experience of Prayer," 59–61; Runehow, *Sacred or Neural?*

communities that admit the possibility of a God or god(s) with whom one might interact. Hence, a religious experience is an experience interpreted as religious within a certain community and in terms of its traditions. For example, our capacity to identify changes in neural activity in cases of glossolalia[8] is consistent with a variety of interpretations, including but not limited to the view that the speaker's brain and body have come under the influence of a deity, that speaking in tongues is nothing but a human activity reducible to synaptic firings in the brain, or that it is the consequence of a ritualized pattern of worshipful activity. Different communities will assess the same phenomenon differently.

On the one hand, then, a religious experience belongs to the category of all human experiences that are embodied and have a neural basis. On the other hand, they are "religious" when they are experienced as an encounter with the divine and interpreted as such within the traditions of one's religious community.

Second, not least on account of the influence of William James, the notion of religious experience is often narrowed to the interior of an individual—that is, to intensely personal and mystical (and, typically, extraordinary) phenomena like visionary experiences or speaking in tongues. Such a view could be used with reference to first-century Jews and Christians only anachronistically. This is because, for God's people in antiquity—and, indeed, for many religious people today—religion refers to an entire way of life. The modern separation of sacred and secular runs counter to traditions that actually refuse attempts to limit "religious" to "something that can be confined to a special private realm or removed from life altogether."[9] Accordingly, "religious" experiences belong to a category that is at once both more expansive and more mundane, including daily prayers, expressions of hospitality like community meals, baptism, and economic sharing, for example.

Third, religious experiences are difficult to study from a neurobiological perspective. After all, neuroscientists work with protocols typically associated with all scientific investigation, requiring phenomena that are not only observable but also capable of being assessed according to some metric and repeatable. As impressive as new technologies for studying the brain might be, our access to neural processes remains limited, with the result that it is difficult to fulfill all of these requirements. Let us suppose, for example, that the necessary equipment had been available to study Saul's neural activity just prior to, during, and immediately following his famed experience on the

8. E.g., Newberg et al., "Regional Cerebral Blood Flow during Glossolalia."
9. McIntire, "Transcending Dichotomies," 86.

Damascus Road, as Luke narrates it in Acts 9:1–8.[10] How would the technicians have been able to anticipate when Saul might have had this visionary experience in order to have their equipment in place? How would the presence of the technicians and equipment have mitigated (or even contravened the possibility of) the experience? And, since no one else in the narrative of Acts has an analogous experience, what would be the utility of any conclusions that might be drawn from this series of brain scans? In fact, in a recent essay, Kelly Bulkeley confesses that we presently have no neuroscientific research directly addressing the topic of religious conversion.[11]

Accordingly, Anne Runehow concludes that neuroscientists can explain religious experiences only "in a methodologically restricted way and to a methodologically limited extent."[12] Whatever technological innovations might overcome those restrictions in the future, this is the state of play today. Although limited, we are not without possibilities for exploration and significant explanation, however. In what follows, I will reflect on the contribution of neuroscientific investigation to the concerns of this chapter with embodiment, and particularly the embodiment of the self and embodied religious experience. Along the way, I hope to demonstrate that a wide range of studies, even some not concerned with religious experience per se, have transferable significance for our ruminations.

The Body and the Self

> A moral man, Phineas Gage,
>> Tamping powder down holes for his wage,
> Blew the last of his probes
>> Through his two frontal lobes;
> Now he drinks, swears, and flies in a rage.[13]

This anonymous limerick summarizes what is probably the most famous case of survival after a massive brain injury as well as a classic exemplar for demonstrating that a person's mind—that is, human personality, affect, exercise of volition, and so forth—has a neural basis. It also illustrates the

10. Of course, the nature of my example requires my readers' indulgence on another, contested point, namely, that we overlook the historical issues associated with Luke's threefold recounting of Saul's experience and with the lack of direct testimony to this event on the part of Paul himself. In other words, let us also suppose that Luke's account refers to an actual experience of the historical Saul, one that theoretically could be measured scientifically.

11. Bulkeley, "Religious Conversion and Cognitive Neuroscience," 240.

12. Runehow, *Sacred or Neural?*, 228.

13. Cited in Macmillan, "Restoring Phineas Gage," 46, italics removed.

unfortunate reality that many significant advances in neuroscience are the consequence of things having gone terribly wrong. Advances in brain scanning techniques, such as positron emission tomography (PET) scanning and magnetic resonance imaging (MRI), have allowed researchers a fresh window into brain structures and activity. Additionally, we can learn a great deal from comparative neurology when the brain structures of other mammals parallel those of humans. However, ethical commitments prevent purposeful injury to the brain for experimental purposes, with the result that we are dependent to a significant degree on what we can learn from neural deficits, whether these are due (for example) to congenital issues, injury, or surgery to mitigate serious neurological problems.

Phineas Gage was a twenty-five-year-old railroad employee preparing the roadbed for the Rutland and Burlington Railroad outside Cavendish, Vermont. In the late summer of 1848, he and his gang were cutting through a large rocky outcropping. His job entailed placing dynamite into the holes drilled in the rock, then tamping it down with a tamping iron—a tool weighing just over thirteen pounds, forty-three inches long, one and a quarter inches in diameter but tapered at one end. While he was tamping down the combustible powder, an accidental explosion drove the iron rod through Gage's head. The rod entered below his left cheekbone, penetrated his skull, traversed the front part of his brain, exited through the top of his head, and landed some twenty-five to thirty yards behind him. Gage apparently never lost consciousness, but was helped to an oxcart in which he rode into town to receive medical attention. Although he survived the accident, his personality underwent a dramatic change. Known previously as a responsible, efficient, energetic, and capable person, he was described afterward as irresponsible and careless, given to raucous profanity, socially backward, and emotionally stagnant. Simply put, "Gage was no longer Gage." Though largely intact physically (the accident left him blind in one eye), he suffered a significantly diminished capacity with regard to social behavior, ethical comportment, and decision making oriented toward his own flourishing or even survival.[14]

The particulars of Gage's case have been widely circulated and its significance repeatedly explored, but his experience is not unique. James Stone has reviewed twelve analogous cases in which persons experienced transcranial injuries—with foreign bodies (like rods and pipes, but not bullets or shrapnel) penetrating the brain through and through—and survived.[15] Depending on the

14. Gage's case is the centerpiece of Antonio Damasio's book *Descartes' Error*, esp. 3–33. For a reconstruction of Gage's case, see Macmillan, "Restoring Phineas Gage."

15. Stone, "Transcranial Brain Injuries."

nature of the injury, patients generally suffered a variety of mental (as well as other) deficits, including losses of memory, organizational ability, and perceptual skill. Steven Anderson and his colleagues have described an analogous set of cases in which lesions to the orbitofrontal cortex in childhood were shown to lead to lifelong social and moral behavioral problems resistant to corrective interventions.[16] Their findings are consistent with the determination that the orbitofrontal cortex is implicated in the modulation of antisocial behavior.[17] Persons suffering brain damage in this area, then, have typically been found to have difficulty regulating their behavior in relation to acceptable social norms.

Having studied individuals with injury to the orbitofrontal cortex, Antonio Damasio and his colleagues have proposed the importance of somatic markers for life navigation and decision making. Somatic markers are physiological reactions that tag earlier emotionally significant events, which then provide subtle emotional and intuitive direction in the future. They resemble "gut feelings" of attraction or repulsion in the face of competing choices. Damage to the orbitofrontal cortex interrupts this signal with the result that present behavior is no longer anchored in previous experiences (nor in anticipated future consequences based on those prior experiences). Instead, behavior appears whimsical and impulsive. In short, even when capacities for memory and abstract reasoning are intact, robbed of the biasing function of emotional responses, persons prove to be incompetent decision makers.[18]

A range of disorders of volition have been studied.[19] Pathological lying has been tied to abnormality within the prefrontal cortex.[20] Focal bilateral damage to the ventromedial prefontal cortex, an area of the brain implicated in the generation of social emotions, has been shown to produce an abnormally utilitarian pattern of moral judgment.[21] In a collection of studies, an interdisciplinary cast of scholars reported on persons who evidenced a "sick will" (e.g., inactivity, lack of ambition, autistic behavior, depressive motor skills, and behavioral inhibition), correlating those symptoms with subnormal activity in the prefrontal cortex.[22] Disorders of volition also appear among persons suffering from depression, a condition in which the inability of patients to initiate new goal-oriented activity is correlated with inhibition in those parts of the brain implicated in executive functioning, namely, the

16. Anderson et al., "Impairment of Social and Moral Behavior."
17. See the discussion by Blair, "Roles of Orbital Frontal Cortex."
18. See Damasio, *Descartes' Error*; also, e.g., Bechara et al., "Insensitivity to Future Consequences"; Bechara, "Role of Emotion in Decision-Making."
19. For the catalog that follows, see Sebanz and Prinz, eds., *Disorders of Volition*.
20. E.g., Yang et al., "Prefrontal White Matter."
21. Koenigs et al., "Damage to the Prefrontal Cortex."
22. Libet et al., eds., *Volitional Brain*; see also Goldberg, *Executive Brain*.

brain's frontal lobe and anterior cingulate cortex. And volitional impairment arises in instances of addiction and substance abuse as regions of the brain related to signaling immediate pain or pleasure override those regions related to future prospects.

If the case of Phineas Gage is famous for demonstrating the neural basis of such human attributes and capacities as personality, affect, and exercise of volition, the case of the London taxi drivers has become a modern classic for demonstrating neural transformation in response to environmental factors. In 2000, Eleanor A. Maguire and her colleagues reported on a fascinating study of London taxi drivers.[23] Their work capitalized on two well-known facts: first, that one important role of the hippocampus is to facilitate spatial memory in the form of navigation (i.e., the storage and use of mental maps of our environments); and second, that licensed London taxi drivers are renowned for their extensive and detailed navigation experience. Using structural MRIs, these researchers compared the brains of a select group of taxi drivers with those of matched control subjects who did not drive taxis. They found that the posterior hippocampi of the taxi drivers were significantly larger relative to those of control subjects. Moreover, hippocampal volume correlated with the amount of time spent as a taxi driver. This led to the conclusion that day-to-day activities are capable of inducing changes in the morphology of the brain.

In a follow-up study, Maguire and her colleagues demonstrated that these differences in hippocampal volume were causally related to the detail and/or duration of acquired spatial representations and not to innate navigational expertise.[24] They also demonstrated that intensively acquiring a large amount of knowledge—say, in the medical profession—does not correlate with hippocampal gray matter volume. This led to the conclusion that the previously documented changes in volume were in fact associated with spatial layout.[25] In a further study, they compared London taxi drivers and bus drivers in order to test whether the previously observed differences in hippocampal volume could be traced to driving experience, stress, or self-motion. Their increasingly fine-grained results demonstrated that the differences were in fact due to increased spatial knowledge.[26] Most recently, Maguire and her colleagues conducted a longitudinal study that followed a group of seventy-nine aspiring London taxi drivers for four years, measuring the relative growth of their hippocampi with magnetic resonance imaging. This allowed her to demonstrate

23. Maguire et al., "Navigation-Related Structural Change."
24. Maguire et al., "Navigation Expertise and the Human Hippocampus."
25. Woollett et al., "Non-spatial Expertise."
26. Maguire et al., "London Taxi Drivers and Bus Drivers."

conclusively that their intensive training was responsible for their hippocampal growth.[27] By addressing a series of alternative explanations of their original study in this way, Maguire and her colleagues have demonstrated a measurable environmental impact on brain morphology.

The embodied nature of human life can be further demonstrated in scores of other ways, though some of the more interesting data come from what Todd Feinberg calls "altered egos." "Patients with altered egos" are those who, because of brain damage, "experience a transformation in the *personal*, the aspects of identity that are most significant to the self."

These persons might reject one of their arms, disown a spouse, or claim nonexistent relationships to strangers. They might have imaginary brothers, children, or alter egos. There is much to be learned from these cases. As slicing an apple reveals its core, the neurological lesion, or damage, in these patients opens a door into the inner self; it provides an opportunity to examine the physical structure of the self and to see how the self changes and adapts in response to the damaged brain.[28]

Feinberg recounts the stories of a wide range of persons who have suffered brain damage, leading to a wide range of ways in which persons have experienced an altered sense of the self. These include the following:

- In cases of asomatognosia, patients fail to recognize a part of their own bodies and may even reject it completely—so that, for example, a woman neglects her own arm and, when asked about it, refuses to recognize it or insists that it belongs to someone else (e.g., to the physician or even to a deceased husband). These are instances in which brain pathology contributes to the fragmentation of the self.

- In cases of Capgras Syndrome, a delusional misidentification syndrome, a person holds that a friend, spouse, or other close family member has been replaced by an imposter who looks exactly like the misidentified person. Here is an example of the loss of a sense of the personal relatedness on which our identities depend.

- In cases of Alien Hand Syndrome, a person has a hand that acts beyond the subject's conscious, voluntary control. One hand seems to function on its own accord, answering the phone, for example, choosing a shirt from the closet, or even attempting to strangle the subject during sleep. Here is an example of how brain lesions can result in disorders related to our basic sense of personal agency and volition.

27. Woollett and Maguire, "Acquiring 'the Knowledge' of London's Layout."
28. Feinberg, *Altered Egos*, 2.

These and a host of other cases lead Feinberg to the conclusion that the mind is "a nested hierarchy of meaning and purpose" created by but not reducible to the brain. "The brain creates the unity of the self by producing a nested hierarchy of meaning and purpose, where the levels of the self, and the many parts of the brain that contributed to the self, are nested within all other levels of the hierarchy. The brain has no pinnacle of consciousness, but we experience ourselves as unified because our meanings and our actions are unified within the nested self."[29]

The Bodily Human

Feinberg's is one of a number of ways neuroscientists, theologians, and philosophers have attempted to make sense of the embodied self. Taken at its simplest level, his thinking coheres with a range of proposals for understanding the human person that require no second, metaphysical entity, such as a soul or spirit, to account for human capacities and characteristics, while at the same time insisting that human behavior cannot be explained exhaustively with recourse to genetics or neuroscience. These include philosophically sophisticated proposals, like nonreductive physicalism,[30] as well as less elegant but more descriptive proposals that account for humans as complex, emergent, developmental, linguistic, relational, neurophysiological beings.[31] From perspectives like these, the phenomenological experiences that we label "soul" are neither reducible to brain activity nor evidence of a substantial, ontological entity such as a "soul," but rather represent essential aspects or capacities of the self.

This emphasis on the embodied character of human capacities and characteristics is not limited to recent findings in the neurosciences but dates back to the very origins of neurology as a discipline in the 1600s in the work of Thomas Willis.[32] Although it is true that this seventeenth-century medic and celebrated founder of neurology referred in his published works to the "Rational Soul" (that is, the immaterial and immortal soul of humans, as opposed to the material soul common to both humans and nonhuman animals), it is difficult

---

29. Ibid., 149.

30. See Murphy, *Bodies and Souls, or Spirited Bodies?*; Murphy and Brown, *Did My Neurons Make Me Do It?*

31. See Brown and Strawn, "Self-Organizing Personhood."

32. Green, "Science, Religion, and the Mind-Brain Problem"; more extensively, Zimmer, *Soul Made Flesh*. I do not mean to imply that the roots of study of the brain can be traced to the seventeenth century, since these run much deeper—see, e.g., Finger, *Origins of Neuroscience*. I refer instead to the place of Willis at the emergence of the systematic study of the brain and larger nervous system as a disciplinary expression of the "new science."

to identify its significance. Traditionally, "soul" (for Willis, the "Rational Soul") had referred to the essential self in which resides what is distinctively human: human personality, consciousness, volition, relatedness, and the like. But Willis's diverse approaches to neurology—comparative anatomy, human necropsy, physiological experimentation, astute history taking and clinical observation, and postmortem investigation of his own patients, allowing for clinicopathological correlations—both weakened any meaningful distinction between humans and nonhuman animals on these points and began to demonstrate the neural basis of these capacities and attributes. In other words, Willis anticipated by more than three centuries the claims of a recent article in the *New York Times*, that scientists are challenging the view "that humans are not, physically or even mentally, in a class by themselves."[33]

Having acknowledged an immortal soul, a move that allowed Willis to avoid clashing with ecclesiastical authorities, Willis then devoted himself at length to the function and properties of the "animal soul," which he also called the "soul of brutes." This allowed him to include psychical issues within the competence of medicine and to present a coherent psychophysiological approach to human capacities and behaviors. As Paul F. Cranefield summarizes, "The soul of brutes, in the hands of Willis, really seems to be simply a handy name for the assemblage of anatomical and physiological mechanisms which underlie psychological processes."[34] Willis writes:

> The Brain is accounted the chief seat of the Rational Soul in a man, and of the sensitive [soul] in brute beasts, and indeed as the chief mover in the animal machine, it is the origine and fountain of all motions and conceptions. But some Functions do chiefly and more immediately belong to the substance of this, and others depend as it were mediately and less necessarily upon it. Among these, which of the former sort are accounted the chief, are the Imagination, Memory, and Appetite. . . . The rest of the Faculties of this Soul, as Sense and Motion, also the Passions and Instincts merely natural, though they

33. Dean, "Science of the Soul?" I mention Willis in order to counter the argument of some contemporary theologians and philosophers who urge that we ought not to embrace the theological and philosophical ramifications of neuroscience because the results of scientific study are forever in a state of flux. This is simply not the case when it comes to the long-standing and growing evidence of the neural basis of the capacities and attributes associated with what it means to be human—evidence that began to surface already in the seventeenth century. Indeed, in the mid-twentieth century, the historian Walther Riese asserted that the human soul had been eliminated in the 1800s (*History of Neurology*, 19–48). Riese's hyperbole does not detract from the fact that the neuroscientific evidence to which the aforementioned theologians and philosophers are reacting is "new" only in its specificity and not in the general directions to which it points.

34. Cranefield, "Seventeenth Century View of Mental Deficiency and Schizophrenia," 306.

depend in some measure upon the Brain, yet they are properly performed in the oblong Marrow [i.e., spinal cord] and Cerebel [cerebellum], or proceed from them.[35]

That is, Willis identifies the brain as the origin of all motions and conceptions. He locates in the brain or spinal column not only reflexes and sensory and motor centers but also cognition, imagination, volition, and affect. He assigns thought to the cerebrum, voluntary movement to the cerebral hemispheres, perception to the corpora striata, imagination to the corpus callosum, memory to the cerebral cortex, instinct to the midbrain, and involuntary regulation to the cerebellum. Consider this: *if* human identity is grounded in consistency of memory; *if* the differentiating marks of the human person are the development of consciousness, individuality within community, self-consciousness, the capacity to make decisions on the basis of self-deliberation, planning and action on the basis of a decision, and taking responsibility for decisions and actions;[36] *and if* these all have neural bases, then the concept of a soul, as traditionally understood in theology and popularly conceived as a person's "authentic self," has little to offer.[37] It would be too much to say that Willis is responsible for all of this. However, given the view that emerged in his work, that cognitive and psychological processes are dependent on neural activity—and, more specifically, his location of thought, volition, perception, affect, imagination, and memory in the various structures of the brain—it is easy to see that Willis set neurobiology firmly on the path that would lead to our current emphasis on embodied human life.

Two more threads of evidence will not only secure this emphasis on the essential embodiment of the human self but also prepare for our more focused interest on embodied religious life. I refer to recent studies of psychotherapy and meditation. For example, Jeffrey M. Schwartz shows the effectiveness of behavioral therapy in the treatment of patients with obsessive compulsive disorder (OCD)—displaying this transformation both in terms of an observable reduction in obsessive tendencies and with reference to a decrease of metabolic activity in those brain areas implicated in the disorder.[38] Veena Kumari surveys psychiatric research that utilized neuroimaging techniques to investigate neural

35. Willis, *Anatomy*, 91.
36. This list comes from Hefner, *Human Factor*, 118–19.
37. That is, the "Rational Soul" seems to have been relegated to the status of an epiphenomenon, not involved causally in bringing about the actions attributed to it and so without real explanatory force.
38. See Schwartz and Begley, *Mind and the Brain*.

events associated with both therapeutic and psychopharmacological interventions in a number of psychiatric disorders.[39] This research included cases of depression, panic disorder, phobia, OCD, and schizophrenia. According to the studies examined, clinical improvements were correlated with regional and/or system changes in the brain. With reference to these two studies, the one by Schwartz and the other by Kumari, then, we find that therapeutic interventions have actually resulted in physiological changes in the brain.

Similarly, in the last five years meditative practices have begun to be studied with an emphasis on their associated neurological changes. Researchers had already observed the role of meditation in decreasing stress, improving mood, and boosting immunity but had not identified transformations in brain structure that might correlate with these reported improvements. Scientists from Massachusetts General Hospital have now shown that practicing mindfulness meditation thirty minutes a day increased hippocampal volume (an area implicated in learning and memory) and decreased density in the amygdala (an area implicated in anxiety and stress response).[40] This research underscores again the correlation of feelings with brain structure but also demonstrates the role of practices like meditation in ongoing neural change. This finding is consistent with other studies.[41] This kind of evidence gains significance for us when we recognize that different meditation traditions express themselves as modified states of consciousness that emphasize attention, concentration, and the letting go of thoughts—a description very much at home in references to certain religious experiences, including religious meditation and visionary experiences.

Embodied Religion?

Although it would be a mistake to limit the category of religious experience to extraordinary phenomena like visionary experiences or speaking in tongues, it is nonetheless true that these are the religious experiences that have attracted most of the scholarly attention.[42] I will introduce visionary experiences more generally in the Lukan narrative before focusing on the particular experience Paul recounts of his being "caught up to the third heaven" (2 Cor. 12:1–4).

39. Kumari, "Do Psychotherapies Produce Neurobiological Effects?"
40. Hölzel et al., "Mindfulness Practice."
41. E.g., Luders et al., "Underlying Anatomical Correlates"; Manna, "Neural Correlates."
42. For an older survey of exegetical, historical, theological, psychological, and sociocultural perspectives on glossolalia, see Mills, ed., *Speaking in Tongues*. On the neurobiological front, see, e.g., Newberg et al., "Regional Cerebral Blood Flow during Glossolalia"; Newberg and Waldman, *Why We Believe What We Believe*, 191–214. For glossolalia in the NT and Hellenistic world, see Forbes, *Prophecy and Inspired Speech*, 44–187.

Dreams and Visions

The narrative of Luke-Acts is peppered with dreams and visions, and these have been usefully studied from a narrative-critical perspective by John Miller.[43] He demonstrates the ubiquity in Roman antiquity of the view that life was engaged by divine forces, so that most experience was for the ancients religious. His study finds that visions in the Lukan narrative demonstrate the activity of God in and behind the course of human events and are often understood as important components of religious experience by which people accessed divine guidance and made sense of their encounters with God.

In fact, however, Luke gives us very little basis for an analysis of the religious experience of vision and ecstasy. We read little if anything about them as subjective experiences, we have no firsthand accounts, and the evangelist reports their having occurred with little fanfare. They apparently constitute events no more extraordinary to his universe of experience than, say, Jesus passing through Jericho or Paul speaking before the Ephesian elders. The world shared by Luke and his model readers[44] is such that the character and credibility of these visionary experiences can simply be taken for granted. It remains noteworthy, though, that visionary and revelatory experiences in Luke's narrative are often associated with such ritual behavior as prayer (e.g., Luke 3:21–22; 9:28–36; 22:39–46; Acts 10:3,[45] 9–17; 11:5; 22:17–21), worship (Acts 13:2), and fasting (Luke 4:1–13; Acts 13:2).[46] This is remarkable because such ritualized behaviors are capable of preparing—one might say "tuning"— the nervous system for an altered state of consciousness.[47]

In other words, Luke's first-century narrative on these points is congruent with the expectation among neuroscientists of twenty-first-century study of altered states of consciousness.[48] Note that to refer to visionary experiences

43. Miller, *Convinced That God Had Called Us*; see also Miller, "Dreams/Visions and the Experience of God in Luke-Acts."

44. By "model reader," I refer to Umberto Eco's notion of the reader posited by the intention of the text, whose competence is generated by the text and who collaborates in actualizing the content of the text. See, e.g., Eco, *Role of the Reader*, 7–11; and Eco, "Portrait of the Elder."

45. The term "prayer" is missing but is implied by Luke's reference to "three o'clock in the afternoon" (i.e., the time of prayer); cf. Acts 3:1.

46. See also Acts 10:9–17; Peter is also hungry, a form of deprivation that can be related to the experience of an altered state of consciousness.

47. See d'Aquili and Newberg, *Mystical Mind*.

48. Admittedly, "altered state of consciousness" is a contested term, dependent on how one understands "consciousness," and, then, on how one experiences what might be called a "normal state of consciousness." For our purposes, we can refer to attentional changes related to the interruption of the normal ebb and flow of activity in the parasympathetic and sympathetic nervous systems, leading either to extraordinary relaxation or to ecstasy in which other stimuli are blocked.

as altered states of consciousness is not to explain them away but rather to insist that they, too, are embodied.

Paul's Visionary Experience

The only autobiographical report of a visionary experience in the NT is found in 2 Cor. 12:1–4:[49]

> It is necessary to boast; nothing is to be gained by it, but I will go on to visions and revelations of the Lord. I know a person in Christ who fourteen years ago was caught up to the third heaven—whether in the body or out of the body I do not know; God knows. And I know that such a person—whether in the body or out of the body I do not know; God knows—was caught up into Paradise and heard things that are not to be told, that no mortal is permitted to repeat.

The history of interpretation of this text has surfaced a number of issues that continue to attract critical debate, but only one of these is central to my concerns. This is the nature of Paul's experience, and particularly the character of this experience as an embodied one.[50] What is remarkable in this text is that Paul twice admits his agnosticism regarding the bodily basis of his experience:

I know a person in Christ . . .	I know that such a person
was caught up to the third heaven	was caught up into Paradise
whether in the body or out of the body I do not know; God knows	*whether in the body or out of the body I do not know; God knows*

The basis of Paul's emphatic agnosticism regarding his bodily state has attracted a variety of explanations, with a number of scholars suggesting that Paul's apparent indifference is integral to his rhetorical responses to his opponents at Corinth.[51] According to this view, if the apostle had identified himself as having had a heavenly journey, he would have played into the hands of those who claimed for themselves elevated status on the basis of revelatory experiences. Alan Segal theorizes instead that the mystical guild had not yet

49. The material that follows is adapted from Green, "What about . . . ?"

50. I assume with most scholars that Paul's reference to "a person in Christ . . . such a person" is a self-reference; see, e.g., Baird, "Visions, Revelation, and Ministry," 653–54; Forbes, "Comparison, Self-Praise, and Irony"; Lietaert Peerbolte, "Paul's Rapture," 163; Tabor, *Things Unutterable*, 114–15; and among recent commentators, e.g., Furnish, *II Corinthians*, 543–44; Harris, *Second Epistle to the Corinthians*, 835. See, however, Goulder, "Vision and Knowledge."

51. See, e.g., Furnish, *II Corinthians*, 545; Tabor, *Things Unutterable*, 121; Baird, "Visions, Revelation, and Ministry," 654; Lincoln, *Paradise Now and Not Yet*, 71–86.

reached clarity on the nature of ecstatic journeying and that this ambiguity is reflected in Paul's statement. "Paul's confusion over the nature of his ecstatic journey to heaven provides a rare insight into first-century thinking, since it demonstrates either a disagreement in the community or more likely a first-century mystic's inability to distinguish between bodily and spiritual journeys."[52] Irrespective of how we negotiate these options, what we cannot escape is what Paul himself not only recognizes but actually emphasizes: he simply does not know the status of his body during this episode.[53]

We cannot escape the further reality that major streams of the traditions of philosophical anthropology and of interpretations of mystical experiences of ascent would have given Paul everything he needed in order to interpret his experience. Analogous reports in the wider world are mixed, with some reports clearly identifying the heavenly journey in terms of soul flight and others in terms of embodiment.[54] In terms of the latter, for example, the *Testament of Abraham* (recension B) has it that the Lord's directions to the angel Michael, "Go and take up Abraham *in the body* and show him everything," are followed with the narrative report that "Michael left and took Abraham up onto a cloud *in the body*" (8.1–3).[55] In material influenced more by Platonic dualism, however, ascension took the form of soul flight apart from the body (e.g., Philo, *Dreams* 1.36). As a general rule, reports of rapture experiences in the Jewish tradition speak to the embodied nature of the phenomenon, whereas those in the Hellenistic tradition trace the journey of the disencumbered soul. Interestingly, in the early history of reception of Paul's autobiographical note, the tendency was strong, though not unanimous, to read Paul's experience as an ascension apart from his body. In circles where human physicality was valued negatively (such as gnostic communities), the tendency was strong to interpret Paul's visionary experience as a disembodied one. Alternatively, in communities where the human body was appreciated as part of God's creation (as in catholic Christianity), Paul's visionary experience was understood as a bodily one.[56]

Indeed, given the definitive categories of Platonic dualism, had Paul been working from within that anthropological framework, he would have known

52. Segal, *Paul the Convert*, 39; cf. Segal, "Paul and the Beginning of Jewish Mysticism," 109.
53. If someone were to argue that Paul seems able at least to entertain the possibility of a disembodied state ("whether . . . out of the body"), it must also be affirmed that he seems not to imagine that an embodied state ("whether in the body") would be a hindrance to even this elevated form of religious experience.
54. For assessment, see Culianu, *Psychanodia I*; Lohfink, *Die Himmelfahrt Jesu*, 32–41; Dean-Otting, *Heavenly Journeys*; Segal, "Heavenly Ascent"; Himmelfarb, *Ascent to Heaven*.
55. ET in E. P. Sanders, "Testament of Abraham," 899, emphasis added.
56. See the analysis in Roukema, "Paul's Rapture to Paradise."

with certainty whether it was in or out of the body. Similarly, given the ample literary evidence of soul ascent, had Paul experienced this "vision and revelation" as soul flight, he would certainly have had the categories for declaring it in just these terms. In the more forceful words of Alan Segal, had Paul been influenced at this point by Platonic dualism, "he would have known quite well that the only way to go to heaven, to ascend beyond the sublunar sphere, is by leaving the body behind."[57]

Someone might urge that Paul's confusion on the question of the status of his body was due to the perplexity accompanying an "out-of-body experience." This view could not be dismissed as a case of wrongly imposing a contemporarily studied phenomenon on a first-century autobiographical account. After all, reports of out-of-body experiences are well known from ancient times up to the present in folklore, mythology, and religious narratives.[58] Indeed, these experiences may have led people long ago to think of themselves as a soul or spirit inhabiting a body since they represent in phenomenological terms a kind of disembodied version of what we would eventually come to know as Cartesian dualism.

Out-of-body experiences are typically brief episodes in which a person's conscious self seems to take leave of the body and to look back on the body as though it belonged to someone else. People talking about their out-of-body experiences report that their "selves" are temporarily not bound to the limits of their bodies. The mind seems to take up a position above or to the side of the body from which the mind is able to see the body in its former position, whether standing or sitting or lying down.[59] Out-of-body experiences are surprisingly common. Many of us tend to think of out-of-body episodes as the product of a brain disorder, like epilepsy or schizophrenia, or as the result of a hallucinatory drug.[60] However, most reports of out-of-body experiences come from ordinary people in ordinary life circumstances, with estimates of the prevalence of out-of-body experiences ranging from some 10 percent of the general population to 25 percent among students. (This is a reminder

57. Segal, "Afterlife," 22.

58. For bibliography, see Blanke et al., "Linking Out-of-Body Experience and Self Processing," 551; Blanke et al., "Out-of-Body Experience," 244.

59. For definitions, see Metzinger, *Being No One*, 489; Blanke et al., "Out-of-Body Experience," 243; De Ridder et al., "Out-of-Body Experience," 1829; Braithwaite and Dent, "New Perspectives."

60. In 2009, a religious group in Oregon that blends Christian and Brazilian indigenous religious beliefs won the right to import and brew a hallucinogenic tea for its religious services ("Ashland Church Can Brew Hallucinogenic Tea"). The tea, brewed from the ayahuasca plant, contains trace amounts of the chemical dimethyltryptamine or DMT, which can cause psychedelic phenomena, including the visual and audio sensations characteristic of an out-of-body experience.

that a subjective experience may or may not be regarded as a religious experience, depending on whether it is understood as an experience of the divine and interpreted as such within the traditions of one's religious community.)

Even though we have reports of out-of-body experiences from ancient times, they have been studied only in recent decades. The results might read like science fiction, but they are very much a part of contemporary brain science. A part of our brains known as the temporal-parietal junction is known to play a key role in the experience of embodiment—that is, the sense of being spatially situated within one's body—which is itself a key element of selfhood. Studies have shown, then, that one's imagined self-location and actual body location share neural mechanisms.[61] A Swiss neuroscientist, Olaf Blanke, observed that, when he electrically stimulated this part of the brain, a patient with no prior history of out-of-body experiences now experienced one. Blanke's experiment was conducted with the patient fully awake and aware of her surroundings. Nevertheless, she informed the researchers that she could now see the world, including herself lying on the bed, from an elevated perspective.[62] Similar results were reported by Dirk De Ridder and his colleagues, who documented the case of a sixty-three-year-old man who presented with intractable tinnitus—that is, a persistent ringing in the ears in the absence of external sound. Stimulation with implanted electrodes overlying the temporal-parietal junction on the right side as a means of suppressing his tinnitus induced out-of-body experiences.[63]

Recently, neuroscientists have induced out-of-body sensations less invasively, through events of multisensory conflict. The brain processes sensations from multiple sources (say, seeing, hearing, and touching) to determine the placement of the body in a particular space. What happens when those multiple sources disagree? A person's in-body experience is interrupted, and they experience themselves occupying space separate from their body.[64]

Of course, this conclusion departs from the popular notion that out-of-body and near-death experiences demonstrate the ability of a disembodied soul to vacate the body, whether temporarily during one's life or permanently upon one's death. This interpretation of these experiences has now been subjected to thoroughgoing analysis by Michael Marsh, whose study is now the definitive work on the subject.[65] Interrogating accounts of what he calls

61. E.g., Arzy et al., "Neural Basis of Embodiment"; Braithwaite et al., "Cognitive Correlates of the Spontaneous Out-of-Body Experience (OBE)."
62. Blanke et al., "Stimulating Illusory Own-Body Perceptions."
63. De Ridder et al., "Out-of-Body Experience."
64. See Ehrsson, "Experimental Induction"; Lenggenhager et al., "Video Ergo Sum."
65. Marsh, *Out-of-Body and Near-Death Experiences*. On near-death experiences, see too the research summary in Mobbs and Watt, "There Is Nothing Paranormal about Near-Death Experiences."

"extra-corporeal experience," he finds that these narratives are idiosyncrati-cally fashioned, drawing on the memories of each individual. Accordingly, "these aberrant mental images are not culled from any other-worldly journey but as a thorough-going, this-worldly event," occasioned by the "chaotic process of re-perfusion and re-oxygenation, terminating abruptly as con-scious-awareness fully re-emerges from the world of subconscious, dream-like mentation."[66] In other words, the basis of an "extra-corporeal experience" can be explained in neurophysiological terms.

These findings do not rule out additional interpretations that draw on one's beliefs, feelings, and interpretive communities. Rather, this brief discussion of out-of-body experiences leads to a simple, ironic conclusion: out-of-body experiences are generated in our bodies, by our brains. Far from proving that there is an ethereal self that can separate itself from our material bodies, out-of-body experiences demonstrate rather the wonderful complexity of our brains as they situate us in time and space in ways that we mostly take for granted.[67]

If reference to out-of-body experiences does not move us beyond Paul's agnosticism regarding the state of his body during his visionary experience, it at least pushes us in a helpful direction of inquiry. That is, it suggests the prudence of thinking about the ecstatic experience of the body in relation to normal or typical body consciousness.

Studying Religious Experiences

In fact, neurobiological study has documented a wide range of extraordinary phenomena under the general category of "disorders of body perception."[68] The result of these studies, often focused on patients with disorders,[69] is the identification of areas of the brain implicated in processing perception of one's body. And this has opened fresh paths for scientific exploration of the nature of religious experience, and particularly the neural correlates of religious, spiritual, and/or mystical experiences.

Examples are increasingly available. Andrew Newberg and his colleagues have conducted several related studies. These include, for example, a single photon emission computed tomography (SPECT) brain imaging of accom-plished Tibetan Buddhist meditators, which yielded results compatible with

66. Marsh, *Out-of-Body and Near-Death Experiences*, 259.
67. See Cheyne and Girard, "Unbound Body."
68. See Goldenberg, "Disorders of Bodily Perception."
69. Many of these stories make for fascinating reading. See, e.g., Sacks, *Man Who Mistook His Wife*; and Feinberg, *Altered Egos*.

deafferentation of (or blocking neural input to) the posterior superior parietal lobe and parts of the inferior parietal lobe during profound unitary states. This provided the neural basis of a seemingly timeless and spaceless loss of a differentiated sense of self that, among Christians, would be experienced as a sense of mystical union with God, but among Buddhists would be experienced nonpersonally as nirvana.[70] They have also conducted a SPECT study measuring cerebral blood flow in Franciscan nuns in meditative prayer. This study found increased activity in the prefrontal cortex, and the inferior frontal and inferior parietal lobes, with changes in the prefrontal cortex reflecting an altered sense of body consciousness during the prayer state.[71] Similarly, Mario Beauregard and Vincent Paquette conducted a functional magnetic resonance imaging (fMRI) study of the brain activity of fifteen cloistered Carmelite nuns while the nuns were subjectively in a state of union with God, and on this basis the researchers reported that mystical experiences are mediated by several brain regions and systems.[72]

Although he is not concerned with the neurobiological substrates of Paul's experience, Bert Jan Lietaert Peerbolte does locate Paul's account in 1 Cor. 12 within this same category of "an altered state of consciousness." Thus, Paul was confused about the status of his body, implying that the boundaries of his self had been blurred, and he interpreted his experience as a revelation from outside himself and as a journey into the divine realm.[73] Colleen Shantz, who is concerned with the neurobiology of Paul's experience, reaches an analogous conclusion.[74]

We conclude this section by underscoring two central motifs:

- Human experience, even religious experience, is fully embodied.
- To identify the neural correlates of religious experience is not to explain that experience fully but only to demonstrate that it is an embodied experience.

Neurobiology and Conversion

Guy Nave's recent narrative-critical assessment of conversion and repentance in Luke-Acts comes after his lengthy survey of the usage of the terms μετανοέω (*metanoeō*, "to change one's mind," "to repent") and μετάνοια (*metanoia*,

---

70. Newberg et al., "Regional Cerebral Blood Flow during the Complex Cognitive Task of Meditation."

71. Newberg et al., "Cerebral Blood Flow during Meditative Prayer."

72. Beauregard and Paquette, "Neural Correlates of a Mystical Experience."

73. Lietaert Peerbolte, "Paul's Rapture," 169–73; cf. Segal, "Afterlife," 23.

74. Shantz, *Paul in Ecstasy*, 87–108.

"change of mind," "repentance," "conversion") in Luke's world, that is, in Greek and Hellenistic Jewish literature, and in NT and other early Christian literature apart from Luke-Acts.[75] This allows him to reject earlier claims about the unprecedented character of Jewish or Christian views of the meaning of repentance and to document contextual influences on how Luke and his audience might have understood the motif. He finds evidence for several trajectories. Practically from the coining of the terminology of *metanoeō* and *metanoia*, the primary sense of these words centered on a "change in thinking," though, he says, this sense expanded to "a change of mind, heart, view, opinion or purpose," often in tandem with feelings of remorse due to the perception of having acted or thought wrongly, inappropriately, or disadvantageously. *Metanoia*, if it were genuine, would be accompanied further by a will to make right the wrong committed or to change the situation that eventuated in the wrongdoing with a concomitant alteration of future behavior. Sometimes *metanoia* was the result of divine and/or human chiding. Ultimately, *metanoia* would lead to forgiveness and reconciliation. This underscores in a helpful way our earlier observation that an experience is deemed "religious" in relation to a community and its traditions. In the ancient world, a conversion need not be identified as "religious," just as today we find references to someone's being "converted" to a hybrid vehicle or a vegetarian diet quite apart from any notion that such a conversion is a "religious" experience.

This is helpful background, but we cannot overlook the ease with which Nave's findings could be interpreted in relation to twenty-first-century categories rather than those of antiquity. Accordingly, we might misconstrue movement from one "philosophy" to another in antiquity as a reference to one's leaving behind one way of thinking for another, imagining that, for the ancients as in modern usage, "philosophy" could signify no more than a disembodied system of thought, ivory-tower intellectualizing. To the contrary, this sort of change—that is, "converting" to a philosophy—would entail entire patterns of living: thinking, believing, feeling, and behaving. Words, deeds, and principles flowed together indiscriminately, inseparably. Josephus, for example, can refer to four Jewish philosophies, then describe them variously with regard to diet, respect for the aged, worship practices, economic sharing, and so on, as well as beliefs (*Ant.* 18.9–25). Thinking and living were not segregated.[76] For our present purposes, this invites reflection on the neurobiological correlates of the human experience of change.

75. Nave, *Repentance in Luke-Acts*, 39–144.
76. For an overview, see Fitzgerald, "Greco-Roman Philosophical Schools." This has been emphasized for study of Acts in Rowe, *World Upside Down*; Rowe, "Grammar of Life."

Remolding the Brain

Although early development of the cerebral cortex is largely genetically determined, environmental factors are key in the newborn and continue their influence throughout an individual's life. This is partially due to neurogenesis (i.e., the generation of new brain cells, or neurons), which persists even in adults, but is especially realized in the generation and pruning of synapses, those points of communication among the cells of the brain. In this way, formative influences are encoded in the synapses of the central nervous system. Hence, although our genes bias our dispositions and character, the neuronal systems and pathways responsible for much of how we think, feel, believe, and behave are shaped by learning. In our first two years (and beyond), far more synapses are generated than are needed. Those neural connections that are used are maintained and remodeled, while those that fall into disuse are eliminated. Fresh connections are generated in response to our experiences, even into adulthood, until the very moment of death.[77] This "learning" (or "training") is the product especially of interpersonal experiences, which directly shape the ongoing development of the brain's structure and function. Jim Grigsby and David Stevens summarize:

> Personality is shaped by the interaction of constitutional processes and the experiences of individuals in unique environments. In other words, we are, at least in part, who we learn to be. As a result of these experiences, learning drives the acquisition and refinement of a wide repertoire of enduring perceptions, attitudes, thoughts, and behaviors. The relative permanence of learning and memory reflects the operation of processes that modify the microscopic structure of the brain, yielding changes in different aspects of functioning over time as a result of the individual's interactions with the world.[78]

In short, we are always in the process of becoming, and this "becoming" is encoded in our brains by means of synaptic activity as both nature and nurture yield the same effect, namely, sculpting the brain (and thus shaping the mind) in ways that form and reform the developing self.

Conceptual Patterns

This is not to say that humans fit the profile of the proverbial wax nose, twisting this way or that with every influence. Predisposed genetically to respond in certain ways and shaped as we are in relation to our environments

77. See further Huttenlocher, *Neural Plasticity*.
78. Grigsby and Stevens, *Neurodynamics of Personality*, 39.

over time, we develop patterns for making sense of the world and patterns of response that bias our dispositions and behaviors at a basic level. We are hardwired, for example, to respond at a preconscious level to fearful stimuli like the sight of a snake or anything that at first glance looks like a snake. We develop neural equipment with a greater capacity to recognize faces belonging to our own "clan," a bias that expresses itself in modern life by the relative ease with which we differentiate the facial features of persons who share our ethnicity as opposed to the difficulty we might experience when trying to differentiate the facial features of other ethnic groups.[79] Our neural systems are "wired" in relation to environmental experiences for a lifetime of conceptualizing our worlds and responding to them.

Borrowing a principle from the neuropsychologist Donald Hebb, known as Hebb's rule, we know that *neurons that fire together wire together*—with the result that, over time, our brains make connections on the basis of which we make sense of the present and predict the future in light of past experience. And in cases where we experience a deficit of incoming sensory data necessary for an unambiguous interpretation of the object of our perception, we "fill in" on the basis of what we expect. Our inferences about life, then, are biased by what we take to be probable or possible. This explains why we find a human face in the full moon, recognize dogs and rabbits in cloud formations, see words rather than individual letters when we read, generally apply old paradigms in new contexts, or prejudicially categorize people by any number of criteria (e.g., accent, hair color, gender, race, or the condition or color of their teeth).[80]

Daniel J. Siegel writes of the coercive power of ingrained brain states as they impinge on human responses.[81] He uses the term "enslavement" to describe large-scale dynamics established by earlier experience and embedded in beliefs in the form of patterns of judgments about good and bad, right and wrong. This is not all bad, he notes. "We must make summations, create generalizations, and initiate behaviors based on a limited sampling of incoming data that have been shunted through the filters of these mental models. Our learning brains seek to find the similarities and differences, draw conclusions, and act."[82] However, the consequence can be an internalized set of "shoulds" that can be destructive of personal well-being and human community. As an antidote, he

79. The neural correlates of this long-observed phenomenon have been explored in Vizioli et al., "Neural Repetition Suppression."

80. See, e.g., Susa et al., "Recognition of Own- and Other-Race Faces"; Kinzler et al., "Accent Trumps Race."

81. Siegel, *Mindful Brain*.

82. Ibid., 135.

offers reflective thinking, mindful learning, and mindful awareness—that is, a reconfiguration of neuronal processes through conditional learning.

Various terms name the structures by which we "fill in"—"imagination," for example, that is, "a basic image-schematic capacity for ordering our experience."[83] Another is "conceptual schemes": patterns that are at once conceptual (a way of seeing things), communal (a set of beliefs and values to which a group and its members are deeply attached), and conative (action generating).[84] To put it differently, in order to make life events meaningful, we must conceptualize them, and in doing so we make use of already-established neural pathways in the service of imaginative structures or conceptual schemes that we implicitly take to be true, normal, and good.

Our neurohermeneutical equipment, then, is formed at the synaptic level, is capable of reformation, and is even now providing the conceptual schemes or imaginative structures by which we make sense of the world around us. My perception of the world is based on a network of ever-forming assumptions about my environment and on a series of well-tested assumptions, shared by others with whom I associate, about "the way the world works."

Antonio Damasio's reflections on the nature of belief gain traction in this context. For him, "belief" refers to the attribution of truth value to a particular datum: "As I see it, to believe is to qualify a perception or recollection as true, false, or something in between. . . . The believer is confident of the qualification. Belief belongs in the same family of meanings as conviction and certainty." In this reckoning, as with human experience more generally, the difference between belief and religious belief is an interpretive one. The neurobiology of belief is the same either way. Damasio goes on to observe, though, that we come to hold beliefs even in the absence of all the relevant data that might be useful to support that belief. "In fact, even on occasions in which we have relevant facts potentially available, we nonetheless shortcut to the concluding belief without coactivating the facts, let alone operating logically on them. . . . Our neural and cognitive systems allow us to jump to a conclusion or even to an action without relying on intervening cognitive steps."[85] Accordingly, belief helps us to structure how, at a preconcious level, we make sense of the world as well as animates our characteristic behavior in the world.

We have thus underscored the neurobiological correlates of moral formation and transformation, together with our growing awareness that a person's

83. M. Johnson, *Body in the Mind*, xx.
84. See Flanagan, *Problem of the Soul*, 27–55.
85. Damasio, "Thinking about Belief," 326–27.

understanding of and responses in the world follow those well-worn grooves in his or her moral cognition. Accordingly, ongoing behavioral change is the correlate of character transformation. The kind of change entailed by conversion, then, necessarily involves bodily existence centered on a change of dispositions and behavior. From a cognitive perspective, this change is facilitated through relational interaction and engagement in the practices of one's group of reference. Put sharply, conversion involves human biological metamorphosis, transformations at the level of neural networks.

Conclusion

From a cognitive perspective, all of human life is really embodied life—bodily life nested in a web of relationships. This is true of all sorts of human capacities and experiences, including those we might understand in specifically religious terms. This raises questions immediately about some of the dichotomies that might guide study of conversion. Is conversion a moral or a cognitive phenomenon? Is conversion an internal experience or an external one? Simply put, such questions might make sense in a modern era governed by a Cartesian segregation of mind and body but have little purchase once the essentially embodied character of the mind is recognized and taken seriously. The evidence we have surveyed in this chapter presses our categories in this direction even in the case of religious conversion. From this perspective, there can be no conversion that is not conversion of the self, understood in relationally extended, embodied, holistic terms.

The question remains whether this emphasis on embodiment is at home within the Lukan narrative, and particularly with Luke's portrayal of conversion. In what follows, I will demonstrate that this is indeed the case, not because the third evangelist was a cognitive scientist born out of time, but because his conceptual patterns held together what subsequent portraits of human nature (especially those influenced by René Descartes in the modern West) have pulled apart.

3

✻

Orienting Conversion

Conversion constitutes a central motif for Luke's theology—this is widely recognized. From this common observation arises a host of questions about how best to understand the contours of Luke's theology of conversion. What approach shall we take? What does conversion look like? I have already begun to insist that *embodiment* is key, so it is crucial that I begin to make good on this proposal by means of detailed engagement with the Lukan narrative itself. Accordingly, my primary concern in this chapter is an analysis of Luke 3:1–14. This text provides the staging point where we find a basic orientation to conversion or repentance and from which we may launch into further explorations of Lukan material. But before moving more directly into a discussion of conversion as this first opens up for Luke's readers in Luke 3:1–14, two more overarching issues require attention.

Preliminary Considerations: Patterns and Lexemes

Patterns of Conversion in Luke-Acts

Previous studies of conversion in Luke's narrative have either assumed or attempted to identify patterns in Luke's conversion accounts. For Luke's

Gospel, for example, Méndez-Moratalla claims to have identified a conversion paradigm:[1]

- divine initiative, especially among the marginal
- conflict or polarized responses to God's plan
- the universal need for a response of repentance
- the expression of repentance in the proper use of possessions
- the offer of forgiveness (sometimes expressed in joy and table fellowship)
- a climactic statement regarding the nature of Jesus's ministry

Working first with ancient conversion stories and then turning to the Acts of the Apostles, Talbert thinks in terms of a consistent form:[2]

- context
- catalyst leading to conversion
- obstacles to conversion
- the conversion itself
- postconversion confirmation of the authenticity of the conversion

Focusing in particular on household conversion narratives, David Matson recognizes a household evangelism taxonomy.[3] For him, this Lukan type scene consists of three parts:

- entering homes of economically established householders
- proclaiming the message of salvation
- remaining in those homes in order to join in table fellowship

Dennis Hamm finds parallels among three Lukan texts that for him identify a conversion story (Luke 5:27–32; 15:1–32; 19:1–10):[4]

- table fellowship
- murmuring against Jesus's behavior
- Jesus's defense

---

1. Méndez-Moratalla, *Paradigm of Conversion*.
2. Talbert, "Conversion in the Acts of the Apostles," 135n2. He refers to Acts 2:1–47; 3:1–4:37; 8:4–25, 26–40; 9:1–22; 10:1–48; 13:13–52; 16:11–15, 25–34.
3. Matson, *Household Conversion Narratives in Acts*.
4. Hamm, "Luke 19:8 Once Again," 436–37.

- images of salvation
- rejoicing

Other examples could be given as well, though already the differences among these attempts at identifying a conversion "form" in Luke's narrative are telling. Will the real Lukan conversion paradigm show itself?

Such attempts to classify and order Luke's material on conversion face three immediate obstacles. First, strangely, with one exception, none demonstrates how the whole of Luke-Acts might fare in terms of this pattern-seeking agenda. Even among scholars who are ready to affirm the unity of Luke-Acts, these patterns are exclusive to a single "half" of the Lukan narrative, either Luke's Gospel or the Acts of the Apostles. The one exception is Matson's study, since he derives the pattern first from Jesus's instruction to the seventy-two in Luke 10:5–7, shows how Jesus exemplifies the pattern in his encounter with Zacchaeus (19:1–10), and then traces how the pattern is implemented in the household conversion stories of Cornelius (Acts 10:1–11:18), Lydia (16:11–15), the Roman jailer (16:25–34), and Crispus (18:1–11). This is less an exception than it might seem, however, since Matson has not attempted to find a pattern for conversion stories more generally, but only for household conversions.

Second, at junctures, some of these attempts seem more deductive than inductive, with the result that they raise the question of whether Luke evidences such a pattern or whether the Lukan data have been pressed into a preformed mold. This is especially problematic in the case of Méndez-Moratalla's study, where aspects of the pattern are sometimes at best implicit. But even the rather minimal taxonomy that Matson has identified raises questions of this kind. For example, in the absence of explicit textual evidence documenting Jesus's proclamation of a salvific message of peace to Zacchaeus and his household (Luke 19:1–10), Matson can only urge that this must have been the case. To come at this issue from another vantage point, we cannot overlook the fact that prior decisions to interpret an episode as a conversion account have guided some of this pattern making. Again, Méndez-Moratalla's work is illustrative, since his exegetical examination of accounts of conversion in the Gospel of Luke includes an obvious choice like the conversion of Levi (5:27–32) but also a text in which the demands of repentance are highlighted (3:1–17) but no conversion(s) is actually recounted, as well as some accounts that are less obviously conversionary (e.g., 7:36–50; 19:1–10; 23:39–43).

The third difficulty arises from the presence of dueling patterns. Depending on the lens adopted, different patterns will emerge. For example, we might refer to a small series of Lukan stories as "potential conversions." They are "potential" since Jesus sets before certain audiences the possibility of a change of heart and life, but Luke's narrative accounts come to premature conclusions before the stories are finished. For example, we might say that Jesus sets before Simon the Pharisee the opportunity to align himself with the woman from the city who demonstrated great love in her hospitality toward Jesus, but the story comes to an end before we hear Simon's response (7:36–50). Similarly, Jesus invites Pharisees and scribes concerned about his comportment with tax collectors and sinners to adopt a heavenly perspective and join in celebrating the finding of the lost, but we are not told how they respond (chap. 15). Again, a rich ruler is saddened when Jesus counsels him to sell everything he has and to distribute the proceeds to the poor in order to gain heavenly treasure, but we do not learn from Luke's account whether the rich ruler followed or refused this directive (18:19–23).

Similarly, we might classify some texts as accounts of "prior conversions." I have in mind those episodes in which people within Luke's narrative behave as people who have already aligned themselves with God's kingdom, who respond as persons who seem to have the status of an "insider" to God's kingdom, but whose conversion (apparently) lies outside Luke's narrative. When and on what basis were the sins of the woman from the city forgiven (7:36–50)? Luke's account picks up the story of her relationship to Jesus at midpoint, so to speak; that is, the woman's hospitality toward Jesus and Jesus's words regarding the woman logically presuppose an encounter to which Luke has not given his readers access. How does one of the criminals crucified with Jesus exercise correct insight into Jesus's innocence and his relationship to the kingdom, such that Jesus promises him a place with him in paradise (23:40–43)? Luke says nothing of the criminal's conversion, suggesting that he, like the woman from the city, occupies the margins of conventional society yet has (already) aligned himself with Jesus. But this is presupposed, not recounted, by the account Luke gives us. Depending on how we understand 19:1–10, the same could be said of Zacchaeus, who is regarded by some onlookers as a "sinner" but whose characteristic behavior qualifies as the "fruit of repentance," according to criteria set forth earlier in Luke's Gospel (3:8, 11–13). According to this reading, we simply do not know when Zacchaeus ordered his life thus in relation to God's kingdom; rather, as was the case with the woman from the city, we pick up the story in midstream. Likewise, how are we to understand Jesus's apparent expectation that the seventy-two sent to extend Jesus's ministry of proclaiming the kingdom and healing the sick will encounter people who (already!) share God's peace (10:5–6)? "Son of peace" (υἰὸς εἰρήνης, *huios eirēnēs*) could refer to someone predisposed to welcome both the messengers and the message of salvation, but it could also signify someone whose life is already characterized by the salvific message carried by Jesus's emissaries.[5] Is this the beginning of a conversion account, or is it an instance, such as we read of the centurion in 7:1–10, where, through means unknown to readers of Luke's narrative, there are those who already embody faithful beliefs and practices consistent with Jesus's message?

Taken together, these considerations underscore the wisdom of Gaventa's position, that Luke's approach to conversion is not really conducive to contemporary concerns with technique or taxonomy.[6] Indeed, if we want to consider Luke's perspective on repentance and conversion, our gaze must include but cannot be narrowly focused on so-called conversion accounts. This is because of the difficulty that resides in predetermining what constitutes such an account. To this we should add that the use of the typical terms for repentance and conversion extends far beyond conversion accounts. Moreover, the relevant evidence extends beyond even the use of particular terms like μετάνοια (*metanoia*, "repentance"), μετανοέω (*metanoeō*, "to change one's course"), ἐπιστροφή (*epistrophē*, "a turning [toward]"), or ἐπιστρέφω (*epistrephō*, "to turn around"). Luke's perspective on conversion may be anchored by such terms but reaches beyond them so as to permeate his narrative.

It is true that searching for type scenes and step-by-step conversion processes can lead to useful ways of organizing the evidence Luke provides. However, these attempts at finding order are costly in terms of their tendency to accord privilege to some data while turning a blind eye to others. My own point of departure will be the first extended discussion of repentance or conversion in the Lukan narrative, namely, Luke 3:1–14. This will set the stage for tracing significant motifs (though not patterns) Luke develops elsewhere.

Repentance or Conversion?

Thus far, I have used the terms "repentance" and "conversion" interchangeably, a practice that flies in the face of the view of some, that conversion constitutes (only) a crossing of religious boundaries. According to this view, repentance would be expected of the Jewish people, conversion of gentiles.[7] Is this a viable distinction?

Some evidence, especially within the speeches of Acts, might initially support this view. Peter and Paul call their Jewish audiences not to serve a new

---

5. On this expression, see Klassen, "'Child of Peace'"; Wolter, *Das Lukasevangelium*, 379. For the view that Jesus refers to those who are ready to receive salvation, see, e.g., Fitzmyer, *Gospel according to Luke*, 2:848; Marshall, *Gospel of Luke*, 420.

6. Gaventa, *From Darkness to Light*.

7. See Nave, *Repentance in Luke-Acts*.

God but to return to the God of their ancestors.[8] As Odil Steck has shown, prophetic speeches that call Israel to repentance follow a well-established tradition in Israel's Scriptures and the literature of Second Temple Judaism,[9] and the preaching of Peter and Paul among Jewish audiences in Acts shares similar emphases.[10] Conversely, in those situations in which Paul addresses specifically gentile audiences, he refers to "the living God" (as opposed to worthless idols; Acts 14:15) and proclaims that this God "commands everyone everywhere to repent" (17:30). At Lystra and Athens, that is, Paul's concerns are more narrowly theological, focused as they are on God's character and activity, while among Jews, one might argue, both Peter's and Paul's addresses are more christologically inspired. For Jews, the needed response is a reorientation toward the God of Israel and his purposes, manifest in Jesus Christ. For gentiles, the needed response is a departure from idolatry in order to join the people of the God who raised Jesus from the dead.

As helpful as such a distinction might be, though, it is not without its problems. From a cognitive perspective, it is probably unsustainable.[11] At the level of neuronal processes, the one metamorphosis is unlikely to be qualitatively different from the other. This is only to be expected, of course, since, as we noted in chap. 2, how best to construe the religious significance of an experience is left to interpretive communities and not to brain scans. More importantly, Luke's terminological preferences provide no support for this distinction. Μετάνοια/μετανοέω (*metanoia/metanoeō*) is used with reference to the responses of both Jews (e.g., Luke 3:3, 8; Acts 5:31) and gentiles (e.g., Luke 24:47; Acts 11:18). Μετάνοια/μετανοέω is used interchangeably with ἐπιστροφή/ἐπιστρέφω (*epistrophē/epistrephō*) in Luke 17:3–4 as well as in a clear reference to Jewish response in Acts 3:19. And ἐπιστροφή/ἐπιστρέφω is used of Jews in Acts 9:35; 28:27 but of gentiles in 14:15; 15:3, 19. Clearly, Luke does not reserve one set of terms for Jewish people, another for gentiles.

On other grounds, too, the distinction between repentance and conversion proves to be wrongheaded as a way of making sense of Luke's perspective. Thus, in addition to (1) terminological considerations, (2) many gentiles within the narrative of Acts need no conversion to the God of Israel per se but, like the exemplary Cornelius (10:1–4), already worship this God. Such gentiles are so prevalent in Acts that Jacob Jervell exaggerates only a little when he

---

8. See Acts 2:38; 3:17–20; 5:31; 13:38–41. Martin Dibelius observes that the exhortation to repentance is stereotypical in the speeches of Acts ("Speeches in Acts," 165); cf. Pokorný, *Theologie der lukanischen Schriften*, 122–24.

9. Steck, *Israel*. See, e.g., Jer. 3:12–16; 7:3–25; 14:6–7; Ezek. 18:30; Zech. 1:3; 7:8–10; Mal. 3:7.

10. See Bayer, "Preaching of Peter," 262–65.

11. I say "probably" because this has not been experimentally demonstrated.

insists that, for Luke, gentile God-fearers and Jews constitute the church—
that, in the narrative of Acts, apart from gentile God-fearers, gentiles do not
convert.[12] Accordingly, gentile conversion in Acts is less movement from one
religious affiliation to another and more movement more deeply into faith
commitments already embraced.

(3) What is more, gentiles and Jews share the same status as recipients of
the gift of repentance. As the apostles and other Christ-followers in Jerusalem
announce, "Therefore, God has given even to the gentiles the repentance
[μετάνοια, *metanoia*] that leads to life" (11:18), a claim that parallels Peter's
pronouncement regarding Jesus, that "God exalted him at his right hand as
Leader and Savior that he might give repentance [μετάνοια, *metanoia*] to
Israel" (5:31).

(4) In Israel's Scriptures, a major component of conversion among God's
people is movement away from idolatry.[13] David Pao underscores the degree to
which an anti-idolatry polemic is integral to Isaiah's vision of a new exodus
(Isa. 40–55) and, then, to the narrative of Acts.[14] This is true, as one might
anticipate, in the case of Paul and Barnabas's words among the inhabitants
of Lystra (Acts 14:15–17) and with respect to Paul's speech on the Areopagus (17:24–31), that is, among gentiles. However, polemic against idolatry
in Acts extends also to the Jewish people. Thus, Stephen's selective rehearsal
of Israel's history reaches its climax as it casts the Jerusalem leadership as
idolaters and the temple they hold in their clutches as the center of idolatry
(cf. 7:48–50; 17:24–25).[15]

(5) When Paul recounts before Agrippa the circumstances and nature of his
commission, he proclaims that Jesus rescued Paul from Paul's own people, the
Jews, as well as the gentiles, and gave him this charge: "to open their eyes so
that they might turn [ἐπιστρέφω, *epistrephō*] from darkness to light and from
the power of Satan to God" (26:17–18). The metaphor of movement from
darkness is used elsewhere in Second Temple literature of religious conversion,[16]
though in this case, Paul's words situate that metaphor in relation to a cosmic
battle of competing kingdoms. Importantly, according to this text, gentiles
and Jews alike need deliverance from darkness (cf. Luke 1:78–79).[17] As Paul

12. E.g., Jervell, "Church of Jews and Godfearers"; Jervell, *Theology of the Acts of the
Apostles*.
13. This is observed by C. Wright, "Implications of Conversion," 15, 18.
14. Pao, *Isaianic New Exodus*, 181–216.
15. See Green, "'They Made a Calf.'"
16. E.g., Isa. 42:7, 16; *Jos. Asen.* 8.10; 15.12; Luke 2:32; Eph. 5:8; Col. 1:12–13; 1 Thess.
5:4–7; 1 Pet. 2:9. See also Hamm, "Sight to the Blind."
17. Some scholars (e.g., L. Johnson, *Acts*, 436–37) take Luke's εἰς οὕς (*eis hous*, "to whom")
as a reference to the gentiles alone, but a Pauline mission inclusive of gentiles and Jews is

goes on to observe, obedience to the heavenly vision entailed declaring "first to those in Damascus, then in Jerusalem and throughout the region of Judea, and also to the gentiles, that they should repent [μετανοέω, *metanoeō*] and turn [ἐπιστρέφω, *epistrephō*] to God and behave in ways consistent with repentance [μετάνοια, *metanoia*]" (Acts 26:19–20). The same response is expected of Jew and gentile alike.[18]

(6) Finally, we should note that in Israel's Scriptures the call to radical and ongoing conversion is addressed above all to God's people. They may serve as agents for the conversion of others, but they themselves have a continuous need for conversion.[19] This is an important point on which Nave's study requires correction. He rejects a connection between the use of the term for repentance in Israel's Scriptures (שׁוּב, *šûb*, "to turn back") and Luke's understanding of repentance. The result is a useful emphasis on Greco-Roman background, which overturns earlier scholarly allegations about the uniqueness of the concept of conversion in Lukan or early Christian usage. But this view fails to recognize that the relevant terms—שׁוּב (*šûb*), the *niphal* form of נָחַם (*niham*, "to be sorry," "to relent"), μετανόεω/μετάνοια (*metanoeō/metanoia*), and -στρεφω (*strephō*, "turn") verbs—overlap in their usage. It is true that the LXX does not translate שׁוּב (*šûb*) with μετανόεω/μετάνοια (*metanoeō/metanoia*), but this is likely due both to the relatively infrequent usage of these Greek terms in classical Greek and to the general sense of "mind" or "reason" signaled by the terms μετανόεω/μετάνοια (*metanoeō/metanoia*), as opposed to the directional sense of the term שׁוּב (*šûb*).[20] Nave thus vacates Luke's concept of its covenantal basis in Yahweh's initiative and call, and problematically so.[21]

In short, it will not do to drive a wedge between the two terms, "repentance" and "conversion," and I will use them interchangeably.[22] This does not mean

---

supported by the Isaianic echoes and by Luke 1:78–79; 2:32; Acts 9:15; 26:20, 23; cf. Jervell, *Apostelgeschichte*, 594; Fitzmyer, *Acts*, 759–60.

18. This is emphasized in Stenschke, *Luke's Portrait of Gentiles*; Méndez-Moratalla, *Paradigm of Conversion*.

19. This is emphasized by C. Wright, "Implications of Conversion"; see also Walls, "Converts or Proselytes?," 3.

20. Graupner and Fabry, "שׁוּב" (on the LXX, see 514). The LXX generally uses -στρεφω to translate שׁוּב (*šûb*) and μετανόεω (*metanoeō*) to translate נָחַם (*niham*). However, note, e.g., the terms used to refer to Nineveh's "turning": μετανόεω (*metanoeō*) in Luke 11:32; and, in Jon. 3:8, 10, שׁוּב (*šûb*) in the MT and ἀποστρέφω (*apostrephō*) in the LXX. See the summary comments in Lunde, "Repentance," 669.

21. Kim-Rauchholz (*Umkehr bei Lukas*, 8–38) concludes that the background of conversion in Luke-Acts derives especially from the OT (and especially prophetic) use of שׁוּב (*šûb*). This motif is emphasized by Ravens, *Luke and the Restoration of Israel*, 139–69; Pao, *Isaianic New Exodus*, e.g., 118–20, 138–40.

22. See the similar conclusion in Böhlemann, *Jesus und der Täufer*, 97–99.

that we cannot or should not distinguish between what conversion might entail for Jewish people and what it might entail for gentiles. It only means that this difference is not easily lexicalized and certainly is not tethered to particular terms drawn from Luke's dictionary. Moving from one religious affiliation to another or transformations in one's understanding and embodiment of one's long-held religious commitments—both fall under the heading of "conversion."

Luke 3:1–14: Restoration and Repentance

Luke 3:1–14 is rife with images of embodied transformation. These include the setting within which transformation is proclaimed and enacted, the metaphors by which Luke (drawing especially on Isaiah) articulates the nature of transformation, baptism as the signifying practice of transformation, and the behaviors by which transformation is enacted and displayed.

Orientation

With its prominent geopolitical and chronological markers, Luke 3:1–2 signals a fresh beginning in the Lukan narrative. After recounting the births and summarizing the childhoods of John and Jesus, Luke moves John onto center stage, sketching the character of his prophetic ministry in preparation of Jesus's public ministry (3:1–20). We are concerned especially with John's ministry of renewal and transformation, which comes into focus in the précis Luke provides of John's ministry: "He went throughout the region of the Jordan, declaring a repentance-baptism for the forgiveness of sins" (3:3); in words descriptive of John's work, borrowed from Isaiah: "Prepare the way for the Lord; straighten his paths" (3:4; cf. Isa. 40:3); in John's words to the crowds, "produce fruit that demonstrates repentance" (3:8); and in John's spelling out for the crowds behaviors that would in fact demonstrate repentance (3:10–14).

The importance of this repeated emphasis on repentance-baptism in relation to John's ministry is underscored by the way it is woven into the fabric of the narrative of Luke-Acts.[23] Thus, in the third Gospel:

- The job description given John even before he is conceived is that "he will turn [ἐπιστρέφω, epistrephō] many of the people of Israel back to the Lord their God. With the spirit and power of Elijah, he will go before him, to turn [ἐπιστρέφω, epistrephō] the hearts of fathers back to their

23. Cf. Luke's repeated use of Isa. 40:3–5; see Snodgrass, "Streams of Tradition," 36–40; Pao, *Isaianic New Exodus*, 40.

children and the disobedient back to righteous patterns of thinking, to prepare a people ready for the Lord" (1:16–17).

- Zechariah, his father, underscores the nature of John's anticipated ministry when he pronounces that John "will go before the Lord to prepare his ways" (1:76).

- Twice in Luke's Gospel, the character of John's work is summarized with reference to John's baptism—in a narrative aside that takes accepting John's baptism as the measure by which people embrace (or refuse) God's ways (7:29–30)[24] and in a dispute about whether John's prophetic ministry originated with God (20:3–7).

In the Acts of the Apostles:

- References to John's baptism occur in 1:5, 22; 10:37; 11:16–18; 13:24–25; 18:24–26; 19:1–7.

- With language that mirrors what we find in Luke 3:3, John's baptism is characterized as a "repentance-baptism" in Acts 13:24; 19:4—in geographical regions far removed from the region encompassing the Jordan River (Antioch in Pisidia, Ephesus).

Moreover, just as the ingredients of John's ministry—proclamation, repentance, and forgiveness—come to expression centrally in John's baptism, so also are these motifs interrelated in the work of the missionaries in Acts.

Structure and Setting: Conversion and the Turn of the Ages

Key to grasping the significance of the introduction to John's mission in Luke 3:1–6 is the structure of this pericope and particularly the way Luke has set in parallel both sociopolitical (vv. 1–2) and redemptive-historical (vv. 4–6) contexts. These two are mutually interpretive, and together they provide the frame for our viewing of Luke's summary depiction of John's ministry in 3:3 (see diagram).

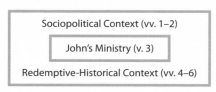

24. How to read ἐδικαίωσαν τὸν θεόν (*edikaiōsan ton theon*) in Luke 7:29 is controverted. My reading assumes that v. 29, the response of the tax collectors, is set in apposition to the response of the Pharisees and legal experts in v. 30: "they rejected God's purpose for themselves." These valuations find their focus in whether people undergo John's baptism.

Verses 1–2 provide geopolitical markers reminiscent of Greco-Roman historiographers, as well as OT figures—national leaders and especially prophets.[25] If Luke's primary agenda in vv. 1–2 had been to provide us with a precise dating for the onset of John's ministry, then he has not been very successful. This is because the collocation of rulers he mentions supports only a rough estimation, a situation helped only a little by the apparently specific reference to "the fifteenth year of the rule of Tiberius Caesar" (v. 1). Since Tiberius was coemperor with Augustus for two years, from 12 CE, the beginning of Tiberius's reign might be dated as early as 12 CE or as late as 14 CE, after Augustus's death. (These dates assume the calendar introduced by Julius Caesar in the mid-first century BCE.) The consequent range of years for dating the beginning of John's ministry would be sometime between 27 and 29 CE. From a calendrical viewpoint, we gain nothing further from Luke's references to Pilate or Herod, or even to Annas and Caiaphas. This raises suspicions against the view that 3:1–2 was written *primarily* to locate John's ministry on the calendar. Rather, Luke uses this list of rulers in order to situate John's prophetic appearance in a particular sociopolitical setting.[26]

Whatever else it does, v. 1 provides a stark reminder of the situation in which Israel finds itself: under foreign rule. And given the judgment on the powerful and wealthy portended in Mary's song earlier in the Lukan narrative (1:52–53), it is surely damning that the temple dynasty represented by Annas and Caiaphas (v. 2a) receives mention in the same breath with Rome's emperor and appointed rulers. This narrative assessment coheres with the political power exercised historically by the high priesthood until the Roman era and, during the Roman era, with the twin facts that the Romans appointed and dismissed high priests (who, then, served at the behest of the Romans) and that high priests continued to preside over the nation's civil affairs.[27] The scene John enters is an oppressive, top-heavy one. Nevertheless, he does so as God's representative, God's prophet. It is to him—not rulers, nor even ruling priests—that God's word comes. And he is in the wilderness, not the urban centers of the civilized world where an emperor or a governor might make his home.

25. Greco-Roman historiography: e.g., Thucydides 2.2; Polybius 1.3; Josephus, *Ant.* 18.106. OT national leaders: e.g., Isa. 1:1; Amos 1:1. OT prophets: e.g., Jer. 1:1–4; Ezek. 1:1–3; Hosea 1:1; Joel 1:1; Jon. 1:1; Mic. 1:1; Zeph. 1:1; Hag. 1:1; Zech. 1:1.

26. The emphasis here is on "prophetic setting"; that is, although, like Greek and Roman historiographers, Luke situates his story in world history, he is closer to Israel's Scriptures in his emphasis on what God is doing in this world. See Marguerat, *First Christian Historian*, 1–25; Yamazaki-Ransom, *Roman Empire*, 74–78.

27. See Schürer, *History of the Jewish People*, 2:227–28, 230.

Intimations of what is to come are found in Luke's reference in v. 2b to John's presence "in the wilderness." Luke thus recalls John's wilderness location in 1:80 ("in the wilderness"),[28] a geographical note that might suggest that, with the onset of his ministry, John would have *departed* the wilderness. Thus it reads in the NRSV, "he was in the wilderness until the day he appeared publicly to Israel." Similarly, one might imagine that, in 3:3a, John departed "the wilderness" before going throughout the region of the Jordan River. This reading seems pivotal to Michael Fuller's thesis that, for Luke, "wilderness" is a metaphor for Israel's sinful and exilic situation, requiring that John exit the wilderness at the outset of his ministry.[29] But this reading is problematic in that it actually seems important to Luke that John exercised his prophetic commission "in the wilderness" (3:4). Moreover, when people came out to see the prophet John, they did so by going "into the wilderness" (7:24). The preposition ἕως (*heōs*) in 1:80 could signify that John was in the wilderness "until" his public ministry (and not thereafter), but it need not do so. Indeed, 1:80 need not be read as saying anything about John's whereabouts after he appeared publicly to Israel. Similarly, the phrase "he went" in v. 3 does not signify John's departure from the wilderness, but his traffic in the vicinity of the Jordan River. In other words, throughout his ministry, John is located in a space, the wilderness, symbolically related to Israel's formative experience of exodus.

This persistent connection of John with the wilderness is important for the association of this prophet with earlier, exuberant visions of God's intervention *in* the wilderness to lead a second exodus *through* the wilderness. Consider, for example, these words from Isaiah, which explicitly tie expectations of deliverance from Babylon to memories of Israel's formation as a people and liberation from Egypt:

> Thus says the LORD,
>   your Redeemer, the Holy One of Israel:
> For your sake I will send to Babylon
>   and break down all the bars,
>   and the shouting of the Chaldeans will be turned to lamentation.
> I am the LORD, your Holy One,
>   the Creator of Israel, your King.
> Thus says the LORD,
>   who makes a way in the sea,
>   a path in the mighty waters,

28. Luke 3:2: ἐν τῇ ἐρήμῳ (*en tē erēmō*); 1:80: ἐν ταῖς ἐρήμοις (*en tais erēmois*).

29. Fuller, *Restoration of Israel*, esp. 222–23. "Luke's most important means of describing Israel's continual exile is his characterization of Israel as a 'wilderness' (ἔρημος)," he writes (211), but where in Luke-Acts is Israel thus designated?

> who brings out chariot and horse, army and warrior;
>> they lie down, they cannot rise, they are extinguished, quenched
>>> like a wick:
> Do not remember the former things,
>> or consider the things of old.
> I am about to do a new thing;
>> now it springs forth, do you not perceive it?
> I will make a way in the wilderness
>> and rivers in the desert.
> The wild animals will honor me,
>> the jackals and the ostriches;
> for I give water in the wilderness,
>> rivers in the desert,
> to give drink to my chosen people,
>> the people whom I formed for myself
> so that they might declare my praise. (Isa. 43:14–21)

God may be about "to do a new thing," as Isaiah puts it, but at key, recognizable points, this new thing resembles the old—including making Israel a people, Israel's sea crossing and the chaotic destruction of Israel's enemies, and divine protection and provision in the wilderness (cf. Exod. 15; 17; 19). Similarly, imagining the return from exile as a new exodus, Isaiah has it that God provides for his people in the wilderness just as he did before (e.g., Isa. 48:20–21; cf. Exod. 17:1–7). In such ways as these, restoration from exile recapitulates exodus from Egyptian slavery. The wilderness was to become the site of rejoicing, the land would be fertile and the people safe from wild animals, and God's people restored would see the Lord's glory (e.g., Isa. 35; Ezek. 20:33–44; Hosea 2:14–23). These and related texts ground wilderness thematically in expectations of restoration from exile.[30]

"Wilderness" could signify rebellion, danger, testing, and punishment, to be sure,[31] but this is hardly the only option. Philo clearly states what could be implicit in Luke, namely, that "wilderness" is the antithesis of "city," the latter characterized by distractions and corruption that make withdrawal to the wilderness a prerequisite to purification and new life (see Philo, *Decalogue* 10–11). John is made a prophet in the wilderness, and he conducts his ministry in the wilderness; the crowds encounter him in the wilderness and in the wilderness hear his message of transformation. As in Philo, might it be in Luke that cleansing and purification are unimaginable unless people

---

30. See Mauser, *Christ in the Wilderness*, 44–58; Talmon, "'Desert Motif.'"
31. E.g., Num. 14:32–33; 27:14; Sir. 8:16; 13:19; 1QM 1.3; Heb. 3:7–11.

first remove themselves from the ways of their hometowns? "Wilderness" could also be understood as the venue of divine revelation and action, the locus of God's past deliverance as well as the space within which God would reveal and enact liberation.[32] So profoundly was this the case that the Qumran sectarians made their home in the wilderness,[33] a space that allowed them to pursue a lifestyle marked by religious purity (1QS 8.12–16) and thus to cultivate among themselves a community that embodied the Isaianic call to prepare the way of the Lord.[34] "As they awaited the end, as they prepared the Lord's way, they situated themselves in the very place where God's salvation would become manifest."[35] A similar correlation of the theologically charged notion of wilderness with geophysical space occurs in references in both Josephus and Luke to failed efforts at the prophetic restoration of God's people in the wilderness.[36]

Verses 1–2 locate John on a map, therefore, but not a typical one. In fact, to use Edward Soja's categories, we might say that, thus far, Luke has done little to give us John's geophysical coordinates in terms of Firstspace, that is, with reference to a locale that we might map empirically.[37] We must wait until v. 3 to find him in the region of the Jordan River (though even this gives us little by way of coordinates for pinning John to a map). Instead, initially, Luke has been more adept at describing John's appearance in Secondspace terms, that is, in terms of the cognitive maps by which we might locate John sociopolitically: distant from the halls of both imperial and temple-based processes and decision making, divorced from urban life. But Secondspace quickly gives way to Thirdspace, with its imaginative interpretive possibilities. On the one hand, a Thirdspace perspective is realized in John's presence in the wilderness, that is, apart from the conventions of urban social exchange. As such, the wilderness serves as contra-space—not simply as an expression of the well-known and pervasive dichotomy between city and wilderness, but as a space where patterns of social life characteristic of the *polis* simply have no traction. (Power and privilege have little currency in the wilderness.) Such space is conducive to John's

32. On these three uses of "wilderness" in Second Temple Judaism, see Najman, "Concept of Wilderness"; cf. Schofield, "Wilderness."

33. This self-understanding depends on the Hebrew text of Isa. 40:3, in which a voice announces that the way of the Lord is to be prepared "in the wilderness"; cf. the LXX, which has it instead that the wilderness marks the location of the voice crying out.

34. VanderKam, "Judean Desert"; cf. Snodgrass, "Streams of Tradition," 28–31; Davis, *Name and Way of the Lord*, 78–82.

35. VanderKam, "Judean Desert," 171.

36. See Josephus, *Ant.* 20.97–99, 169–72; *J.W.* 2.259, 261–62; 7.438–39; Acts 21:38.

37. See Soja, *Thirdspace*; and the groundwork laid earlier in Soja, *Postmodern Geographies*.

asceticism (cf. 1:15) and growth in the Spirit (1:80),[38] that is, to his formation as one who, having been "filled with the Holy Spirit even before his birth" (1:15), would "go before the Lord to prepare his ways" (1:76). On the other hand, we have begun to see the degree to which John's wilderness venue participates in a wider discourse regarding Israel's hoped-for liberation. This underscores the theological potency of Luke's geographical markers in vv. 1–2.

These hints regarding the significance of John's wilderness location are like sparks that, when tended, erupt into a blaze in vv. 4–6. This means that Luke introduces his citation from Isa. 40 not as a counter to but as an interpretive correlate of the calendar of rulers in vv. 1–3. John's prophetic ministry is thus contextualized with reference to the exilic situation of God's people. To be more specific, John's prophetic ministry marks the conclusion of exile and so introduces the anticipated restoration. Moreover, the introduction of Isa. 40:3–5 in Luke 3:4–6 certifies that the shape of the events Luke will relate, their significance, while located profoundly in the world of human affairs and of human distribution of power (Luke 3:1–2), is determined by the outworking of God's saving purpose.[39]

Although the use of Isa. 40 with reference to John's ministry is witnessed in all four NT Gospels (Matt. 3:3; Mark 1:1–3; Luke 3:4–6; John 1:23), Luke's citation is the most extensive of the four. The Isaianic material on which he draws is found in the prologue of this new section of the book, in which God announces a new era for his people. Negatively, this is the cessation of exile. Positively, it signals restoration, forgiveness, salvation, the coming of the Lord in strength. Issues concerning the authorship of this section of Isaiah aside, recent scholarship has underscored the thematic coherence of Isa. 40–55,[40] particularly vis-à-vis a constellation of images drawn from Israel's memory of exodus now recast in anticipation of new exodus. Max Turner summarizes this pattern with reference to the following motifs:

a. God calls for a "way" for the Lord to be prepared in the wilderness for his saving activity ([Isa] 40.3–5; 43.19).

b. His advent "with might" as the divine warrior will defeat Israel's oppressors and release the oppressed (40.10–11; 42.13; 51.9–16; 49.9, 24–25).

---

38. According to Bovon, "Πνεύματι ('in spirit') is perhaps intentionally ambiguous, i.e., in his human spirit and in God's Spirit" (*Luke 1*, 77).

39. Ibid., 121; Yamazaki-Ransom, *Roman Empire*, 77.

40. See the brief summary of historical-critical study of Isaianic unity in Childs, *Isaiah*, 289–91.

c. The Lord will lead the glorious procession out of captivity along "the way" through the wilderness, his presence before and after them (52.11–12), through water and fire (43.1–3), and he will shepherd them along the way (40.11).

d. He will sustain them in the wilderness more fully than in the Exodus, ensuring they do not hunger, and providing streams in the desert (41.17–20; 43.19–21; 49.9–10). The very wilderness will be transformed to celebrate the release of God's people (43.19; 49.10–11; 55.12–13).

e. God will pour out his refreshing and restoring Spirit on his people (44.3) so that they own him as their Lord (44.5); he himself will teach them and lead them in "the way" (54.13; 48.17), so opening the eyes of the blind and the ears of the deaf.

f. The final goal of this New Exodus is God's enthronement in a restored Zion/Jerusalem (44.26; 45.13; 54.11–12). The announcement of this "good news" to her is her "comfort," the occasion for her bursting into song to celebrate her salvation (40.1, 9–10; 52.1–10).

g. These things will be accomplished at least in part through a somewhat enigmatic servant figure with "Israel," kingly and prophet-liberator traits.[41]

This constellation of images, most of which are anticipated already in Isa. 40:1–11, serves as the backdrop by which Luke contextualizes John's ministry in Luke 3; indeed, Luke exploits the concerns of Isa. 40 in his presentation of John's mission.

Compared with the quotation of Isa. 40 in the other three NT Gospels, the inclusion of additional material in Luke's extended citation highlights three emphases. First, it sketches what takes place in the wilderness in terms of transposition (or reversal):

> Every ravine shall be filled up,
>   and every mountain and hill be made low,
> And all the crooked ways shall become straight,
>   and the rough place shall become plains. (Isa. 40:4 NETS)

Elsewhere, Luke will interpret such images of transposition in terms of status transformation and ethical comportment (see already 1:52–53; 2:34), and this is how he develops those images in the present context as he shines the

---

41. Turner, *Power from on High*, 246–47. Presumably, the obscurity surrounding the servant figure rests at least in part in the postponement of the new exodus, with the servant replacing Cyrus as Yahweh's agent of liberation. See R. Watts, "Consolation or Confrontation?"

spotlight on what a "people prepared" (1:17) looks like. Second, the Isaianic citation names the consequence of these preparations as salvation (σωτήριον, *sōtērion*), and, third, it extends the scope of this salvation universally (πᾶσα σάρξ, *pasa sarx*, "all flesh" or "all humanity").[42]

Luke's dependence on Isaiah is programmatic for his portrayal of John. This is established primarily by the formulaic phrase "as it was written in the book of the words of the prophet Isaiah" (Luke 3:4a). For Luke, John's mission as this is spelled out in 3:3 must be understood within the framework of Isaiah's pronouncement of restoration. We easily identify the correlations between John's repentance-baptism (v. 3) and the messenger's summons to "prepare the way of the Lord" (v. 4), and between John's proclamation of the forgiveness of sins (v. 3) and the messenger's promise of salvation (v. 4). Pushing harder, a case could be made, too, that the prologue of Isa. 40:1–11 shapes the broad contours of the whole of Luke's précis of John's ministry. In this case, Isa. 40:3–5 would introduce the nature of John's call for conversion (Luke 3:1–14), and the proclamation of good news (εὐαγγελίζομαι, *euange-lizomai*, Isa. 40:9) and the coming of God in strength in Isa. 40:6–11 would stand behind both John's words regarding the coming, powerful one (Luke 3:15–18)[43] and Luke's summary of John's mission as one of "proclaiming good news" (εὐαγγελίζομαι, *euangelizomai*, v. 18).

Against this backdrop, it remains to discuss more fully the metaphor of "the way" Luke introduces with his dependence on Isa. 40 and the nature of John's ministry. Before turning to these issues, though, we should underscore what we have seen thus far, namely, that Luke has situated John's ministry, including his conversionary rhetoric, in a world of earthy expectation. From what we have seen thus far, we should anticipate the fully embodied character

---

42. Compared to the present version of the LXX, Luke's citation lacks phrases from Isa. 40:5a and c ("Then the glory of the Lord shall appear," "because the Lord has spoken," NETS), presumably in order to highlight all the more the climactic phrase in Isa. 40:5b ("and all flesh shall see the salvation of God," NETS).

43. This way of construing the potential influence of Isa. 40:1–11 on Luke 3:1–18 turns on Luke's christological reading of the Isaianic text, in which the LXX phrase εὐθείας ποιεῖτε τὰς τρίβους τοῦ θεοῦ ἡμῶν (*eutheias poieite tas tribous tou theou hēmōn*, "make straight the paths of our God," Isa. 40:3) is transformed in Luke as εὐθείας ποιεῖτε τὰς τρίβους αὐτοῦ (*eutheias poieite tas tribous autou*, "make straight his paths," Luke 3:4), so that the antecedent of αὐτοῦ (*autou*, "his") is the ambiguous κύριος (*kyrios*, "lord"), which identifies the way of the Lord (Jesus) with the way of the Lord (Yahweh). (For incontrovertible references to Jesus as κύριος [*kyrios*] thus far in the Lukan narrative, see 1:43; 2:11. On κύριος [*kyrios*] in 3:4, see Rowe, *Early Narrative Christology*, 70–77.) Similarly, then, the identity of "the Lord [who] comes with strength" (κύριος μετὰ ἰσχύος ἔρχεται, *kyrios meta ischyos erchetai*, Isa. 40:10) would for Luke embrace the one more powerful than John who is coming (ἔρχεται . . . ὁ ἰσχυρότερος, *erchetai . . . ho ischyroteros*, Luke 3:16).

of the conversion and salvation proclaimed by John—which, then, must never be reduced to the realm of the "spiritual" (or "ethereal," "heart," "mental," "soulish," etc.), as though this were somehow separable from either embodied response or embodied experience of divine restoration. How could it be otherwise for a prophet whose proclamation focuses on baptism, manifestly a bodily act?

Conversion as Journey

A disputed issue concerning John's baptism has to do with its origin(s), its etiology. Should we trace its roots in Jewish purification washings, in Jewish proselyte baptism, or in some other background? We return to this question below, but here it is important to recognize that Luke's own clarification comes in the form of the collocation of baptism with "repentance" or "conversion" (μετάνοια, *metanoia*). What kind of baptism? John's is a repentance-baptism. Etymologically, μετανοέω (*metanoeō*) refers to "knowing after," and, early on, took its significance from a change of mind that resulted from this afterthought.[44] This might lead one to think of conversion primarily in terms of a change of mind, that is, an abstract, cognitive act. Such a move would be shortsighted, however. On the one hand, as we observed in chap. 2, "conversion" between philosophies was not simply an exchange of one worldview for another. Conversion could never be reduced to an internal realignment of the intellect but rather signified movement from one way of living to another. This was a transformation of *habitus*, a transformed pattern of life. On the other hand, Luke's own understanding of conversion refuses this sort of reductive approach.

The first time Luke presents John's mission, he invokes a journey frame.[45] The journey frame encompasses the entire process of movement from one place to another and includes a range of constituent features: e.g., a path, a traveler, an itinerary, fellow travelers, mode of transportation, obstacles encountered, starting point and destination, and traveling paraphernalia. The journey frame is integral to a range of common metaphors, such as LOVE IS A JOURNEY or A CAREER IS A JOURNEY, which capitalize on the primary metaphor LIFE IS A JOURNEY.[46] The metaphor LIFE IS A JOURNEY invites correspondences such as the following:

44. MHT 2:318; *TLNT* 2:472.
45. On "frame," see chap. 1 above; also Evans and Green, *Cognitive Linguistics*, 222; cf. Fillmore, "Frame Semantics"; Croft and Cruse, *Cognitive Linguistics*, 7–14.
46. See Lakoff and Turner, *More Than Cool Reason*, 3–6. Cognitive linguists use capital letters to identify conceptual metaphors.

Source Domain: Journey	Target Domain: Patterns of Life
Traveler	Person living a life
Destination	Purpose
Road, way	Means for achieving purpose
Obstacles	Impediments to achieving purpose
Landmark	Metric for measuring progress toward purpose
Crossroad	Choice in life

This chart exemplifies mapping between two conceptual domains. This is important for our larger thesis regarding embodiment since conceptual metaphor theory recognizes that metaphor is not linguistic decoration, as though metaphor were an unnecessary but ornamental or stylistic feature of language, but is actually characteristic of thought itself. Semantic structure mirrors conceptual structure as we conceive the world around us by projecting patterns from one domain of experience in order to structure another domain. The one is a source domain, the other a target domain, and studies have shown that where these two domains are active simultaneously, the two areas of the brain for each are active. Phrases like "She uncovered the truth" or "I am struggling with a problem" recruit bodily actions in relation to abstract concepts, and neuroscientists have demonstrated that phrases like these arise through relatively constant mappings across brain functions. Brain imaging has shown, for example, that when we use auditory-related words, we experience increased blood flow to the areas of our brains implicated in auditory processing; the same is true of sight-related terms or words related to speech, and so on.[47] Hence, conceptual metaphor theory is grounded in the embodiment of the patterns by which we conceptualize the world, which we share with people across cultures, and which drive our responses to the world around us. Essentially all of our abstract and theoretical concepts draw their meaning by mapping to embodied, experiential concepts hardwired in our brains.[48] In this case, I am claiming that Luke portrays conversion in a way that triggers the journey frame. Accordingly, we find that Luke conceptualizes conversion in terms of the metaphor LIFE IS A JOURNEY.

The metaphor LIFE IS A JOURNEY has been studied extensively and has proved to be highly complex. It comprises a number of related metaphors, including STATES ARE LOCATIONS, CHANGE IS MOTION, MEANS

47. Posner and Raichle, *Images of Mind*, 115. On this point more generally, see, e.g., Ramachandran, *Brief Tour*, esp. chap. 4; Feldman, *Molecule to Metaphor*; Gibbs, *Embodiment*, 158–207.
48. Yu, "Metaphor from Body and Culture," 248.

ARE PATHS, DIFFICULTIES ARE OBSTACLES TO PROGRESS, and so on.[49]
How this works out with reference to Luke's account will become clear shortly.

In Luke 1, John's mission and its anticipated outcomes are articulated above
all in terms of movement. Thus, in 1:16 the key verb is ἐπιστρέφω (epistrephō),
"to turn back" or "to return," with the extended sense "to change belief or
course of conduct, with focus on the thing to which one turns" (in this case,
"to the Lord their God").[50] Thus "*He will turn* many of the people of Israel
to the Lord their God" (1:17) functions epexegetically, sketching with three
infinitive clauses how John will accomplish the commission summarized
in v. 16:

> *to go before* him, endowed with the spirit and power of Elijah,
> *to turn* the hearts of fathers to their children, and the disobedient to
>   the wisdom of the righteous,
> *to make ready* a people prepared for the Lord.

Of these three, the first is interesting for the way it articulates John's purpose
in terms of a journey: "to go before." Since the third is related intertextu-
ally to Isa. 40:3–5, cited in Luke 3:4–6, we will return to it shortly. Though
less explicitly, it too is tied to the journey frame: people prepare for travel.
The second is central in terms of identifying the anticipated outcome of
John's mission in journey-related terms: ἐπιστρέφω (epistrephō), "to turn
back" or "to return," with reference first to the hearts of fathers returned to
their children and then to the "disobedient" or "unbelieving"[51] returned "to
righteous patterns of thinking" (CEB). Here, change is cast in directional
terms that assume motion toward an objective. It is worth noting, too, that
ἐπιστρέφω (epistrephō) is explicitly collocated with patterns of thought, thus
denying in Lukan usage an easy distinction between conversion-as-motion
and conversion-as-change-of-mind.

A similar move is found in Luke 3:3–6, where a noticeable consequence of
Luke's use of Isa. 40 is that the language of "repentance" or "conversion"
(now μετάνοια, metanoia) is tied to a reference to "the way [or "road," ὁδός,
hodos] of the Lord" (v. 4), then developed in terms of "paths" (τρίβος, tribos,
v. 4) and "roads" (ὁδός, hodos, v. 5). Here, then, we have the frame, change of
direction, which assumes a turn, a new vector, and continued travel on this
new trajectory. At the same time, Luke's language engages the frame of the

---

49. See Evans and Green, *Cognitive Linguistics*, 299–300.
50. BDAG 382.
51. Ἀπειθής, *apeithēs*, can signify the disobedient or the unbelieving (LSJ 182); cf. Bläser,
"ἀπειθέω."

traveler: someone on a journey, typically planned in advance with a purpose in mind, perhaps accompanied by fellow travelers, and so on. This leads to a consideration of "conversion" in relation to the metaphor CHANGE IS MOTION and the metaphor system LIFE IS A JOURNEY.

An outstanding question is how Luke's dependence on Israel's story, and especially Isaiah's vision of restoration, thickens his description of repentance in Luke 3:3–6. In Israel's story we find both a basic image for portraying the ongoing character of one's life—traveling or journeying, or simply walking—and a strong paradigm identifying the destination of God's people in terms of liberation from oppression and taking up residence in the promised land.

First, with regard to the conventional metaphor, LIVING IS WALKING, we may observe frequent references in Israel's Scriptures to the life of persons and of the nation itself as a "journey" or a "walk." In Israel's Scriptures, "way" (דרך, *drk*) is the most common term for lexicalizing the concept of life, and "walk" (הלך, *hlk*, rendered in the LXX by πορεύομαι [*poreuomai*, "to walk"] in about two-thirds of its fifteen hundred occurrences in the Hebrew Scriptures) is the most common term for "the act or process of living."[52] This usage is hardly surprising among a nomadic people: "they live 'on the move.'"[53] Day-to-day experience provides images for abstract concepts: human life is a journey.

What is more, since the outcome of the journey depends on the manner of the travelers' conduct, "to walk" can refer more broadly to "the process of living according to behavioral norms congruent with a particular goal." Several hundred of the more than fifteen hundred occurrences of the verb carry this metaphorical sense—famously of David, who walks "through the valley of the shadow of death" (Ps. 23:4) or with reference to lives of obedience and disobedience vis-à-vis Yahweh (e.g., Lev. 19:3; 1 Kings 3:3). What does the Lord require "but to do justice, and to love kindness, and to walk [MT: הלך, *hlk*; LXX: πορεύομαι, *poreuomai*] humbly with your God" (Mic. 6:8)?

This metaphor is not limited to Israel's Scriptures, but is also pervasive in early Christianity. For example, Paul articulates the Christian life as a step-by-step affair, that is, as walking (περιπατέω, *peripateō*) "in the Spirit" (Gal. 5:16; cf. Rom. 8:4). "As you have therefore received Christ Jesus the Lord, continue to walk [περιπατέω, *peripateō*] in him" (Col. 2:6, my translation). The Australian NT scholar Robert Banks theorized that, with this metaphor, Paul was dependent not only on precedent in Israel's Scriptures and Second Temple Jewish literature but also on the character of much of

52. Merrill, "הלך," 1032.
53. Helfmeyer, "הלך," 389.

Paul's life as an apostle, his itinerancy. This led Banks to refer to Paul as a walkabout theologian.[54] In Luke's birth account, the evangelist echoes biblical usage when he writes of Zechariah and Elizabeth, "They were both righteous before God, walking [πορεύομαι, *poreuomai*] blamelessly according to all the commandments and regulations of the Lord" (Luke 1:6). Similarly, Luke reports that "the church throughout Judea, Galilee, and Samaria had peace, . . . walking [πορεύομαι, *poreuomai*] in an attitude of reverence for the Lord and equipped with the Holy Spirit's reassurance" (Acts 9:31).

Second, the notion that exodus serves as a paradigm of salvation for God's people pervades Israel's Scriptures and hardly requires much by way of demonstration or development.[55] In the Scriptures, exodus is alive in the memory of God's people not only as a historic event but also as a lens through which to make sense of present experience and as the matrix within which to shape future hopes. In the Psalms, for example, hymns of praise celebrate exodus (e.g., Pss. 66; 68; 105), and psalms of lament appeal to God's mighty act of deliverance (e.g., Pss. 74; 77; 80). The prophets paint Israel's infidelity with patterns taken either from Egypt or from Israel's rebellion in the wilderness, while portraying Yahweh as the liberating God who would restore Israel.

Efforts at casting the hope of Israel as a new exodus reach their high point in Isaiah. In Isa. 40 we find a message centered on the imagery of the highway: "prepare the way," "make straight a highway" for the coming of "our God." Appropriating the language of the exodus from Egypt (e.g., 11:16; 51:9–11; 52:8–15), the prophet envisions a road for the return of the exiles. The return of Yahweh marks the return of his people. Earlier, the prophet had imagined a road through the wilderness:

> A pure way shall be there,
>   and it shall be called a holy way;
> and the unclean shall not pass by there,
>   nor shall be there an unclean way,
> but those who have been dispersed shall walk on it,
>   and they shall not go astray.
> And no lion shall be there,
>   nor shall any of the evil beasts come up on it
> or be found there,
>   but the redeemed shall walk on it. (Isa. 35:8–9 NETS)

---

54. Banks, "'Walking' as a Metaphor of the Christian Life."
55. See, e.g., Larsson, *Bound for Freedom*; R. Watts, "Exodus."

Observe the fivefold repetition of the adverb "there" (ἐκεῖ, *ekei*) in these two verses, designating the wilderness itself as the place where God saves.[56] This coheres with our earlier observation concerning the transformation of the notion of wilderness in a number of texts, from a place of judgment to one of blessing. Note, too, that these verses are closely tied intratextually to, and anticipate, the material on which Luke explicitly draws in Isa. 40:3–5.[57] Of particular interest, of course, is how Isaiah draws on the age-old image LIVING IS WALKING to portray God's people as walking in God's holy way.[58]

One might imagine a certain tension between Isa. 35 and Isa. 40 since, in the former, the "way" (ὁδός, *hodos*) is simply "there," whereas in the latter the "way" (ὁδός, *hodos*) requires preparation. These texts represent differences of emphasis, to be sure, but in the end the distinction is not dramatic. Isaiah 40 also assumes the presence of a "way" or a "road," but here the road is an obstructed one. It is an uneven road, a crooked one, when what is needed is a road that is smooth (or level) and straight (cf. Isa. 26:7; 33:15; 40:3, 4; 42:16; 45:13; 59:14). Roadwork is needed, and this is the significance of the call for preparations to be made. What form might this road construction take? It is none other than repentance, of course, following the well-established pattern of sin leading to exile, and repentance leading to restoration.[59] Accordingly, Isaiah's reference to the Lord's way can signal at one and the same time God's restoration of his people (new exodus) and the way of life embraced by those people whom God restores. The same is assumed in the case of Isa. 35, however, where we are told that the road in question is for those who return from the dispersion and a holy way on which only the "clean" shall walk.[60] In both instances, the road is not for everyone but only for those who have adopted God's ways as their pattern of life and who are continuing to live according to God's ways.[61] Conversion thus refers to an ongoing journey on an obstructed path requiring ongoing roadwork. CONVERSION IS A JOURNEY.

Building on Isaiah, Luke's portrait is not simple, and can be understood in terms of walking the wrong path, or of walking on a path that needs reconstruction, or walking in the wrong direction. However the problem is conceived, the point is that a change is required, and this change is not simply

---

56. See J. Watts, *Isaiah 34–66*, 15–16.

57. F. Delitzsch urges that Isa. 35 is a "prelude" to Isa. 40–66 (Keil and Delitzsch, *Commentary on the Old Testament*, 7:80); cf. Childs, *Isaiah*, 249–50, 299.

58. Childs, *Isaiah*, 298–99.

59. For this pattern, see Fuller, *Restoration of Israel*.

60. It is hard to understand why it would be necessary, with Øystein Lund (*Way Metaphors*), to choose between these two options.

61. See Motyer, *Isaiah*, 219–20. Cf. the further development of these images in Isa. 57:14–21.

from one state to another, but from one kind of journey to another. That is, conversion signifies a continued journey in the right direction down a road under reconstruction. Borrowing from and building on Isaiah's portrait, repentance entails roadwork (that is, engaging in transformed patterns of life) as well as journeying along the road (that is, ongoing life oriented toward God's purpose). Conversion thus exemplifies the metaphor LIFE IS A JOURNEY. To anticipate only slightly our further work with Luke 3, we can provide a partial map of this metaphor (see table).[62]

Source Domain: Journey	Target Domain: Patterns of Life
Journey, path, way	Pattern of life
Straight, level path	Path of conversion
Crooked, uneven path	Path refusing conversion
Traveler	People (or community of people)
Movement	Purposeful action toward a destination
Destination	For the repentant, salvation; for the unrepentant, divine wrath

According to Luke's presentation, the current path on which God's people are walking is uneven and crooked, and they are moving in the wrong direction. In other words, they are pursuing ways of life and life goals antithetical to the life purposed for them by God. If this is true, then we might expect the ensuing Lukan narrative to underscore this journey motif.

In fact, the importance of journeying for Luke is incontrovertible. Statistically, this is illustrated by the prominent use of such terms as πορεύομαι (*poreuomai*, "to walk"; 88 of 153 uses in the NT) and ὁδός (*hodos*, "way"; 40 of 101 uses in the NT) in Luke-Acts.[63] Even more compelling are the following data:

- Luke's thematic use of ὁδός (*hodos*) in Luke 3:4 (cf. 7:27) to identify obedience as a "going" and God's will as a "path"
- Luke's identification of God's purpose as "the way" (ὁδός, *hodos*; Luke 20:21; Acts 18:25, 26)
- Luke's use of the language of traveling with reference to Jesus's journey to Jerusalem in the service of God's saving agenda (Luke 9:52; 10:38; 13:22, 33; 17:11; 19:4; cf. Acts 20:22), including Jesus's assessment of

62. The map is partial because I am excluding features that are less relevant to Luke's portrait.

63. Since Luke-Acts constitutes some 27 percent of the NT, in terms of word counts, these statistics are telling. Luke is responsible for 58 percent of the uses of πορεύομαι (*poreuomai*) and 40 percent of the uses of ὁδός (*hodos*).

his journey through rejection and death to his exaltation as an ἔξοδος (*exodos*, "departure"; Luke 9:31)

- Luke's identification of the community of Jesus's followers as ἡ ὁδός (*hē hodos*), "the Way" (Acts 9:2; 19:9, 23; 22:4; 24:14, 22)
- Luke's identification of the gospel as a "way of salvation" (ὁδός σωτηρίας, *hodos sōtērias*) in Acts 16:17, and related references to "the way of the Lord" in 18:25 (ἡ ὁδὸς τοῦ κυρίου, *hē hodos tou kyriou*) and to "the way of God" in 18:26 (ἡ ὁδὸς τοῦ θεοῦ, *hē hodos tou theou*)

If Jesus's life and mission constituted a journey, so also would that of his followers. Indeed, the coming of a powerful savior is to this end: "to guide our feet in the way [ἡ ὁδός, *hē hodos*] of peace" (Luke 1:79). As Robert Maddox has summarized, for Luke "the story of Jesus and of the church is a story full of purposeful movement."[64]

Although our survey has taken us well beyond the boundaries of Luke's presentation of John's mission, we have seen that "the way," programmatically introduced with reference to John's ministry and tied to his mission of proclaiming repentance, is paradigmatic for the narrative as a whole. Luke's understanding of conversion is thus framed in terms of travel and builds on metaphors grounded in common, embodied human experience. Conversion entails movement, so it is conceptualized as a journey. What is more, Luke roots his presentation in Isaiah's anticipation of a new exodus, which is itself rooted in pervasive scriptural portraits of exodus and of walking in the ways of God, thus biasing his audience to identify themselves positively with John's conversionary rhetoric. After all, the way of conversion follows the well-worn pattern from sin to exile, from exile to repentance, and thus to restoration. Conversion is tied to God's peace, God's salvation. Luke thus imaginatively shapes his readers' understanding of conversion so as to participate in the identity-forming history and hope of God's deliverance from exile and promised restoration.

Baptism, Conversion, Forgiveness

In Luke 3:1–20, the evangelist presents John as one who proclaims a baptism more than as one who baptizes.[65] The significance of this introduction notwithstanding, John is known throughout the Lukan narrative as one who baptizes. This conclusion takes seriously the name by which John is known:

---

64. Maddox, *Purpose of Luke-Acts*, 11.
65. Böhlemann, *Jesus und der Täufer*, 100; Hartman, *Baptism*, 19.

"John the Baptizer" (7:20, 33; 9:19); the identification of John with his baptism
(Luke 20:4; Acts 1:22; 10:37; 18:25; 19:4); and the contrast between John and
Jesus articulated in terms of their respective baptisms (Luke 3:16; Acts 1:5;
11:16; cf. 19:4–5).[66] This emphasis coheres with Luke's observation in 3:7 that
it was in order to be baptized by John that the crowds journeyed out to him.
Recognition of baptism as John's characteristic activity has led to ongoing
discussion about the particular historical antecedent(s) of John's baptism—
whether Jewish proselyte baptism, for example, or Jewish ritual washings, or
some other.[67] This inquiry has been stymied primarily by the lack of any clear
parallel in contemporary Jewish practice. Thus, for example, in purification
rites and in proselyte baptism (if, indeed, proselyte baptism can be regarded as
a Jewish practice *contemporary* with John),[68] individuals bathed themselves,
whereas John administered baptism on behalf of others; ritual purification
was directed toward specified contaminants, whereas John's baptism was
nonspecific and focused on the remission of sin; and ritual washings occurred
again and again, whereas John's baptism seems to have been nonrepeatable.[69]

The significance of this general lack of definitive, precursory practice should
not be overdrawn, since one might justifiably postulate a common disposition
underlying all such practices. I refer to embodied cognition and particularly
to the grounding of relatively abstract concepts like morality in concrete
experiences of physical cleanliness. In fact, a growing literature highlights
the embodiment of the moral-purity metaphor in expressions of physical
cleanliness. Examples include the following:

- A series of experiments conducted by Simone Schnall and her colleagues
  demonstrated that surreptitiously activated cognitive concepts related
  to purity influenced moral decisions, that exposure to physical dirtiness

66. On this point, see Green, "Significance of Baptism."

67. E.g., Barth, *Taufe*, 29–33; Webb, *John the Baptizer*, chap. 4; C. Brown, "John the Baptist,"
38–44; J. Taylor, *Immerser*, esp. 15–100; Ferguson, *Baptism*, 84–89.

68. Judith 14:10 is formulaic regarding the conversion of Achior: "he believed firmly in God.
So he was circumcised, and joined the house of Israel, remaining so to this day"; there is no
reference to immersion. Karen Pusey, to cite one example, urges on the basis of circumstantial
evidence that baptism was integral to proselyte conversion in the first century CE ("Jewish
Proselyte Baptism"; cf. the earlier arguments of Jeremias, "Der Ursprung der Johannestaufe";
Jeremias, "Proselytentaufe"), but the data are far from straightforward, both in terms of relative
chronology and similarity vis-à-vis John's baptism. Concerning Jeremias's argument, see the
response by Smith, "Jewish Proselyte Baptism"; more generally, cf. McKnight, *Light among the
Nations*, 82–85; Webb, *John the Baptizer*, 122–30; Ferguson, *Baptism*, 76–82.

69. The question might be raised whether these differences are due, at least in part, to the
conforming of John's baptism to the practice of Christian baptism to which it led in Christian
memory. Since my concern here is less with the historical John and his baptism and more with
Luke's representation of John, such a concern is irrelevant.

shaped moral evaluations, and that physically cleansing oneself after experiencing disgust modulated the severity of moral judgments.[70]

- Reporting in 2010 on two related experiments concerned with how embodiment shapes cognition, Katie Liljenquist, Chen-Bo Zhong, and Adam D. Galinsky demonstrated that clean smells motivated virtuous behavior.[71]

- Zhong and Liljenquist collaborated in other studies that demonstrated that the simple act of copying an immoral story increased the participants' desire for cleaning products, especially products directed at the external world (e.g., detergents, disinfectants), that those who thought about moral transgressions were more likely than those who thought about morally upright behavior to request an antiseptic cloth, and that using an antiseptic cloth after recollecting one's own past immoral behavior resulted in the apparent alleviation of guilt. They concluded that exposure to one's own or another's moral failure posed a moral threat and stimulated the need for physical cleansing.[72]

- Spike W. S. Lee and Norberto Schwarz have taken a step further, demonstrating that physical cleansing removes traces of past decisions, reduces the need to justify those decisions, and can have the effect of wiping the slate clean.[73]

In their analytical inventory of their own and others' recent work, Lee and Schwarz concluded:

> These findings show that the psychological impact of cleansing goes beyond the conceptual metaphor of moral cleanliness. The metaphoric notion of washing away one's sins seems to have generalized to a broader conceptualization of "wiping the slate clean." This allows people to remove unwanted residues of the past, from threats to a moral self-view to doubts about recent decisions and worries about bad luck. . . . *In sum, physical cleansing removes not only physical contaminants but also moral taints and mental residues.*[74]

Given these basic observations around embodied cognition, we should not be surprised to find in Israel's Scriptures and in Second Temple literature the

70. E.g., Schnall, Benton, and Harvey, "With a Clean Conscience"; Schnall, Haida, Clore, and Jordan, "Disgust as Embodied Moral Judgment."

71. Liljenquist, Zhong, and Galinsky, "Smell of Virtue."

72. Zhong and Liljenquist, "Washing away Your Sins." Cf. Lee and Schwarz, "Dirty Hands and Dirty Mouths."

73. Lee and Schwarz, "Washing away Postdecisional Dissonance."

74. Lee and Schwarz, "Wiping the Slate Clean," 309–10, emphasis added.

correlation of washing with ethical comportment. In the opening chapter of Isaiah, for example, we read, "Wash yourselves; make yourselves clean; remove the evil of your doings from before my eyes; cease to do evil, learn to do good; seek justice, rescue the oppressed, defend the orphan, plead for the widow" (1:16–17). This compact, staccato-style series of commands is the divinely scripted antidote to a series of practices the consequence of which is graphically portrayed with these words: "your hands are full of blood" (NRSV) or, as the CEB puts it, "Your hands are stained with blood" (Isa. 1:15c). External cleansing is internally efficacious and leads to new behaviors—a reformation not only for individuals but for Israel as a people.[75] Ezekiel envisions the regathering of God's people with these words:

> I will sprinkle clean water upon you, and you shall be clean from all your uncleannesses, and from all your idols I will cleanse you. A new heart I will give you, and a new spirit I will put within you; and I will remove from your body the heart of stone and give you a heart of flesh. I will put my spirit within you, and make you follow my statutes and be careful to observe my ordinances. Then you shall live in the land that I gave to your ancestors; and you shall be my people, and I will be your God. (36:25–28)

External cleansing is collocated with a religious-ethical new beginning, completing the pattern: sin-exile-conversion-restoration. Similarly, Zechariah anticipates the day when "a fountain shall be opened for the house of David and the inhabitants of Jerusalem, to cleanse them from sin and impurity" (13:1). Again, the metaphor is explicit in 1QS 3, where we read, in part, "And when his flesh is sprinkled with purifying water and sanctified by cleansing water, it shall be made clean by the humble submission of his soul to all the precepts of God."[76] The clearest evidence for this phenomenon in Luke-Acts comes in Paul's testimony in Jerusalem concerning the words of Ananias to Paul, following Paul's visionary experience on the road to Damascus: "Why delay? Get up! Have yourself baptized and your sins washed away,[77] as you call on his name!" (Acts 22:16).

In fact, this emphasis on moral cleansing is precisely what we might have anticipated from our reading of Luke 3, where John's proclamation serves to specify the nature of the "washing" he practices. His is a repentance-baptism

---

75. See Motyer, *Isaiah*, 47.

76. ET in Vermes, *Complete Dead Sea Scrolls*, 101.

77. Βάπτισαι (*baptisai*, "to baptize") and ἀπόλουσαι (*apolousai*, "to wash") stand in parallel: middle imperative verbs with a causative or permissive force; cf. 1 Cor. 6:11; Bruce, *Acts*, 457–58; BDF §317; Robertson, *Grammar*, 808.

whose aim is forgiveness of sins (3:3).[78] In Luke's presentation, this purpose is juxtaposed to the closing phrase of the Isaianic citation that follows in vv. 4–6: "All humanity will see God's salvation" (σωτήριον, *sōtērion*). Thus, "forgiveness of sins" and "salvation" stand in parallel. Interestingly, the only reference to "forgiveness of sins" found earlier in the Lukan narrative also stands in parallel with "salvation" (σωτηρία, *sōtēria*); there, in 1:77, the result of John's mission is that God's people will experience salvation as the forgiveness of sins. Against attempts to read this language primarily in existentialist, individualist terms,[79] the cotext provided by both Zechariah's song (1:68–79) and the introduction to chap. 3 calls for an eschatological reading centered on the restoration of God's people.[80]

The prospect of salvation is firmly rooted in God's formation of a people in exodus and, then, their expectation of salvation-as-new-exodus. Consider a few examples of ways in which Zechariah's song is rich in echoes of (new) exodus:

Zechariah's Song	(New-)Exodus Material
"Bless the Lord God of Israel, because he has *come to aid* and brought *redemption* to his people" (Luke 1:68).	"The people believed and rejoiced because God *came to* Israel's *aid* and had seen their affliction; then they bowed down and worshiped" (Exod. 24:31, my translation).
	For *redemption*, see Exod. 6:6; Deut. 7:8; 9:26; 13:6; 15:15; 21:8; 24:18.
	Cf. the celebration of exodus in Ps. 105 LXX (106)— e.g., "*come to* our *aid* with your salvation" (v. 4, my translation).
". . . *salvation* from *our enemies* and *from the hand of* all *who hate* us" (v. 71).	"And he *saved* them *from the hand* of people *who hate* and *redeemed* them from an *enemy's hand*" (Ps. 105 LXX [106]:10, my translation).
"He has shown mercy . . . and remembered his holy covenant . . . that we, having been *rescued from the hand of our enemies*, might *serve* him without fear" (vv. 72–74).	For *rescue* from Egypt, see, e.g., Exod. 6:6; 14:30. For *hand of our enemies*, see Luke 1:71; Ps. 105 LXX (106):10. In Exod. 7:16, the Lord directs Moses to tell Pharaoh, "The Lord, the God of the Hebrews, has sent me to you, saying, 'Send away my people so that they may *serve* me'" (NETS; cf. Exod. 7:26; 8:16; 9:1; Josh. 24:14).
"You will go before *the Lord* to *prepare his ways*" (v. 76).	"*Prepare the way of the Lord*" (Isa. 40:3 NETS).

78. An alternative interpretation has sometimes been championed; see, e.g., J. Taylor, *Immerser*, 88–100. This is the view that, for John, repentance leads to the forgiveness of sins, which leads to baptism. As Taylor's argument itself makes clear, this view is based less on the Lukan narrative, however, and more on a supposed Qumranic background, a reading of Josephus, and her understanding of the Aramaic possibly underlying the NT portrayals of John. See the discussion in Ferguson, *Baptism*, 93–95.

79. See Bovon, *Luke 1*, 75; his reading is representative of many.

80. As in discourse analysis more generally, I use "cotext" to refer to linguistic material surrounding a text.

These parallels are symptomatic of the degree to which Zechariah's song is embedded in exodus memory.[81]

Were we to use a wide-angle lens, we would see additional reverberations of exodus hope in the infancy narratives of Luke 1–2. "Salvation" in these chapters is spelled out above all in the Lukan hymns—for example, in the language of reversal characteristic of Mary's song (1:46–55), with reference in Zechariah's song (1:67–79) to divine rescue from oppressive enemies in order to live lives shaped by worship of God, and in terms corresponding to Isaianic hopes for Israel's renewal in Simeon's song (2:28–32; cf. Isa. 42:6; 49:6, 9). Luke captures this vision in an economic way in Anna's report concerning Jesus "to everyone waiting expectantly for Jerusalem's redemption" (2:38). Turner helpfully summarizes this vision of salvation as "the special presence and blessing of God that enables a radically transformed community existence."[82] The new era of salvation—a state of "peace" (1:79; 2:14; cf. 7:50; 8:48; 19:38, 42; 24:36; Acts 9:31; 10:36; 16:36) in which the deathly threats of darkness and shadow are turned back by the light of "the heavenly dawn" (1:77–79; cf. Acts 26:18)—is dependent on, and inaugurated by, God's forgiving the people's sins. This is the object of John's baptism.

That "forgiveness of sins" ought to be understood in such a holistic way, and, indeed, as a virtual stand-in for "God's act by which Israel is restored," has been well documented by N. T. Wright. For him, *forgiveness of sins is another way of saying 'return from exile.'*[83] The logic of the association of forgiveness and Israel's restoration is straightforward and rests on the people's sinfulness as the impetus for exile in the first place. Lamentations 1:8 is illustrative: "Jerusalem sinned grievously, so she has become a mockery." That is, this view takes seriously the widespread perception among the exilic prophets that Israel's exile was divine punishment for its sins—a state of affairs, then, that could be overturned only by the cessation of punishment, that is, by God's forgiveness of Israel's sins. In support of these associations, Wright refers to Lam. 4:22: "The punishment of your iniquity, O daughter Zion, is accomplished, he will keep you in exile no longer." He also points to Jer. 31:31–34:

> The days are surely coming, says the LORD, when I will make a new covenant with the house of Israel and the house of Judah. It will not be like the covenant

81. This is not to say that echoes of exodus constitute the whole of Luke's indebtedness to Israel's Scriptures. One also finds significant play with OT Davidic material. Many of the data are conveniently charted (though not fully explored) by R. Brown, *Birth of the Messiah*, 386–89. See the insightful discussion of Israel's destiny in Luke 1–2 in Ravens, *Luke and the Restoration of Israel*, 24–49.

82. Turner, *Power from on High*, 325.

83. N. T. Wright, *Jesus*, 268, emphasis original.

that I made with their ancestors when I took them by the hand to bring them out of the land of Egypt—a covenant that they broke, though I was their husband, says the LORD. But this is the covenant that I will make with the house of Israel after those days, says the LORD: I will put my law within them, and I will write it on their hearts; and I will be their God, and they shall be my people. No longer shall they teach one another, or say to each other, "Know the LORD," for they shall all know me, from the least of them to the greatest, says the LORD; *for I will forgive their iniquity, and remember their sin no more.* (emphasis added)

Wright draws attention to additional texts[84] to support his conclusion that, for Second Temple Judaism, forgiveness of sins cannot be reduced to a private blessing. "Since covenant renewal means the reversal of exile, and since exile was the punishment for sin, covenant renewal/return from exile *means* that Israel's sins have been forgiven—and vice versa."[85]

For our purposes, this identification of forgiveness and restoration is secured above all by the intertextual frame within which Luke has sketched John's appearance and mission. As we have seen, in myriad ways Luke has underscored the significance of John's prophetic aims in terms of Israel's restoration. The words Luke borrows from Isa. 40 to describe John follow and are predicated on God's announcement that the time of Israel's punishment is over and that Israel's sins are forgiven (Isa. 40:2; cf. 51:17). And, though "salvation" can refer to a range of benefactions, for Isaiah, as for Luke 1–2, the focus is above all on Israel's restoration from exile.[86]

One more line of evidence points in the direction of understanding "forgiveness of sins" and its correlate "salvation" in terms of Israel's restoration. Luke's citation of Isa. 40 extends to 40:5, which reads, "the glory of the Lord shall appear, and all flesh shall see the salvation of God, because the Lord has spoken" (40:5 NETS). Read against the backdrop of Isa. 35, this reference to "seeing" actually signifies a return of vision, since God's judgment was experienced as blindness: "Look, our God is repaying judgment; yes, he will repay; he himself will come and save us. Then the eyes of the blind shall be opened" (vv. 4–5 NETS). As quickly becomes evident, Luke understands

84. E.g., Jer. 33:4–11; Ezek. 36:24–26, 33; 37:21–23; Isa. 40:1–2; 43:25–44:3.
85. N. T. Wright, *Jesus*, 269, emphasis original.
86. See Preuss, *Old Testament Theology*, 2:274–77; Middleton and Gorman, "Salvation": "Beneath the OT's use of explicit salvation language lies a coherent worldview in which the exodus from Egyptian bondage, followed by entry into the promised land, forms the most important paradigm or model" (45); van der Watt, ed., *Salvation in the New Testament*; Colijn, *Images of Salvation*. The last two books sketch something of the variety of ways in which salvation is portrayed in the NT, but neither Colijn nor Steyn ("Soteriological Perspectives," in *Salvation in the New Testament*, 67–99) develops much the significance of forgiveness of sins vis-à-vis Israel's restoration.

the "all" who will "see salvation" in two interrelated ways. First, as in Isaiah so in Luke, "all" refers to the faithful remnant (cf., e.g., Isa. 12–13; 56)—or, perhaps better in Luke, the remnant who display their faithfulness through undergoing a repentance-baptism and living conversionary lives. Although Isaianic influence is self-evident in this presentation, it should not be overlooked that Luke's portrait actually inverts the Isaianic pattern. For Isaiah, judgment gives way to salvation, whereas for Luke the advent of salvation occasions judgment.[87] John addresses all Israel (3:3, 15, 18, 21), even if his doing so segregates the repentant from those who refuse to flee "the coming wrath" (3:7; cf. 3:9). Second, as in Isaiah so in Luke, "all" includes gentiles (e.g., Isa. 49:6; 51:5; 60; 62), an emphasis associated in Luke more with the mission of Jesus and the church (e.g., Luke 2:14, 31–32; Acts 13:47). John's mission is more narrowly directed toward God's people, Israel, but it is integral to God's larger agenda, his salvific agenda for all humanity. Accordingly, the central emphasis in John's ministry of conversion cannot be segregated from its twofold embodiment—in the physical act of baptism and in the sociopolitical ramifications of God's restoration of his people. Regarding the former, Luke's summary of John's ministry participates in a universal exemplar of embodied cognition: the embodiment of the moral-purity metaphor in expressions of physical cleanliness. Regarding the latter, "forgiveness of sin" and its correlate "salvation" cannot be reduced to an interior, subjective experience but must be understood eschatologically and in terms of God's faithfulness to Israel.

Conversion Embodied

For Luke, John's proclamation is integrally tied to his baptismal work. In fact, in the present cotext the third evangelist expends far more energy disclosing the character of John's proclamation than sketching the nature of the baptismal act or experience itself. This may leave Luke's interpreters in a state of uncertainty regarding the mode of John's baptism. (At the same time, Luke's readers are uncertain whether the act of baptism itself communicated any sort of symbolic meaning such as would become important in later ecclesial discussions of baptism.) Nevertheless, Luke's portrait of John serves to highlight John's identity as the Isaianic harbinger of good news (cf. Isa. 40:1–9; Luke 3:18).

From the standpoint of ritual studies,[88] it is easy to find in Luke's presentation a portrait of baptism as an initiatory rite of passage. Thus, people (1) temporarily withdrew into the wilderness, away from their life routines and habitations,

---

87. This is also observed in Pao, *Isaianic New Exodus*, 108.
88. The classic study is van Gennep, *Rites of Passage*.

in order to participate in John's ministry through baptism (*separation*), (2) underwent a repentance-baptism signifying their (re)new(ed) devotion to God's aims (*transition*), and (3) returned to their everyday lives as pilgrims together on a conversionary journey (*incorporation*). This points already to an understanding of the embodied character of conversion, locating conversion in human practices that are more than activities arising from covenant relationship but which themselves constitute the very character of that relationship. Hence, the practices Luke describes in 3:7–14 are means by which God's restorative aims are brought to expression within human community. One's status (baptized or not) is inseparable from one's practices, with covenantal membership constituted by conversionary behaviors. Put sharply, according to John's proclamation, changed hearts and lives are the basis on which judgment will be executed.

Klaus Berger's work represents one path into this decidedly non-Cartesian way of seeing the world.[89] His investigation of the historical psychology of the NT texts repeatedly underscores the problem of anachronistic assumptions about the nature of humanity. Among these is the ease with which modern people assume of these ancient texts a conventional, but modernist, separation between being and doing, identity and behavior, internal and external. Similarly, we saw already in chap. 2 that, from the perspective of cognitive science, there can be no (trans)formation that is not fully embodied. Therefore, the now-popular distinction between "being" and "doing" is problematic, since the "me" who is "being" is nothing other than the "me" implicated in the "doing."[90] It will not do, then, to think of the behaviors John countenances as though they were supplementary to conversion or as though they were nothing more than conversion's accessories.

For assistance in grasping the embodied character of practices, we can turn to the reflexive sociology of Pierre Bourdieu, whose work emphasizes the importance of the body and practices in social interaction. Bourdieu concerns himself with accounting for the practical competence of human agents and the social conditions within which those encounters find their meaning. In his theory of practice, he gives special attention to the concept of *habitus*, those dispositions that incline agents to respond and act in certain ways without those actions and responses being ruled by external authorities or even coordinated by thoughtful decision making. *Habitus* thus refers to

systems of durable, transposable dispositions, structured structures predisposed to function as structuring structures, that is, as principles which generate and

89. K. Berger, *Identity and Experience*.
90. This is not to deny the possibility of a disconnection between what one claims to be and what one is; this is the problem of human integrity implicated in sin (see James 1:21–27).

organize practices and representations that can be objectively adapted to their outcomes without presupposing a conscious aiming at ends or an express mastery of the operations necessary in order to attain them. Objectively "regulated" and "regular" without being in any way the product of obedience to rules, they can be collectively orchestrated without being the product of the organizing action of a conductor.[91]

For Bourdieu, then, human dispositions are (1) *inculcated*—that is, they are acquired through a gradual process by which they assume the status of second nature; (2) *structured*—that is, they reflect the social conditions within which they are acquired; (3) *durable*—that is, they are stable schemes of attentiveness and perception; and (4) *transposable*—that is, relocated to new settings, they (might) generate alternative practices.

On two points that have bearing on our discussion, Bourdieu's presentation is subject to criticism. First, we need to take issue with what Bourdieu refers to as the *durability* of dispositions, which I take to refer to their relative stasis: once formed, always formed. Even when he insists on *habitus* as "an *open system of dispositions* that is constantly subjected to experiences, and therefore constantly affected by them in a way that either reinforces or modifies its structures" and of their "*relative reversibility*,"[92] we may wonder from his publications more generally whether he does not place more emphasis on "irreversibility" than on "relative." From the perspective of cognitive science, this fails to give sufficient weight to continuous neurogenesis (the ongoing production of neurons, even in adults) and to neural plasticity (the ongoing sculpting of neuronal connections within the brain, which provide the neural basis of learning or training, including religious formation). Moreover, when we contemplate the possibility and significance of the conversionary journey, even the relative fatalism of this model is problematic, even if it usefully underscores how far-reaching, or radical, the work of conversion must be. Indeed, the degree to which we are able to judge Luke-Acts as a conversionary narrative is predicated on the possibility among human beings of destabilizing long-held dispositions and, over time, developing alternative ones. Second, it is worth asking whether Bourdieu has exaggerated the degree to which practices are the *outgrowth* of the interaction of *habitus* and specific social contexts—and, then, whether practices are not also *generative* of the dispositions that form the heart of Bourdieu's proposal.

With these two caveats in hand, we return to underscore what is central to Bourdieu's thesis, namely, that dispositions are *embodied history*, internalized,

---

91. Bourdieu, *Logic of Practice*, 53.
92. Bourdieu and Wacquant, *Invitation to Reflexive Sociology*, 133, emphasis original.

and so operative at a preconscious level, and that practices are integrally related to this "second nature" in its interaction with one's particular social contexts. Behavior is not an add-on to conversion, then, not even an important one. Rather, conversionary practices are constitutive of conversion. This is because conversion refers to transformed patterns of human life, that is, to transformed patterns of thinking, feeling, believing, and behaving. Practices serve not only as the window through which one's deepest commitments are on display, therefore, but also as the per se embodiment of those commitments. In the present case of the Lukan narrative, perhaps this is nowhere more apparent than in the reality that judgment is tied to conversion's fecundity: "Every tree that fails to produce good fruit will be chopped down and thrown into the fire" (3:9).

John's message turns on an *organic* metaphor, not a *mechanical* one. The resulting frame has no room for prioritizing inner (e.g., "soul" or "mind" or "heart") over outer (e.g., "body" or "behavior"), nor of fitting disparate pieces together to manufacture a "product," nor of correlating status and activity as cause and effect. Organic metaphors conjure no images of hierarchical systems but invite images of integration, interrelation, and interdependence. Practices do not occupy a space outside the system of change but are themselves part and parcel of the system. Accordingly, John's agricultural metaphor inseparably binds "is" and "does" together.

What is more, we find in Luke 3 no hint of keeping an accounting of who has or has not been baptized. The act of baptism is thus integral to the ritual of status transformation but not its sum.

The Conversionary Life

The shape of the conversionary life as this is related to John's mission takes multiple forms, two of which we will develop here. The first is only implicit in Luke 3 but becomes increasingly visible later in the Lukan narrative. I refer in this instance to the community that forms in relation to John's baptism. The second is more explicit, grounded as it is in the words of the crowds, tax collectors, and soldiers—respectively, "What should we do, then?" (v. 10), "Teacher, what should we do?" (v. 11), and "What about us? What should we do?" (v. 14). These questions allow John to provide seemingly mundane exemplars of the conversionary life.

CONVERSION AND COMMUNITY

Lars Hartman rightly draws attention to the reality that the NT evidence presupposes a community of John's followers, however loosely organized those followers might have been.[93] This is certainly true with regard to the narrative Luke has provided. Luke refers to John's disciples (e.g., Luke 7:18), and he recognizes that they engage in characteristic behaviors by which they are identified—fasting, for example, and prayer (5:33; 11:1). Luke assumes that they share, or ought to share, a hopeful expectation of the coming of a messiah who will baptize with the Holy Spirit and with fire—and, so, that John's followers ought to become members of the community of Jesus's disciples (3:15–16; 7:18–20; Acts 1:5; 11:16; 13:25; 19:3–4).[94] And Luke presupposes a geographically expansive Baptist movement (Acts 18:25; 19:1–4). Presumably, the community of John's disciples has as its members, too, those who have in common their baptism by John (or by his followers).

The importance of this Baptist community for our discussion of conversion is grounded in two related observations. First, it points to a communal context for identity and moral formation. Recalling our discussion in chap. 2, above, we saw the importance of the patterns of thinking, feeling, believing, and behaving that characterize our lives in the world. Various terms are used to identify the structures by which we make sense of the world, including "imagination," for example, and "conceptual schemes." These conceptual schemes, we noted, refer to patterns that are at once *conceptual* (a way of seeing things), *communal* (a set of beliefs and values to which a group and its members are deeply attached), and *conative* (action generating). Whatever else they are, then, conversionary practices are communally based. A community's common practices help to give it its identity and to identify those associated with that community as its members. Even if the general practices of prayer and fasting characteristic of John's disciples are hardly unique to this apparently loosely organized cadre, they nonetheless serve as identity markers. How such practices might actually distinguish these persons as John's (as opposed, say, to the Pharisees') disciples is unclear. According to Luke 5:33, for example, both sets of disciples are unlike Jesus's followers in that followers of the Baptist and of the Pharisees "fast frequently" and "pray often." At the same time, Luke 11:1 at least opens the possibility of prayer patterns peculiar to John's community.

That John's mission expresses itself communally gains significance, second, insofar as this is congruent with the accent in recent work on the sociology of conversion concerning conversion as *incorporation into a new community*, including adopting the rituals and practices peculiar to or definitive of that new community.[95] In this case, *incorporation* is marked by the initiatory act

93. Hartman, *Baptism*, 15.
94. See Green, "Significance of Baptism."
95. See N. H. Taylor, "Social Nature of Conversion"; Green, "Nature of Conversion."

of undergoing John's baptism. These observations are fully at home with the emphasis thus far in our discussion of conversion relative to the eschatological restoration of a people whose common life puts into practice the aims of Yahweh, rather than an understanding of conversion parsed in primarily individualistic and subjective terms.

A Conversionary Life

Both in Luke 3:7–9 and 3:15–17, the need for readiness is set against the backdrop of impending judgment. Abraham's children will escape the coming wrath, so the critical question is this: Who are Abraham's children? Familial status in this instance is determined not by a paternity test or genealogical record—not, that is, by birth into the covenant community. Rather, how one responds to God's gracious initiative in bringing salvation is determinative. We recognize Abraham's children by means of their family resemblance measured in terms of embodied character.

"Good fruit" (3:9) in this cotext is fruit that has a conversionary quality about it (3:8).[96] The wheat, but not the chaff, escapes the unquenchable fire of judgment (3:17; cf. 3:9; Isa. 66:24; Mal. 4:1). John's graphic warnings are grounded in OT portraits of divine wrath, which is typically (though not always) both a response to Israel's failure to maintain the covenant and a corollary of God's covenantal righteousness.[97] Accordingly, Mark Boda writes, "It is his justice that explains his regular discipline of sin but his grace that offers hope to a disciplined people. His justice has gracious intent, as he seeks to eliminate sin that threatens human existence and severs relationship with him. His grace is seen in his constant mitigation of punishment and expressed in his reticence to discipline."[98] Boda's summary is especially pertinent to the context within which Luke has located John the Baptist. Though he recognizes the complexity of the portrayal of sin and its remedy in the OT, Boda nevertheless finds a normative pattern: human sin leads to divine discipline, divine discipline leads to human response (especially repentance), and human response leads to divine grace.[99] This pattern is easily mapped onto another one: sin-exile-conversion-restoration. In the case of Luke 3, however, conversion is, first, the response appropriate to God's initiative in restoration, and, second, the response that marks one as a member of the

---

96. That is, καρπὸς ἄξιος τῆς μετανοίας, *karpos axios tēs metanoias*, fruit "corresponding to" or "worthy of" conversion (BDAG 94).

97. See Goldingay, *Old Testament Theology*, 2:135–70; Fretheim, "Wrath of God"; Grant, "Wrath of God."

98. Boda, *Severe Mercy*, 522–23.

99. See ibid., 519–22.

restored community (and thus the community of those who avoid the eschatological judgment; 3:7).

Avoiding any possibility that conversion might remain an abstraction (or
be reduced to an interior decision), Luke's account elucidates conversion in
terms of performance. Who are Abraham's children? Since "children of *x*"
are those who share in *x*'s character,[100] the question of Abrahamic qualities
seems particularly apt. In actuality, though, this query comes into play more
fully elsewhere in the Lukan narrative, where that cornerstone of Abraham's
reputation, his practice of hospitality,[101] surfaces as a pervasive conversionary
practice. Here, though, John's counsel takes a different (though related) path,
and is especially marked by its socioeconomic accent. Josephus's summary
of John's message to the people—that "they practice goodness and justice
toward each other" (*Ant.* 18.117, my translation)—is a fitting précis of the
Lukan presentation. It is even more important, though, that we recognize
how much John's instruction is at home in Israel's Scriptures, where covenant
faithfulness takes the form of ethical comportment in social relations (e.g.,
Isa. 1:15–17; 58:7). The result is a focus on life at the local level in which one's
routine network of relationships is touched by an ethical vision that makes
conversion visible in the everydayness of human existence.

"What should we do, then?"[102] The question posed by the crowds to John
(Luke 3:10) is repeated by tax collectors in 3:12, soldiers in 3:14, a legal
expert in 10:25, a rich ruler in 18:18, a Jerusalem audience in Acts 2:37, a
jailer in Acts 16:30, and a zealous Jew in Acts 22:10. With one possible exception (Luke 18:18), the question arises as a response to proclamation or to a
miracle, underscoring the importance of human performance as a response
to the divine initiative. In the present cotext, John has made clear the pivotal
significance of conversionary performance over against any other attempt to
define oneself as Abraham's child. In this way, John articulates the character of
that performance with his charge that the converted, all of them, share what
they have with those who lack the basic necessities of life. The apparently
conventional character of John's directive (conventional, that is, among the
converted) becomes clear elsewhere in Luke's Gospel, where we discover that

100. For example, God's children love their enemies, do good, and lend without expecting
anything in return, and are thus like God, who is kind to the ungrateful and the wicked; they
are told, "Be compassionate, just as your Father is compassionate" (Luke 6:35–36); a "son of
peace" is someone who shares God's peace (10:6); "sons of this age" and "sons of the light"
behave in ways consistent with "this age" and with "the light," respectively (16:8); and a "son
of the devil" is simply diabolical in his practices of deception and unscrupulousness, in his
hostility toward righteousness and his customary twisting of the Lord's ways (Acts 13:10).

101. See Gen. 18:2–8; Heb. 13:2; *T. Ab.* [recension A], 1.1–2; 2.2.

102. On what follows concerning 3:10–14, I am dependent on my work in *Luke*, 177–80.

care for the hungry and naked is nothing more or less than heeding Moses and the prophets (16:19–31). Should anyone imagine that John has thus singled out these behaviors as the basis of membership among God's restored people, this would be due to a fundamental misunderstanding of a psychology, such as we find in Luke 3, that refuses to drive a wedge between one's character and commitments, on the one hand, and one's practices, on the other. A life oriented toward the way of the Lord is one in which the way of the Lord—in this case, care for the have-nots—is in play.

From the general counsel directed to the crowds (3:10–11), the focus moves more narrowly to tax collectors who have come out to be baptized (3:12–13). This second scene amplifies the first, in that it presents a further, concrete instantiation of the words directed to the crowds and turns attention to a particularly offensive subgroup of those who have journeyed out to participate in John's ministry: tax collectors. In two respects, Luke presents the target of John's concern as the practices of these tax collectors themselves rather than the potentially oppressive tax system itself. (Whether the tax system was in fact oppressive depends on how one evaluates the burden it placed on those on whom taxes were levied, an issue concerning which Luke provides no basis for an opinion.) First, the intensive phrase *"even tax collectors"* by which Luke introduces this vignette anticipates the surprise with which Luke's audience might greet the appearance of tax collectors among God's restored people. This is due to the unenviable status shared by tax collectors in wider Roman society, known as they were as snoops, corrupt, dishonest, the social equivalent of pimps and turncoats.[103] Second, John's reply does not actually take aim at the tax system itself; instead, the Baptist challenges his audience with carrying out their duties within the boundaries set for them: "Collect no more than you are authorized to collect" (3:13). How much is this? What percentage? We are told only that, for them, a conversionary life is recognized when they do not exceed the amount set by those in authority over them.[104] Apparently, a conversionary life is possible for tax collectors qua tax collectors. Even so, it should not escape our notice that the emphasis thus falls on day-to-day life as the venue within which conversion is performed.

In 3:14, soldiers are cast in a role similar to that of tax collectors in 3:12–13. They are an assemblage of surprising participants in John's mission whose inquiry sets the stage for yet another concrete instantiation of John's call to bear fruit characteristic of a conversionary life. As with the tax-collecting

---

103. See, e.g., Herrenbrück, *Jesus und die Zöllner*, 60–72; Michel, "τελώνης."

104. Elsewhere, Luke uses διατάσσω (*diatassō*) for activity performed under the authority of another (Luke 8:55; 17:9–10; Acts 18:2; 23:31).

system, so here John's response is not directed against the military complex per se. Instead, he calls for an end to the typical behaviors by which soldiers manipulate the local populace to their advantage. Routine interactions provide the setting for an exegesis of conversion.

It is worth repeating that the behaviors John urges among his audience are not themselves the basis for covenantal restoration. It is better to say that they enact the covenant. Nor should we imagine that John's directives constitute the grand sum of conversionary behavior as this will be developed in the Lukan narrative. What Luke records here are nothing more than exemplars, though they are important as far as they go. They provide a kind of script, one that calls for performance in terms of creative fidelity—"fidelity" in the sense that the notes on the score or words of the play script secure the character of the expected performance, "creative" in the sense that life is too particular and life situations too varied to be carefully and specifically scripted in advance. (Some may therefore prefer the metaphor of "improvisation" over that of "performance.")[105] If crowds and tax collectors and soldiers, what of synagogue leaders and jailers and dealers in purple dye? If John does not specifically address such persons in their day-to-day circumstances, this does not mean that they are left altogether without guidance. This is because John has begun to map the patterns of thinking, feeling, believing, and behaving that deserve the label "conversionary." Such patterns reflect the way of the Lord who brings salvation, who restores his people. Such patterns reach into the day-to-day interactions and affairs of life. Conversion is embodied.

Conclusion

In this chapter, I have attempted to carve out a foothold from which we might reflect on the significance of conversion for Luke-Acts. This has required efforts both deconstructive and constructive. Thus, I have urged that the search for patterns of conversion in the Lukan narrative leads down a cul-de-sac within which it is difficult to escape the view that Luke's variegated accounts have been stuffed into molds not of Luke's making. The search for patterns is problematically presented as an inductive enterprise—problematic because the shape of those paradigms has been predetermined by the requirements of the search itself, and because of the circularity inherent in the prior determination of what counts as a "conversion account." I have

---

105. See Barton, "Performance"; Craig-Snell, "Command Performance."

also counseled against attempts to drive a wedge between conversion and repentance, at least as these terms are found in Luke-Acts. Although certain interpretive communities may find this distinction useful today, Luke provides no linguistic justification for it as a means for analysis of his narrative. Most importantly, though, I have targeted attempts to read conversion in Luke 3:1–14 (together with chaps. 1–2) in ways that reduce conversion to an interior decision, to individualistic decision making, or, indeed, to a (single) event.

Instead, I have followed two of the axioms in discourse analysis by prioritizing study of 3:1–14 as a means for orienting our study of conversion in Luke-Acts, and, with regard to 3:1–14, I have taken seriously the intertextual frames the evangelist has provided. The first axiom I have followed centers on presuppositional pools—that is, the ever-evolving data set by which audiences make sense of a narrative like Luke-Acts. Privilege of meaning is allocated to the lexicon that is supported by and developed within the narrative as one proceeds in the narrative from start to finish. *What comes before constrains the possible meaning of what comes after, within the text.* Accordingly, repentance-baptism as this is portrayed in Luke 3 ought to figure prominently in our analysis of repentance elsewhere in Luke-Acts—an assumption that is supported by repeated recollections of this textual unit elsewhere in the narrative. The second axiom directs attention to the recognition of intertextual frames in the process of meaning making. We make sense of conversion in Luke-Acts on the basis of what we have seen and heard.[106] Sometimes what we have seen and heard before consists of evidence *internal* to Luke-Acts. Hence, as I have already indicated, we read accounts of conversion in Luke 5 or Acts 16 in ways shaped by the horizons of Luke 3. For our reading of Luke 3, however, we have seen the significant degree to which *external* frames are operative with regard to the explicit and implicit use of the LXX and of the story of Israel in exile more generally.

Accordingly, we have found reason to grapple with Luke's theology of conversion in ways that take seriously geographic space as well as the plotline according to which God initiates his restoration of his people through the forgiveness of sins. Conversion is first the story of God's prevenience, God's gracious visitation that opens the way for human responses of repentance. Even the language by which Luke sketches the character of conversion highlights human embodiment, an emphasis further underscored by the human, bodily experience of washing, the windows Luke provides into the community of those being converted, the nature of conversion as a journey, and the

106. See Tannen, "What's in a Frame?"

importance of conversionary practices constitutive of covenant renewal. In this chapter, then, I have attempted from a variety of perspectives to demonstrate the fully embodied character of conversion as Luke understands it. The question remains whether the rest of Luke-Acts will support this limited, albeit programmatic, sounding.

4

✵

Texts and Metaphors

Conversion is programmatic for Luke's narrative. This is clear enough from the initial soundings we have taken from Luke's presentation of the Baptist's context and mission in Luke 3:1–18. Based on the evidence through which we have sifted thus far, we are able to articulate a provisional definition:

> *Converts are those who have undergone a redirectional shift and are now on the move with the community of those faithfully serving God's eschatological purpose.*

This much is evident already, even if we will be able to expand this definition somewhat after examining the Lukan narrative further.

It will be useful, first, to highlight four aspects of this provisional definition. (1) Embedded in the notion of conversion as a journey is a prominent emphasis on directionality. Conversion is not so much an acquiescence to a particular set of faith claims as it is participation in the unfolding of a particular story.[1] (2) Closely related, then, conversion is identified with an orientation toward

---

1. Similarly, Walls ("Converts or Proselytes?," 6) observes: "Conversion . . . is less about content and more about *direction*." This coheres somewhat with Paul G. Hiebert's description of the church as an "extrinsic well-formed (centered) set" defined relationally by its center, Jesus Christ, with Christians identified as those who have entered into the "set" and are moving toward the "center" ("Category of Christian," 122–31). Luke's narrative differs from Hiebert's description in two significant ways, however. First, Hiebert's "center" is focused in an overly narrow way—christologically and confessionally rather than theologically and narratively.

God's eschatological purpose. This means that conversion is deeply embedded in the ancient story of God's dealings with Israel, so that it is to this
God that life is directed; that conversion accounts for a particular reading of
that ancient story, one that insists that God's purpose is being realized in the
ministry of John the Baptist—itself anticipatory of the Messiah's coming;
and, so, that conversion is eschatologically driven, since it is the eschatological
coming of God to restore Israel that marks the turn of the ages, places before
people the word of repentance, and enables conversion. (3) Conversion is basic
to Luke's presentation of God's restoration of God's people; hence, even if
conversion is personal, it is not individualistic. (4) Conversion is inseparable
from the practices constitutive of participation in the remnant representing
God's restored people. Accordingly, Luke grounds conversion in the grand
narrative of God's ancient and ongoing purpose. The first and initiating act
is God's. Conversion is both gracious gift and response. Luke's theology
of conversion refuses any facile distinctions between conversion as act and
process, between cognitive and moral change, between movement from one
religion to another and deepening commitment within one's religion, and
between personal and community formation.

Reading further into Luke's account both solidifies and extends these emphases. The purpose of this chapter, then, is to work with a selection of Lukan
texts in order to demonstrate how Luke's presentation of conversion coheres
with and thickens the orientation he has given us in Luke 3.

Jesus Calls His First Disciples to a Journey (Luke 5:1–11)

Some may find it strange that I have chosen to begin this analysis of selected
Lukan conversionary texts with his account of Jesus's calling of Simon (Peter)
and the sons of Zebedee, James and John. After all, the standard terminology of conversion is missing from this pericope.[2] My choice is deliberate,
however, as I want (1) to provide an example of a Lukan text that narrates
conversion sans the typical language of conversion,[3] (2) to illustrate further
the importance of articulating conversion in Luke-Acts in terms of a process
or journey, and (3) to anticipate an emphasis that grows in importance in the

---

Second, Hiebert apparently prefers to use the term "conversion" for "entering the set," with
"movement toward the center" being a second kind of change.

2. In fact, recent treatments of repentance or conversion in Luke's Gospel have bypassed
this episode in favor of their focus on Jesus's encounter with the tax collector Levi in 5:27–32.
See, e.g., Kim-Rauchholz, *Umkehr bei Lukas*; Méndez-Moratalla, *Paradigm of Conversion*.

3. That is, μετάνοια (*metanoia*) and its verbal form μετανοέω (*metanoeō*), or ἐπιστροφή
(*epistrophē*) and its verbal form ἐπιστρέφω (*epistrephō*).

Acts of the Apostles, namely, the nature of conversionary life as participation in God's mission.

Simon's Transformation

Luke's account begins with a wide-angle lens but quickly centers on the interaction between Jesus and Simon ("Simon Peter" in v. 8)—moving as it does from the lake and crowd to "two boats" (vv. 1–2), before narrowing to Jesus and Simon (vv. 3–9). Simon's "partners" are mentioned in v. 7 and named as James and John in v. 10, but Luke mentions nothing of any interaction between them and Jesus. Moreover, the commission, "Do not be afraid. From now on, you will be fishing for people" (v. 10), is addressed to Simon alone.[4] Within the flow of Luke's narrative thus far, Simon thus serves a paradigmatic role in demonstrating the character of appropriate response to Jesus's mission. That Simon is representative of the others is encouraged by the narrator's reference to them along with Simon as his "partners,"[5] then assured by the communal response of James and John, with Simon, in v. 11: "Leaving everything, *they* followed him."[6]

Luke sets the stage for Simon's response in three ways. First, even if we are given no details, we gather that Simon, with the crowds, is the recipient of "God's word" (vv. 1, 4). This phrase is used in Acts for the good news concerning Jesus, but in Luke for Jesus's own proclamation.[7] Given that Luke provides in v. 1 nothing by way of the substance of Jesus's preaching, we can do little else but assume that it is congruent with the earlier words of the prophet Jesus. Thus, "God's word" would entail "good news to the poor," the coming of "the Lord's favor," the message of God's kingdom (4:18–19, 43). Second, Jesus presses Simon into service, both in Jesus's use of Simon's boat as a speaking platform (v. 2) and in his directive to Simon that Simon maneuver his boat into the deep water and drop his nets (v. 4). Simon performs the first service without demurring but the second only after initial skepticism. Together with Simon's report that the whole night of fishing had been unproductive (v. 5), his

---

4. Both verbs, φοβοῦ (*phobou*, "do not be afraid") and ἔσῃ (*esē*, "you will be"), are in the second-person singular.

5. Note the shift from μέτοχος (*metochos*, "business partner") in v. 7 to κοινωνός (*koinōnos*, "companion") in v. 10.

6. Ἠκολούθησαν, *ēkolouthēsan*, "they followed."

7. Luke 8:11, 21; 11:28; Acts 4:31; 6:2, 7; 8:14; 11:1; 13:5, 7, 44, 46, 48; 16:32; 17:13; 18:11. See also Jeremias, *Sprache des Lukasevangeliums*, 129; and the excursuses in Bovon, *Luke 1*, 168; Klein, *Lukasevangelium*, 207 ("Gottes Wort ist Botschaft von der Annahme der Sünder und zugleich Lehre über das rechte Leben der Christen, den Weg zum Heil" [God's word is the good news of the acceptance of sinners and, at the same time, teaching on the true Christian life, the way to salvation]).

incredulity highlights, third, the miraculous nature of the catch: "so enormous that the nets began to tear" and "they filled both boats with the result that they threatened to sink" (vv. 6–7). This third stage-setting device anticipates the more thoroughgoing emphasis Babu Immanuel discerns in Luke's second volume: miraculous acts lead to conversionist episodes.[8] Word and deed thus prepare for the interaction between Simon and Jesus.

Their interchange is reminiscent of a scene familiar in Israel's Scriptures—more generally the type scene of a commission story but more particularly the call narrative in Isa. 6:1–10 (see table).

Luke 5:1–11	Element	Isaiah 6:1–10
vv. 4–7 (9–10a)	Epiphany	vv. 1–4
v. 8	Reaction	v. 5
v. 10b	Reassurance	v. 7
v. 10c	Commission	vv. 8–10

Unlike Isa. 6, however, Simon's response is immediately documented and is expressive of a far-reaching life transformation (Luke 5:11). That the miraculous catch is epiphanic is evident from the shift in terms by which Simon addresses Jesus. Prior to the miraculous catch, Simon uses the vocative ἐπιστάτα (epistata, "master"; v. 5), a term that in Luke's Gospel conveys distance between the speaker, on the one hand, and Jesus and his aims, on the other.[9] Afterward, he refers to Jesus as κύριος (kyrios, "Lord"; v. 8); moreover, in doing so, he agrees with Luke the narrator regarding Jesus's identity and, as Isaiah had done vis-à-vis the "Lord" (κύριος, kyrios),[10] so Simon Peter confesses his unworthiness in relation to the Lord Jesus. In the face of divine revelation, he can only respond with gestures of humility ("he dropped to his knees") and words that demonstrate his awareness of the contrast between himself, a sinner, and Jesus, the Lord (v. 8). Even if Peter's grasp of the significance of this appellation for Jesus is incomplete, his identification of Jesus as Lord both signifies a profound statement regarding Jesus's status and bespeaks a concomitant life transformation for Simon Peter.

The metamorphosis Simon undergoes is marked, further, in Jesus's commission (v. 10). First, he (and his partners) will no longer sell dead fish in the

8. Immanuel, *Repent and Turn to God*.
9. 8:24 (2x), 45; 9:33, 49; 17:13; and see the discussion in Rowe, *Early Narrative Christology*, 84–89.
10. Isa. 6:1 ("the Lord sitting on a throne, lofty and raised up"), 3 ("Holy, holy, holy is the Lord Sabaoth"), 5 ("the King, the Lord Sabaoth"), 8 ("the Lord") (NETS).

marketplace but will catch people alive, giving them liberty.[11] Jesus himself is first portrayed as a fisherman: proclaiming God's word from a boat and catching Simon and his companions alive; now he promises that they will do the same. Second, Jesus marks a break in Simon's history (as well as in the biography of his partners) with the phrase "from now on." This episode thus exemplifies a key marker of conversion recognized in contemporary social-scientific study: *autobiographical reconstruction*. As Peter Berger and Thomas Luckmann summarize it, "Everything preceding the alternation is now apprehended as leading toward it . . . , everything following it as flowing from its new reality. This involves a reinterpretation of past biography *in toto*, following the formula 'Then I *thought* . . . now I *know*.'"[12] Simon, James, and John thus respond: "Leaving everything, they followed him" (v. 11). Conversion in this instance is realized, then, as a change of vocation and anticipated participation in Jesus's mission, but it also participates in Luke's wider ethics of faith and wealth. As Jesus will later proclaim, "Similarly, whoever among you is not willing to give up everything cannot be my disciple" (14:33), just as Peter will later affirm, "Look, we gave up everything we had to follow you" (18:28). In our present text, indeed, they leave their boats, the enormous catch of fish, and everything associated with their livelihood, in order to follow Jesus.

Peter Begins a Journey

On the most obvious level, these three newly commissioned disciples experience conversion quite literally as journeying with the itinerant Jesus (cf. 4:43). At a second level, though, conversion for them entails a new way of life characterized by a particular comportment vis-à-vis both the material accessories of their former ways of life and a missionary vocation. At a still further level, we find above all in Luke's unfolding portrait of Peter a journey whereby Peter comes to greater and greater insight into Jesus's significance.

For example, Peter's deficit of understanding is obvious in his response to Jesus's transfiguration, words that invite divine correction (9:32–35). Addressing Jesus again with the vocative form of ἐπιστάτης (*epistatēs*, "master"; see above), Peter testifies to his misunderstanding of Jesus. Not surprisingly, then, his bid to construct three shrines on the Mount of Transfiguration is interrupted with the heavenly command that he and his companions should

---

11. The metaphorical use of the language of *fishing* is widely attested: Jer. 16:16; Amos 4:2; Hab. 1:14–15; Mark 1:17; et al. See also Wuellner, *Meaning of "Fishers of Men,"* 64–231, 237–38; *TLNT* 2:161–63.

12. Berger and Luckmann, *Social Construction of Reality*, 160; cf. Snow and Machalek, "Convert as a Social Type," 266–69.

listen to God's Son, the chosen one. Peter's lack of clarity is even more on display, however, when his correct identification of Jesus as God's Messiah (9:20) is set in parallel with his failure to comprehend the nature of Jesus's messiahship. And this latter miscomprehension is nowhere clearer than in Luke's twofold reference to the disciples' obtuseness in the face of Jesus's predictions of his passion—the one located toward the beginning of the journey narrative (9:44–45), the other near its end (18:31–34).

9:44–45	18:31–34
"Let these words sink into your ears: the Human One [or Son of Man] is about to be delivered into human hands." They did not understand this statement, its meaning was hidden from them so they could not grasp it, and they were afraid to ask him about it.	Jesus took the Twelve aside and said to them, "Look, we are going up to Jerusalem, and everything written about the Human One [or Son of Man] by the prophets will come to fruition. He will be handed over to the gentiles, ridiculed, mistreated, and spat on. After beating him, they will kill him. On the third day, he will rise up." The Twelve did not understand any of these things, this statement's meaning was hidden from them, and they did not grasp what he was saying.

This level of misunderstanding is especially perplexing since the journey section of Luke's Gospel, 9:51–19:48, is composed primarily of instruction, with most of that teaching aimed, both directly and indirectly, at the disciples. Whereas we might anticipate the need for further clarity at the beginning of the journey section, it is astonishing that misunderstanding on this central message remains as Jesus and his entourage arrive at Jerusalem's gates.

Why are the disciples, including Peter, so slow to comprehend? Luke explains, twice, that the disciples did not understand Jesus's saying to them because its sense "was hidden from them." Some have attempted to mitigate the scandal of misapprehension by reading these two passive verbs as divine passives; in other words, God must have prevented the disciples from understanding Jesus's words.[13] This reading stands in tension with Luke's portrayal of what the disciples ought to know, however. For example, in the context of revelatory prayer, "turning to the disciples, Jesus said to them privately, 'Happy are the eyes that see what you see!'" (10:23), the disciples are those to whom the kingdom's secrets are revealed (8:10), and Jesus's injunction in 9:44 ("Let these words sink into your ears," or, more idiomatically, "Take these words to

---

13. See, e.g., Schürmann, *Lukasevangelium*, 1:573; Fitzmyer, *Luke*, 1:814. Bovon thinks in terms of both predestination and the disciples' "blindness to salvation history" (*Luke 1*, 393). John Nolland (*Luke*, 2:514) thinks the failure of insight is Satanic.

heart") presumes that they should be able to understand. Nevertheless, Luke's wording in 18:45 is emphatic: they lacked understanding, the meaning was hidden, they lacked perception, and they feared discussing it further. What is more, their failure continues through the entire Gospel of Luke, until the concluding moments of Luke 24, with Luke reporting that Jesus "opened their minds to understand the Scriptures" (24:45). First, though, Jesus scolds two of his followers for their dull minds—a response on Jesus's part that assumes they could have understood and believed. Texts like these make it difficult to trace the disciples' lack of understanding to God's keeping them in the dark.

How, then, might we understand their perplexity in the face of Jesus's teaching and, what is more, Luke's claim that the sense of Jesus's words was unavailable to them? Recall from chap. 1 our discussion of framing, our references to those experience schemas signaled by the introduction of a term, the cascade of associations that come to mind when words or phrases are used. Recalling this, we can see that Jesus and his followers are working with different frames. Simply put, the disciples lack the conceptual equipment necessary to link what Jesus holds together in his passion predictions, namely, his exalted status and impending dishonor.[14] Thus, for example, in 9:43–48 Luke's observation of the disciples' failure to understand Jesus is followed immediately by their arguing over who was the greatest; Jesus's response prioritizes hospitality toward marginal people like little children and includes his pronouncement "Whoever is least among you is the greatest" (9:48). In Luke 18, conventional patterns of thinking and believing are overturned as Jesus prizes a tax collector's humility over a Pharisee's blamelessness, Jesus chides his disciples for standing between himself and parents bringing their babies to receive his blessing, a rich ruler learns that neither his wealth nor his position qualifies him for God's kingdom, and Jesus counters the behavior of those at the front of his entourage (his disciples?) by attending to a blind man calling for mercy. In the midst of this string of episodes, we find that the disciples are flummoxed by Jesus's prediction of his suffering and death.

In other words, the honorifics typically associated with divine blessing and benefaction, or with terms like Human One (or Son of Man) or Messiah—these do not easily signal patterns of belief and thought related to humiliating betrayal and torture. So accustomed are the disciples to imagining God's agenda along a certain set of lines, with different meaning associations, that they now find Jesus's statements about God's ways incomprehensible. The

14. "It is in fact the very revelation of God's 'secrets' (8:10) that leaves them perplexed before the incomprehensible way of God" (Schweizer, *Luke*, 163). For ἵνα as a "marker serving as substitute for the [infinitive] of result, *so that*," see BDAG 477.

disciples are in the dark, so to speak, because they lack the necessary cognitive categories, the required patterns of thought. Like travelers in distant lands who have odd, stomach-turning, perhaps even taboo foods placed before them or who witness seemingly bizarre customs, the disciples are unable to pigeonhole Jesus's words into long-established meaning slots. They cannot integrate in a seamless way how Jesus's messiahship could be defined with respect to both his elevated status before God and his rejection by human beings. Accordingly, they did not, and could not, understand Jesus.

According to this example (and elsewhere in the narrative besides), the primary obstacle to be overcome is ignorance.[15] This point is made more generally for Luke-Acts by Jens-W. Taeger, who sees that the human situation in Lukan thought is one characterized by ignorance needing correcting rather than sin needing forgiveness.[16] Of course, Taeger thus introduces an enigma into our study of the Lukan narrative, since we have already found in Luke's Gospel a heightened interest in forgiveness of sins.[17] But this is because Taeger's view suffers from an anemic understanding of knowledge and ignorance. As we saw in chap. 3, knowledge is embodied, embracing patterns of thinking, feeling, believing, and behaving. Accordingly, we should understand Luke's notion of ignorance less in terms of lacking information and more with regard to faulty conceptual patterns or possessing a faulty imagination. They have information aplenty, but they lack insight. Ignorance would thus be a failure at the most profound level to grasp adequately God's purpose. Accordingly, as long as Jesus's disciples remain embedded in their former ways of construing God's agenda and, then, the nature of life before God, they are blinded to what God is doing. What is needed is a theological transformation: a deep-seated conversion in their conception of God and, thus, in their commitments, attitudes, and everyday practices. Consequently, the resolution of ignorance is not simply amassing facts but *(re)alignment* with God's ancient purpose now coming to fruition (that is, *conversion*) and divine forgiveness.[18]

Note that we are speaking here of Peter and his companions as though they need to discern better and to align themselves with God's agenda. This is important since these people are already Jesus's followers, his disciples, with

---

15. This is true of Jew and gentile alike: see, e.g., Acts 3:17; 17:30. In Luke 9:45: ἀγνοέω (*agnoeō*, "to lack ability to understand") + αἰσθάνομαι (*aisthanomai*, "to understand"), used in the subjunctive with μή (*mē*, "not"). In 18:34: συνίημι (*syniēmi*, "to understand") + γινώσκω (*ginōskō*, "to know"), both used with the negative οὐ (*ou*, "not"). Luke's ignorance motif is helpfully explored in Strahan, *Limits of a Text*, 65–85.

16. Taeger, *Mensch und sein Heil*.

17. See already 1:77; 3:3 (see chap. 3, above), as well as 5:20–21, 23–24; 7:47–49; 11:4; 12:10; 17:3–4; 23:34; 24:47; Acts 2:38; 3:19; 5:31; 10:43; 13:38; 15:9; 22:16; 26:18.

18. Pokorný, *Theologie der lukanischen Schriften*, 62–63, 66–67.

some from the inner circle of the Twelve. Having begun their journey down a conversionary road, they now require further steps. The disciples' quandary, which Luke documents in 9:44–45 and again in 18:31–34, achieves a decisive, if not final, resolution at the pivot point of Luke's two-part narrative, in the postresurrection appearances and at Pentecost (Luke 24; Acts 1–2).

First, the two disciples in Emmaus have Jesus himself as their teacher "opening the Scriptures" to them (Luke 24:32), and indeed they receive Jesus's interpretation of the Scriptures (24:25–27), as do the disciples gathered in Jerusalem (24:44, 46). Note, though, that they have had Jesus as their teacher throughout the Lukan narrative and have witnessed before his expounding Israel's Scriptures. Later, the Ethiopian eunuch will demonstrate that reading the Scriptures cannot be confused with grasping their meaning (Acts 8:27–31), just as Paul will urge in his homily in a synagogue in Pisidia at Antioch that it is entirely possible to hear the scriptural words week after week and fail to understand them (13:27). Clearly, scriptural data are not enough.

Second, the Emmaus disciples have their eyes opened as they share bread with Jesus at the table (Luke 24:30–31, 35), whereas the Jerusalem followers witness proofs of Jesus's resurrection body (24:36–43), after which Jesus "opened their minds to understand the Scriptures" (24:45). If they are to understand, they need something more than syllogistic reasoning, critical analysis, or even a scriptural lesson. They need the Scriptures, to be sure, but genuine, life-forming comprehension—the kind that is realized in and generates testimony, mission, and worship (24:33–35, 47–53)—requires more. For Luke 24, this kind of transformation finds its catalyst in a postresurrection context characterized by assurances to the community of disciples concerning the continuity in Jesus's identity before and after death, by Jesus's own narration of his life in continuity with Israel's Scriptures, and by the communal actions of sharing a common table (24:27, 29–31, 35, 36–43, 44).[19] The first and second of these, concerning Jesus's identity, ensure the authenticity of their encounter with Jesus of Nazareth, Lord and Christ—whose life is inscribed in the ancient story of God's engagement with his people, and whose life brings that story to its climax. The third, comprising communal actions like sharing a meal and worship, enacts the character of that encounter. And all three depend on God's gracious gift whereby they are enabled "to see," "to recognize," and "to understand" (24:16, 31, 45): "their eyes were opened [διανοίγω, *dianoigō*, "to open"]" and "he opened [διανοίγω, *dianoigō*] their minds." These emphases are summarized in Acts 1:3–4, where we find that

19. See Green, *Body, Soul, and Human Life*, 166–70; cf. Laytham, "Interpretation"; Hays, "Reading Scripture."

Jesus "showed them that he was alive by many convincing proofs" and spoke to them concerning God's kingdom, and "they were eating together" (see 10:41).[20]

Third, they are the recipients of the Holy Spirit, who enables inspired interpretation of the Scriptures (Acts 2).[21] Having internalized Jesus's understanding of God's agenda and the means by which God would achieve his purpose in Jesus's suffering, death, and resurrection, they now work with Israel's Scriptures to proclaim, especially through their representative Peter, that, in God's economy, the high status of God's anointed one is not challenged by humiliation and suffering. Rather, with words that recall Jesus's instruction in Luke 24, Peter insists that God foretold this through all of the prophets: "his Christ would suffer" (Acts 3:18; cf., e.g., 2:22–24, 36; 3:12–26; 4:10–11; 5:30–32).

The story continues, of course, and with it Peter's insight into God's purpose continues to evolve. To visit one final, celebrated account, we may refer to Peter's continuing conversion in Acts 9:32–11:18. As we follow Peter into and through the Lukan narrative of his encounter with Cornelius, we recognize that Peter stands in an ambiguous relation to a long-standing ideology grounded in careful demarcations between clean and unclean. On the one hand, he manifests his awareness of and allegiance to such an ideology. This is self-evident in his interaction with the Lord in his vision: "Lord, no! I have never eaten anything that is impure or unclean" (10:14). Later, when relating this vision at Jerusalem, Peter's recollection is even more emphatic: "Lord, no! Nothing impure or unclean has ever entered my mouth" (11:8). Moreover, as Peter readies himself to enter Cornelius's house, he voices a related socioreligious script: "It is forbidden that a Jew associate with or visit a gentile" (10:28). (Compare Jesus's apparent intent to enter the home of a gentile centurion in Luke 7:1–10.) And when Peter returns to Jerusalem after his encounter with Cornelius, he is criticized precisely on this point, for sharing the hospitality of gentiles (11:2–3).

On the other hand, two lines of evidence suggest that Peter is on a collision course with the ideology he has thus espoused. First, from 9:32–43 he has not

20. Συναλίζομαι (*synalizomai*, "to eat with") is sometimes taken as a form of συναλίζω (*synalizō*, "to gather"; e.g., KJV) and sometimes as a misspelling or variant of συναυλίζομαι (*synaulizomai*, "to stay with"; e.g., NRSV). See the discussion in BDAG 964. Elsewhere, Luke notes that the postresurrection Jesus ate with and in front of his disciples (Luke 24:36–38; Acts 10:41); moreover, the translation offered here reflects both classical usage (e.g., Aristotle, *Eth. nic.* 8.3.8 §1156b:24, which correlates genuine friendship with eating together) and the early versions (Latin, Armenian, Coptic, Arabic, Ethiopic, Syriac; cf. Bowen, "Συναλιζόμενος," 248–49).

21. As John R. Levison (*Spirit in First Century Judaism*, 254–59) has demonstrated, the Spirit's role in the interpretation of Scripture is well known in the literature of Second Temple Judaism (e.g., Josephus, Sirach, Philo, and at Qumran).

only departed Jerusalem but has been moving progressively away from the city—from Jerusalem to "traveling throughout the whole region" (9:32), to Lydda, to Joppa, and on to Caesarea. His geographical movement is mirrored in his crossing boundaries of another kind as well, as he takes on the mantle of healer (who of necessity must move among the sick), acquires corpse impurity in order to restore a dead woman to life (cf. Num. 19), and finally takes up lodging with a tanner (whose livelihood would have implicated him perpetually in ritual impurity). Thus, when we find Peter on a tanner's roof arguing with the Lord over issues of ritual purity (10:9–16), we can only wonder at Peter's apparent sanctimony.[22] Indeed, it is perhaps unsurprising that, when Peter relates his story to the Jerusalem believers, he admits only to staying in Joppa (11:5), dropping the not-insignificant detail that he had been enjoying the hospitality of a tanner. From his perch on the roof of a tanner's home, the symbolic distance represented by crossing the threshold of the house of a gentile centurion is after all not so far to traverse. If concerns with purity are correlated with the three matrices of persons, spaces, and foods, then all three are contravened in this narrative sequence, for Peter has moved outside the land of the Jews, is interacting personally with gentiles, and is directed by the Lord to eat animals of all kinds.

The interpersonal interactions on display and broadcast in this account extend acceptance and embrace friendship across deeply rooted socioreligious lines. In the ensuing exchange between Peter and Cornelius, a transformation of conceptual patterns (that is, patterns of thinking, feeling, believing, and behaving) occurs in a progression of steps:

- in Peter's insistence that he is "only a human being" (10:26)
- in Peter's decision to forgo the Jewish ban on sharing hospitality with gentiles (10:28–29)
- in Cornelius's testimony to the vision he has received from God (10:30–33)
- in Peter's recognition that Jesus Christ is indeed "Lord of all" (10:36)
- in the Spirit's coming upon Cornelius and his household (10:44)
- in the water baptism of those who had received the Spirit (10:47–48a)
- in the sharing of household hospitality over the ensuing days (10:48b).

22. Peter's hypocrisy is only "apparent" because he (and with him, others of the Jerusalem community of Jesus's followers, according to Acts) is himself deeply embedded in the ideology expressed in his challenge to the Lord's instructions. His own transformation is ongoing. For good reason, then, study of the Cornelius episode has come to emphasize not only Cornelius's conversion but also Peter's; cf., e.g., Gaventa, *From Darkness to Light*, 107–22; Plunkett, "Ethnocentricity and Salvation History."

Whatever else Luke recounts in this narrative sequence, he represents at least the ongoing conversion of Peter. Peter, and with him the Jerusalem community, progress toward an ever-more-full embodiment of transformed conceptual patterns grounded in and illustrative of the confession that Jesus is, indeed, "Lord of all."

Although I have tended to focus more narrowly on Peter's conversionary journey, the degree to which his is a shared journey is obvious. This is not surprising, since the journey frame (see chap. 3) typically includes traveling companions who share and assist the journey. Moreover, the heavy indebtedness of Luke's journey frame to Israel's story is a barometer of the high degree to which the conversionary journey must be understood as the path or way of a people and not that of an individual. Indeed, within the third Gospel, Luke often refers to "the disciples" without differentiating among them as followers of Jesus. "Grumbling, the Pharisees and their scribes were saying to the disciples . . ." (Luke 5:30). "His disciples were picking the heads of wheat, rubbing them in their hands, and eating them" (6:1). And so on. Even when the spotlight shines most brightly on Peter alone, the story singles him out as a representative of the others. And in the early chapters of Acts, Luke characteristically embeds the apostles, Peter included, in the community of believers. In Acts 1:14; 2:46; 4:24; 5:12; 15:25, he characterizes them with the term ὁμοθυμαδόν (*homothymadon*), "with one heart and mind." Thus, the Eleven, Mary and some other women, and Jesus's brothers are defined by their determined orientation toward a common aim, single-minded in their solidarity, giving themselves to prayer (1:14); the disciples persist in their unity in the temple (2:46); Luke declares their solidarity over against their opponents and associates their unity with the community-defining practice of prayer (4:24); and the disciples' oneness is contrasted with the betrayal of community dispositions by Ananias and Sapphira (5:12). Similarly, Luke uses the phrase ἐπὶ τὸ αὐτό (*epi to auto*, "together") in 1:15; 2:1, 44, 47 to underscore the oneness of the company of believers, both as a consequence of their obedience to Jesus and as an expression of the Spirit's generative work. Reflecting back on Peter's initial encounter with Jesus in Luke 5, we recall that Peter's movement from one form of fishing to another is shared with his mates. Moreover, in Luke 24, community practices of shared meals and shared testimony are integral to the enlightenment that comes in the postresurrection encounters with Jesus.

Importantly, through the entire process we have begun to sketch, Peter never ceases to be a Jew. Conversion for him is not a transformation from one religion to another. It is, rather, a journey by which he and his traveling companions are more and more deeply embedded in a particular way of tracing God's agenda with Israel, a metamorphosis realized in transformed patterns of reflection and practices. The fisherman now fishes for people, to catch them alive and bring them liberty. The owner of a small business now depends on others' hospitality, even that of a gentile centurion and his household, as he participates in announcing the good news. Conversion is a journey into more and more light (enlightenment), as the journey takes one in the direction of the dawning of God's restorative aims.

Conversion as Journey

Thus far, we have found plentiful evidence in the Lukan narrative for grasping "conversion" as a particular way of construing the metaphor LIFE IS A JOURNEY, namely, CONVERSION IS A JOURNEY (chap. 3). Moreover, we have found this to be true in multiple ways in Luke's account of Peter's ongoing transformation. Before taking up another series of Lukan conversionary accounts, we should step back to note some of the myriad ways the evangelist characterizes this conversionary movement, as well as reflect on why the evangelist portrays this movement as he does.

A preliminary linguistic observation will help our thinking about how Luke sketches his perspectives on the movement characterizing conversion. Consider, for example, the language of "entering" God's kingdom (e.g., Luke 18:17, 24, 25) and its corollary that one can be "in" the kingdom (e.g., 7:28; 13:28, 29; 14:15; 22:16; 22:30). The most natural sense of the verb "to enter" portrays God's kingdom as a container. On this accounting, movement would be from one vessel to another. Alternatively, we might think of God's kingdom as a place, as though one might move from one location to another. This portrait does not take us very far toward understanding Luke's theology, however. More helpful would be depictions that enable us to imagine entering the kingdom as entering a sphere, in this case, a sphere or field of influence, activity, or operation. On this view, entering or being in God's kingdom would entail our experiencing, identifying with, participating in, coming under the influence of, and joining the community formed in relation to God's kingdom. This way of thinking makes better sense of the reality that God's kingdom cannot be confined to a particular region or set of borders, since God's rule is not constrained by any geographical boundaries; it cannot be contained. Accordingly, from this point of view, movement from Point A to Point B is less about crossing the boundaries from one place to the next than it is about crossing the boundaries from one complex of conceptual patterns (ways of thinking, believing, feeling, and behaving) to another. It is less like moving geographically from one country to the next and more like exchanging one form of government (with its entailments, like freedom of speech, taxation, health care, or freedom of religion) for another.

Accordingly, Luke portrays conversion as movement from one life situation to another. In what follows, I will sketch three examples of the ways in which Luke presents conversion as movement.

From Darkness to Light

Luke presents conversion as the movement from darkness to light above all in Acts 26:17–18. In his testimony to King Agrippa, Paul represents his commission by recalling the words Jesus spoke to him on the way to Damascus: "I [that is, the Lord Jesus] will rescue you from your people and from the gentiles—to whom I am sending you, to open their eyes so that they might turn from darkness to light and from the power of Satan to God, so that they might receive forgiveness of sins and a place among those who are sanctified through faith in me."

"Darkness" and "light" appear to be universal metaphors in which language and conceptual structure from the source domain of vision, a bodily function, are used to depict the more abstract concepts of the presence or absence of knowledge, understanding, or even wisdom. Accordingly, someone might complain, "Why was I kept in the dark about that decision?" The biblical tradition presses this metaphor further by associating it with knowledge *of God*, or with living in God's light. In Exod. 10:21–23, for example, one of the disasters the Lord brings on Egypt involves three days of darkness, during which time the Israelites enjoy the light. For Isaiah, God forms light/prosperity as well as darkness/doom (45:7), and, at Israel's restoration, God's people are told, "Arise, *shine*; for your *light* has come, and the *glory* of the LORD has risen upon you. For *darkness* shall cover the earth, and thick *darkness* the peoples; but the LORD will arise upon you, and his *glory* will appear over you. Nations shall come to your *light*, and kings to the *brightness of your dawn*" (60:1–3, emphasis added).

We can survey Luke's use of darkness and light as follows:[23]

- Luke 1:77–79: The coming of God's agent of salvation marks Israel's restoration. Darkness is associated with death. Light is associated with salvation, forgiveness, and peace.

---

23. Luke's vocabulary of darkness: σκότος (*skotos*, "darkness") and σκοτεινός (*skoteinos*, "dark"); and of light: φῶς (*phōs*, "light"), ἐπιφαίνω (*epiphainō*, "to shine"), and φωτεινός (*phōteinos*, "full of light").

- Luke 2:32: Light is revelatory and associates the saving work of Christ with gentiles.
- Luke 11:33–36: Light signifies Jesus's message. Light, health, and ethical comportment are correlated, as are darkness, disease, and unethical comportment.
- Luke 16:8: People who belong to the light are contrasted with people who belong to this world.
- Luke 22:53: The supremacy of darkness is realized in Jesus's arrest.
- Luke 23:44–45: Jesus's crucifixion is a time of darkness (see Acts 2:20).
- Acts 2:20: The cataclysm of the end-time includes the darkening of the sun (see Luke 23:44–45).
- Acts 9:3: Light is revelatory.
- Acts 12:7: Light marks divine intervention to liberate Peter from prison.
- Acts 13:11: Divine judgment is realized as darkness.
- Acts 13:47: Paul and Barnabas bring light, that is, the message of salvation, to the gentiles.
- Acts 26:18: Conversion is from darkness/Satan's power to light/God.
- Acts 26:23: Paul's message is light, that is, salvation, to both Jew and gentile.

We find, then, that (1) light and darkness can refer to the presence or absence of sunlight, but even when they do their metaphorical senses are not far from view; (2) light and darkness can be understood as realms to which people belong and according to whose rule people behave; (3) light is typically associated with divine revelation more generally, as well as with the coming or message of salvation more particularly, and thus with illumination, health, the age of salvation, and the Lord's coming or presence; and (4) darkness is typically correlated with divine judgment, and more particularly with death, disease, the devil, cataclysm, and blindness. Conversion, understood in terms of movement from darkness to light, is thus easily understood as movement from a less desirable to a more desirable life situation.

From Crooked to Straight

Conversion as movement from crooked to straight is signified already in Luke's representation of John the Baptist's mission: "Prepare the way of the Lord, make his paths straight. . . . The crooked will be made straight" (Luke 3:4–5, following Isa. 40:4). As we saw in chap. 3, this phrasing does double duty, signifying both the path on which God's restored people walk and the reformed character of the people who walk this path. Luke's language thus signals at one and the same time God's restoration of his people and the way of life embraced by those people whom God restores. This is not surprising since, from the standpoint of cognitive metaphor theory, we find here a conception of well-being and ethical comportment expressed in terms of spatial situatedness.[24] Thus, a moral person might be said to be "following the straight and narrow," and trustworthy people are "straight shooters." Conversely, as the psalmist puts it, "Those who turn aside to their own crooked ways the LORD will lead away with evildoers" (Ps. 125:5).

How are these terms used in Luke's narrative?[25]

- Luke 3:4–5: God's ways are straight paths. The coming of God's salvation is realized in the crooked being made straight.
- Luke 9:41: "Crooked" (or "perverse") characterizes a people who are also faithless (cf. Acts 2:40), a description that recalls Israel in the exodus story (cf. Deut. 32:4–5: "A faithful God, without deceit, just and upright is he; yet his degenerate children have dealt falsely with him, a perverse and crooked generation").
- Luke 13:11, 13: Satan (13:16) has crippled a woman with the result that she is incapable of standing up straight (symptomatic of a state of illness); Jesus releases her from diabolic oppression so that she can stand up straight (symptomatic of a state of wellness) (cf. Acts 14:10).
- Luke 21:28: When people recognize the signs of the end of the age, they should "stand up straight" in anticipation of their redemption.
- Luke 23:2: Jesus is accused of making God's people "crooked," that is, of leading them astray.
- Acts 2:40: This generation is morally corrupt (cf. Deut. 32:5; Luke 9:41).
- Acts 8:21: Simon Magus's heart is "not straight before God."
- Acts 9:11: Ananias will find Saul on "Straight Street."
- Acts 13:8, 10: A false prophet tries to turn Sergius Paulus away from the faith, but Paul confronts him: "Stop twisting the Lord's straight ways into crooked ones!"

24. See Slingerland, "Conceptual Metaphor Theory," 19–20.

25. Luke's vocabulary of crookedness: διαστρέφω (diastrephō, "to make crooked") and σκολιός (skolios, "crooked"); and of straightness: ἀνακύπτω (anakyptō, "to straighten up"), ἀνορθόω (anorthoō, "to restore"), εὐθύς (euthys, "straight"), and ὀρθός (orthos, "straight, correct").

- Acts 14:10: Paul directs a crippled man to stand up straight (cf. Luke 13:11, 13).
- Acts 15:16: David's tent will be restored.
- Acts 16:11: Paul and his entourage travel a straight route.
- Acts 20:30: False teachers will make crooked, or twist, God's word.
- Acts 21:1: Paul and his entourage travel a straight route.

We find that (1) Luke can use the term "straight" in its ordinary sense (e.g., a straight course); (2) "straight" and "crooked" can describe good and bad health, respectively; and (3) attending to God's ways is correlated with the concept of straight, and opposing God's ways is correlated with the concept of crooked. Conversion, understood in terms of movement from crooked to straight, is thus easily understood in terms of movement from an undesirable moral space to a desirable one.

From Outside to Inside

One of the structures by which humans organize experience is by means of spatial orientation. For example, "up" and "down" refer to "more" and "less," whether one is gauging status or the price of eggs. Another example: With the concepts of in and out, we map relationships of inclusion or exclusion, based on our experiences of containment (e.g., in or out of a room, and, then, in or out of a circle of friends).[26] Thus, spatial experience maps onto relational concepts, undergirding the metaphor CLOSENESS IS BELONGING. If the community of believers serves as a point of orientation, a landmark, then we can ask who is in and who is out, and we can think of *conversion* as movement from out to in. (Conversely, again taking the community of believers as the landmark, we can speak of movement from in to out as *deconversion*, about which I will have more to say in chap. 5.) Luke-Acts employs a range of images that exhibit this concern. For example:

- Who are Abraham's children? Those who are included in Abraham's family are those whose lives imitate Abraham's hospitality: sharing with those who have none and practicing what is just (Luke 3:7–14; 19:1–10). In fact, practices of hospitality are characteristic of the baptized, like Lydia (Acts 16:15) and the Philippian jailer and his family (16:33–34), whereas those who refuse hospitality to the needy might refer to Abraham

26. See M. Johnson, *Body in the Mind*, 30–40.

as "father" but find themselves distant from Abraham in the afterlife (cf. Luke 16:19–31).

- Who belongs to Jesus's family? His mother and brothers come to him but stand outside, unable to reach him. Jesus proclaims, "My mother and brothers are those who hear and do God's word" (Luke 8:19–21; cf. 11:27–28).

- Entry into the end-time banquet is through a narrow door, and Jesus advises his audience to make every effort to enter through it. He also warns that some will be surprised to find themselves outside the door, thinking they belonged when they did not (Luke 13:23–30).

- After Peter's Pentecost address, about three thousand people accepted Peter's message, were baptized, were added to the community of Christ followers, and engaged in such Spirit-enabled practices as sharing homes, sharing meals, and sharing possessions (Acts 2:41–47).

In these examples, we find that closeness is worked out in relation to participation in Abraham's family, in the end-time banquet, and in the community of Christ's followers. Those who are close include those who are characterized by faith, baptism, and a range of identifying, formative practices: doing God's word, engaging in hospitality, and so on.

Importantly for Luke-Acts, conversionary movement from out to in is matched by missional movement from in to out. God's promise of the gift of the Spirit, whose coming participates in God's restoration of his people, is both for "you and your children" (Israelites present in Jerusalem and elsewhere besides) and for "all who are far away," a phrase with universalistic innuendo (cf. Isa. 57:19). Both Jews and gentiles are thus called to save themselves "from this crooked generation," that is, to move away from the rebellious practices of one people, a corrupt one, toward the sort of faithfulness that is characteristic of the community of the baptized (Acts 2:39–40).

Lukan Rhetoric

These metaphors lie close to the surface of the Lukan narrative, suggesting that further investigation would bring further metaphors to the surface—including those related to changing sides in a struggle (e.g., Acts 9:26–27), slavery and freedom (e.g., Acts 16:16–17), and more.

Can we say more about the role these metaphors play in Luke's narrative? The language Luke uses to describe conversion as movement must be understood as integral to his narrative rhetoric. These metaphors, we should recall, speak to abstract notions like straight or crooked, or judgment or restoration, by recruiting bodily experiences such as light and darkness, sickness and health. Such metaphors can be and often are associated with visceral responses. As a result, they function as somatic markers that, when activated, promote or fuel certain ways of feeling. (The phrase "somatic markers" refers to bodily mechanisms by which emotions like happiness or disgust influence decision making.) Accordingly, these metaphors play a role in biasing persons, often at an unselfconscious level, in one direction rather than another.[27] If LIFE IS A JOURNEY, Luke's metaphors encourage taking one route rather than another.

By fueling positive or negative feelings, whether consciously or, more likely, unconsciously, metaphors can direct our attention toward a more welcome life situation and thus influence decision-making processes. Consider some of the associations on which Luke draws: Darkness or light? Outcast or intimate? Filthy or clean? Life or death? Such metaphors recruit negative and/or positive associations in order to encourage one form of response over another. Who wants to remain in the realm of Satan? Who wants to live under diabolic oppression? Who wants to live life bent over, unable to stand up straight? Who wants to be on the outside looking in? Luke's conversionary metaphors thus invite conversionary responses at a gut level, through feelings of attraction or repulsion.

Tax Collectors, Sinners, and the Lost: Three Lukan Texts

Luke's Gospel includes three narrative accounts that are joined together by a set of shared, stable features: Levi Responds to Jesus's Invitation (Luke 5:27–32), Rejoicing at the Finding of the Lost (15:1–32), and Jesus Defends Zacchaeus (Luke 19:1–10). All three accounts include the following elements:

- Jesus in the company of tax collectors and sinners; in 5:29–32 and 15:1–2 with specific reference to eating together, and in 19:5–7 with the expectation of doing so.
- Others (Pharisees and their legal experts in 5:30; Pharisees and legal experts in 15:1–2; "those who saw" in 19:7) protest[28] against Jesus's association with such people.
- Jesus responds with reference to the character of his mission: "to call sinners, not the righteous, to conversion" (5:32); to participate in God's

---

27. This is ably argued by Slingerland, "Conceptual Blending." For the role of feelings as embodied cognition in decision making more generally, see Damasio, *Descartes' Error*.

28. Luke 5:30: γογγύζω (*gongyzō*, "to murmur, grumble"); 15:2 and 19:10: διαγογγύζω (*diagongyzō*, "to complain, grumble").

own happiness by celebrating the finding of the lost (15:6–7, 9–10, 32); "to seek and to save the lost" (19:10).

Although no one would imagine that Luke has told the same story three times, when read together, these three episodes demonstrate how Jesus's mission redraws the boundaries around what is acceptable, especially through emphasizing how people are labeled as insiders or outsiders to God's people, and they demonstrate the embodied nature of conversion, particularly with regard to hospitality and possessions.

Labels That Stick

Luke 5:27–32 introduces two important categories of people, "tax collectors" and "sinners," and these same labels are found in 15:1–2 and in 19:1, 8. Both tax collectors and sinners are censured through their pairing in 5:30 and 15:2, and placing tax collectors and sinners side by side clearly identifies tax collectors as sinners. In our third account, a tax collector, Zacchaeus, is subsequently labeled by onlookers as a sinner (19:2, 7).

What can we say about tax collectors? Tax collecting was a form, perhaps the prototypical form, of private enterprise in the Roman Empire. When, long before Luke's Gospel was written, Rome ceased collecting its own taxes, it sold the right to collect taxes to the highest bidder, who himself farmed out the work of collecting taxes to others. We might imagine an ancient precursor to modern companies like Amway or Tupperware: a pyramid structure in which profits from goods sold make their way up multiple levels of businesspeople, with each along the way taking a share of the overage. A major difference, of course, is that private enterprise in the service of the Empire focused on collecting taxes, not selling goods. The tax rate might be set at 10 percent, but this varied widely, and tax collectors often simply took whatever they could get away with. Recall John the Baptist's counsel to tax collectors: "Collect no more than you are authorized to collect" (3:13)—counsel that suggests a tendency among tax collectors to charge too much.

The tax collectors we find in Luke's Gospel typically occupy the front line of the business. They were the public face of the enterprise and as such were tagged with all sorts of insults (as we saw in chap. 3)—thieves, snoops, and corrupt—the social equivalent of pimps and turncoats. Even when these entrepreneurs were wealthy (and it is easier to imagine wealth accruing to the upper echelons of the hierarchy than to the bottom), they occupied lower rungs on the status ladder than their wealth might suggest. Theirs was "new money," the money for which they had to work, and, however necessary it might be, their work was widely detested; contrast this, then, with the money and status of those from old families with vast landholdings. The exception to the typical tax collector in Luke's Gospel is Zacchaeus, whom Luke introduces with a term otherwise unknown in ancient Greek literature: ἀρχιτελώνης (*architelōnēs*), usually translated "chief tax collector" (e.g., NAB, NRSV, TNIV). Although the job title itself reflects Luke's widespread interest in "rulers," including compound words that begin with ἀρχι- (*archi-*, "chief," "ruler," "leader"), here it probably designates Zacchaeus's role as the head of a group of tax collectors, a kind of "district manager," responsible for collecting customs on the lucrative trade route between Perea (to the east) and Judea (to the west), which passed through Jericho.[29] This would help to explain a further term with which the narrator characterizes Zacchaeus: he was "wealthy" (πλούσιος, *plousios*; 19:2).

If "tax collector" thus designates someone of objectionable status in the Roman Mediterranean, his social position would be further threatened by his association in these Lukan texts with sinners. What "sinner" entails is not altogether clear, however, with scholars championing a range of options: the wicked, for example, as well as those who reject the Pharisees' holiness program, the immoral, and so on.[30] The standard Greek-English dictionary gets us close to how Luke uses the term when it recognizes that "being considered an outsider because of failure to conform to certain standards is a [frequent] semantic component."[31] In this case, "sinner" is a relative term, measured in relation to a particular group; "sinners" do not maintain faithfulness in the way "we" measure it. If we take the Pharisees and their legal experts as the landmark, or defining center of faithfulness to God, then it is not surprising that Luke's phrase "tax collectors and *others*" morphs into "tax collectors and *sinners*" (5:29, 30). Jesus's antagonists introduce the term, so we must hear it from their perspective. Whatever else "sinner" might entail, then, this label is a form of socioreligious shunning. It designates people who live outside the landmark group. And in the three episodes we are considering, this ostracism takes two forms: name-calling and (expected) exclusion from the common table. With the label "sinners" introduced by others, Jesus goes on to use the term in 5:31–32, but his usage is ironic, as we shall see.

29. This was suggested long ago by Godet, *Luke*, 2:216. Concerning tax collectors, I have drawn on Herrenbrück, *Jesus und die Zöllner*; Michel, "τελώνης"; Donahue, "Tax Collectors and Sinners"; Badian, *Publicans and Sinners*.

30. See, e.g., Borg, *Conflict, Holiness and Politics*; Sanders, *Jesus and Judaism*; Neale, *None but the Sinners*; Adams, *Sinner in Luke*.

31. BDAG 51. Cf. Dunn, "Pharisees, Sinners, and Jesus," esp. 275–80.

Thus far we have maintained that the terms "tax collector" and "sinner" function as labels and that in normal usage they would have been correlated with marginal status. Hence, tax collectors and sinners were socioreligious outsiders, people to be avoided. What is fascinating, then, is that this is not at all what we find concerning them in Luke's Gospel. Tax collectors come to be baptized (3:12), follow Jesus (5:27), acknowledge God's justice (7:29), are numbered among Jesus's friends (7:34), listen to Jesus and join him at the table (15:1–2; cf. 5:29), come to God in humility (18:9–14), and both seek and welcome Jesus (19:2–3). Tellingly, twice Luke contrasts the Pharisees with tax collectors, since the Pharisees and the legal experts reject God's purpose for themselves (7:30) and a Pharisee prays in a self-exalting manner rather than in humility (18:9–14). Similarly, people regarded as "sinners" in Luke's Gospel are counted among Jesus's friends (7:34), demonstrate great love (7:36–50), repent (15:1–32) and seek God's mercy (18:9–14), and share meals with Jesus (5:29–32; 15:1–2; cf. 19:1–10). If Jesus and the good news (rather than the Pharisees, legal experts, and their characteristic judgments and practices) compose the landmark by which life's orientation and trajectory are traced, then it seems that Luke portrays tax collectors and sinners as those having oriented themselves rightly and now numbered among those faithfully serving God's eschatological purpose. They are converts.

The situation with Zacchaeus is more complex, however, and in some ways his story demonstrates the folly of all human label-making and name-calling. In 19:1–10, three agents label Zacchaeus, as follows:

- Luke the narrator labels Zacchaeus as a *ruler* of *tax collector*s who is *wealthy* (19:2).
- The unnamed onlookers label Zacchaeus as a *sinner* (19:7).
- Jesus labels Zacchaeus as a *son of Abraham* and, by implication, one of the *lost* (19:9–10).

Considering initially those first four labels, we see that they actually provide contradictory ways of portraying Zacchaeus. We have already learned that, within Luke's narrative, tax collectors and sinners are marginalized by others but portrayed positively in terms of their response to the good news. The opposite would hold for people described as "rulers," "chiefs," or "leaders": high priests (3:2; 22:50, 54), synagogue leaders (8:41, 49; 13:14), chief priests (9:22; 19:47; 20:1, 19; 22:2, 4, 54, 66; 23:4, 10; 23:13; 24:20), the ruler of demons (11:15), state authorities (12:11, 58; 20:20), a leading Pharisee (14:1), a "certain ruler" (18:18), and the Jerusalem elite as a group

(23:35).[32] These are uniformly portrayed negatively in relation to Jesus and his message, a reality foreshadowed in Mary's commanding voice concerning God's gracious intervention on behalf of his people:

> He has shown strength with his arm;
>> He has scattered those with arrogant thoughts and dispositions.
> He has pulled the powerful down from their thrones;
>> He has raised up the lowly.
> He has filled the hungry with good things;
>> He has sent the rich away empty-handed. (1:51–53)

As this portion of Mary's song also clarifies, Luke's Gospel is persistent in its negative portrayal of those who carry the label "rich" or "wealthy," too. The fate of the wealthy and for those with plenty is a terrible one (6:24–25; 16:19–31), wealth lures people to pursue prestige and security apart from God (12:13–21, 33–34), and the wealthy who want to enter God's kingdom face insurmountable obstacles, at least from a human vantage point (18:24).

What Luke has given us thus far, then, is a perplexing presentation of Zacchaeus. If Jesus and his message constitute the landmark by which we measure life's orientation and trajectory, then Zacchaeus is a man torn in two directions, nothing short of schizophrenic. He is a ruler, but a ruler of tax collectors. He is rich but regarded by unnamed observers as "a sinner." The usual labels fail in this instance, their paradoxical complexity undermining all attempts to prejudge Zacchaeus's character in the usual way.

We get little help from another set of images Luke uses to tell Zacchaeus's story, those concerned with verticality: up, down.[33] Zacchaeus was "short in stature," he "climbed up" a sycamore tree, Jesus "looked up" and told Zacchaeus to "come down," and Zacchaeus "came down" (19:3–6). At the beginning of this account, Luke has us nodding our heads, up and down, as we follow the action. It all starts with Luke's description of Zacchaeus as "short," though we should not immediately assume that Zacchaeus's problem was his height per se. In fact, Luke's vertical images compete with each other. Humorously, Zacchaeus elevates himself in his quest to see the one whom he addresses with the high-ranking title "Lord." If Zacchaeus is a "ruler," does this mean that his throne is a sycamore tree? What is a grown man doing in a tree? "How childish!" people might say, both then and now.

---

32. That is, anyone identified as an ἄρχων (*archōn*, "ruler") or with a compound using the prefix ἀρχι- (*archi-*, "ruling, leading").

33. Contra Parsons, *Body and Character*, 97–108. I have adapted some of this material from the lengthier treatment in Green, "Hospitality for Kids."

Indeed, we must allow for the strong likelihood that others would have looked down on Zacchaeus. After all, repeated studies have shown that height is a metaphor for power and status, with those who are taller more likely to acquire respect and influence.[34] This is consistent with the way we correlate "up" with "more" and "down" with "less." In Luke's text we have a clear instance of the universal metaphor according to which the physical experience of verticality is mapped on to subjective experiences of quantity, leading to a range of novel associations: UP IS POWERFUL, UP IS IMPORTANT, and so on.[35] Zacchaeus is "down," and so less important, less powerful, of lower status. Given these linkages, we should not allow to escape our attention how Luke thus associates Zacchaeus in chap. 19 with infants in chap. 18—smaller than those around them (19:3) and spurned either by the disciples or more generally by those looking on (18:15; 19:7) but nonetheless recognized and blessed by Jesus as exemplary (18:16–17; 19:9–10).

Zacchaeus, then, is "down" and "out." It is no wonder that Luke writes that Zacchaeus was unable to see Jesus—not because he was short but "because of the crowd" (19:3). As the disciples formed a barrier between Jesus and infants in 18:15, now the crowd forms a barrier between Jesus and Zacchaeus. As those who headed the parade coming into Jericho blocked a blind man's access to Jesus in 18:39, now the crowd blocks Zacchaeus's access to Jesus. Yet Zacchaeus seeks Jesus out and happily welcomes him as his guest. Zacchaeus does not just meet Jesus in the streets and share a meal with him; however meaningful such behavior might be, it does not mark one out as a member of the community of the saved (13:23–30). He goes further, demonstrating through his customary practices of restitution and sharing with the poor that his life is oriented toward God's purpose (19:8; see 3:7–14).[36] Here, then, is the critical point: Zacchaeus displays the character of his life in these ways *and yet* remains on the fringes of his socioreligious world.

This leads to Jesus's own characterization of Zacchaeus. He does not label Zacchaeus as a "ruler," "tax collector," "rich man," "sinner," or a "short" man of low status. Here is Jesus's label for Zacchaeus: "son of Abraham." What might this mean? It does not identify Zacchaeus as a Jew. As his Hebrew name suggests, he is almost certainly a Jew, but, for Luke, no DNA test designed

34. E.g., Egolf and Corder, "Height Differences"; Judge and Cable, "Physical Height"; Schubert, "Your Highness"; Giessner and Schubert, "High in the Hierarchy."

35. Cf. Lindstromberg, *English Prepositions Explained*, 191–202.

36. It will be clear that I regard 19:1–10 as a vindication story: Luke presents Zacchaeus as someone already engaged in a conversionary life, without giving us insight into how or when Zacchaeus converted. Key to this reading are the present-tense verbs in 19:8, "I give" and "I pay back" (cf. KJV, CEB), which most contemporary translations render with a futuristic sense (e.g., NAB, NIV, NRSV). For further discussion, see Green, *Luke*, 666–73.

to determine one's ancestry could prove that someone was Abraham's child. "Don't begin to say among yourselves, 'Abraham is our father,'" John the Baptist had proclaimed (3:8). Reading through Luke's Gospel, we find that Abraham's descendants are the recipients of God's mercy (1:54–55), they "produce fruit that demonstrates repentance"—including the very "fruit" that characterizes Zacchaeus's life (3:7–14; 19:8), they are the marginal who are loosed from bondage (13:10–17), and they are spurned in this life but blessed in the life to come (16:19–31). That is, in Luke's narrative, Abraham's children are understood in two ways: (1) they occupy society's fringes where they are easily ignored, yet are those to whom God responds with fidelity and mercy (e.g., 16:19–31); or (2) they are those who demonstrate their family resemblance with Abraham through their Abraham-like behaviors, parsed in terms of socioeconomic relations and hospitality (e.g., 3:7–14). As if Luke practiced double-exposure photography, we see both portraits in the one image of Zacchaeus. At the end of the day, this label, "Abraham's child," is the only one that matters.

With regard to Zacchaeus one final question remains, namely, what it means for him to be counted among "the lost" whom the Son of Man has come to seek and to save (19:10). Jesus's pronouncement concerning "the lost" is the climax of this narrative account, and it encourages our thinking within the horizons of meaning offered by two other texts—one from within Luke's Gospel, the other from Ezekiel.

In Luke 15, Jesus responds to the indictment brought against him by the Pharisees and legal experts by telling "this parable" (15:3). "This parable" turns out to be three parables, all of which have a similar structure and press toward a single conclusion. The first concerns a lost sheep, the second a lost coin, and the third a lost son. Finding the lost leads to joyous celebration, and the close association of these three parables demonstrates that joyous celebration on earth is nothing less than a mirror of joyous celebration in heaven. In short, Jesus defends his eating with tax collectors and sinners with his claim that his behavior participates in God's actions.

What does it mean to be "lost"? Luke gives us no straightforward answer in these parables. Clearly, the younger son chooses a life apart from his family, community, and religious traditions; Jesus's comment that this younger son journeyed to "a distant country" (15:13) is thus true not only geographically but also in social and religious terms. Also clear is that the younger son came to his senses and returned home, a transparent description of conversion (15:17–20)[37] that parallels references to repentant sinners in the preceding

---

37. The younger son's action illustrates the meaning of repentance in Israel's Scriptures: "having moved in a particular direction, to move thereupon in the opposite direction, the implication

parables (15:7, 10). At the same time, it is difficult to understand how a coin, or even a sheep, might "repent"; they are simply lost, then found, and their finding is celebrated. For his part, the lost son gets no further in his prepared speech than admitting his sin and recognizing his shame before he is restored and the celebrations begin.

Ezekiel 34 is interesting in this respect, since here God's people need to be rescued, or restored, but are not called on to repent. They remain lost, not because of the sinful choices and behaviors from which they need to turn, but because of the failure of their leaders.

> And a word of the Lord came to me, saying: Son of man, prophesy against the shepherds of Israel; prophesy, and say to the shepherds, This is what the Lord says: Oh, you shepherds of Israel, do shepherds feed themselves? Do not shepherds feed the flocks? Behold, you devour the milk and wrap yourselves with the wool and slaughter the fatling, but you do not feed my sheep. You did not strengthen the weakened and did not build up the unwell and did not bind up the crushed and did not turn about the one that strayed and did not seek the lost, and you subdued the strong with hardship. And my sheep were scattered because there were no shepherds, and they were as food for all the animals of the field. And my sheep were scattered on every mountain and upon every lofty hill, and they were scattered upon the surface of every land, and there was not one who searched for them nor one who turned them back. (Ezek. 34:1–6 NETS)

Note the conjunction of these terms in v. 4: "weakened," "unwell," "crushed," "strayed," and "lost." With this list, Judean rulers are indicted for their failure to support the flourishing of society's weakest members. What is more, this failure of leadership was itself responsible for the scattering of the sheep. Therefore, the Lord stands against the shepherds and announces that he will take up the role in which they failed:

> This is what the Lord says: Behold, I will search for my sheep and watch over them. Just as the shepherd seeks his flock by day, when there is thick darkness and cloud in the midst of the separated sheep, so will I seek out my sheep and drive them away from every place, there where they were scattered in a day of cloud and thick darkness. And I will bring them out from the nations and gather

---

being (unless there is evidence to the contrary) that one will arrive again at the initial point of departure" (Holladay, *Root Šûbh in the Old Testament*, 53, italics removed); see also Thompson and Martens, "שׁוּב," 57: "The imagery is one of a person doing a turnabout." Cf. Bailey, *Poet and Peasant*, 173–80; Bailey sees in the younger son's soliloquy evidence of shrewdness, but this overlooks both the way his behavior models conversion and, especially, the importance of 15:7, 10 as parallels for understanding the younger son's action.

them from the countries and will bring them into their land, and I will feed them upon the mountains of Israel and in the ravines and in every habitation of the land. I will feed them in a good pasture; their folds shall be on the lofty mountain of Israel; there also they shall lie down, and there they shall rest in fine luxury, and they shall be fed in a rich pasture on the mountains of Israel. It is I who will feed my sheep, and it is I who will give them rest, and they shall know that I am the Lord. This is what the Lord says: I will seek the lost, and I will turn about the one that strayed, and I will bind up the crushed, and I will strengthen the abandoned, and I will watch the strong, and I will feed them with judgment. (Ezek. 34:11–16 NETS)

The failure to care for society's weakest in v. 4 is recalled in v. 16 as the Lord names those for whom he will care: "the lost," "strayed," "crushed," and "abandoned." By way of analogy, Luke 15 portrays the Pharisees and legal experts as Israel's failed leaders, and tax collectors and sinners as God's scattered people whom God seeks to shepherd. The "lost" would thus be those spurned by Pharisees and legal experts, and so the lost-but-found sheep, the lost-but-found coin, and the lost-but-found son symbolize those tax collectors and sinners with whom Jesus gathers at the table. Similarly, in seeking hospitality with Zacchaeus, who was himself scorned by the crowd and onlookers, Jesus identifies himself with Ezekiel's Lord, who seeks and saves the lost.

"In" and "out"—where one stands in relation to the center—depend on the nature of the center, how the center is identified, and who does the identifying. In Luke's account, an outsider in relation to his own townspeople, yet a man whose life produces fruit associated with a genuine alignment toward God's purpose, Zacchaeus (and with him, his household), is found by Jesus and restored to the community of God's people.

Conversion, Hospitality, Possessions

None of these three narrative accounts explicitly uses the language of repentance or conversion to describe what people do, even if this seems to be implied. Zacchaeus engages in behavior that identifies him as someone who has (at some time in the past) (re)oriented his heart and life toward God's purpose (19:8). Anonymous tax collectors and sinners are associated by way of analogy with repentant sinners (15:7, 10), and a son comes to his senses and returns to his home (15:17–21). And Levi and his banquet guests apparently constitute the sinners for whom Jesus has come to call to repentance (5:32). What conversionary dispositions and/or behaviors do these people display? What can we learn about conversion from them?

LUKE 5:27–32

We are struck in the first instance with the sheer economy of the encounter between Jesus and Levi in Luke 5:27–28. Levi is at his station, a kiosk for tax collection. Jesus speaks two words only: "Follow me." Luke's report is short, clipped, staccato-like: Levi "left everything, got up, and followed him." As it turns out, though, this abrupt and simple sequence sets the stage for a larger scene, in which Levi hosts a large banquet in his home, including numerous tax collectors and "others" (5:29), and this provides the venue for Jesus's give-and-take with Pharisees, their legal experts, and "some people" (5:30–39). Five emphases come to the fore.

1. Luke's readers are given no background regarding Levi, apart from his occupation as a tax collector. This is significant in its own way, insofar as it provides us with insight into the social stigma associated with Levi (see above) and paves the way for his guest list for the banquet he will hold in Jesus's honor. However, we have no insider knowledge of Levi's relationship to the synagogue, regarding whether Levi might have been among the tax collectors who heard John the Baptist's message (3:12–13), or concerning whether he had developed an interest in, or even was aware of, Jesus and his message. We have no basis for imagining that he is a "seeker," and no initial reason to rethink the common caricature of tax collectors as dishonest Roman collaborators. The encounter Luke portrays, then, underscores Jesus's apparently unwarranted initiative, subsequently captured in his mission statement, stated positively: "I've come to call sinners to a change of heart and life" (5:32). In this instance, then, the motivation for conversion comes from outside the converted, entirely at Jesus's initiative.

2. Conversion is realized for Levi in "following" Jesus. This involves accompanying Jesus as one of his entourage, of course, but also embracing his itinerary, obeying his words, and taking on his life habits. Levi's response triggers the journey frame we discussed in chap. 3, so it is not surprising that, in this narrative account, we find some of the characteristics and accoutrements of the journey: taking a path determined by the leader, traveling light, and beginning the journey of following Jesus with an emerging band of "travelers."

3. Leaving everything precedes adopting Jesus's itinerary, so that Levi comes to the expedition of discipleship unencumbered. As Jesus says elsewhere, "Only those of you who give up everything that's yours can be my disciples" (14:33); or as he told a rich ruler, "Sell everything you have, give to the poor, . . . and come, follow me" (18:22). Apparently, this journey requires prior disinvestment, but here is a paradox: How can Levi leave everything *and* throw a party for Jesus at his house? The term "everything" disallows any suggestion that

Levi gives up *only* his station and position as a tax collector. (Moreover, we know from 3:7–14 that one can live a conversionary life as a tax collector.) More generally in Luke-Acts, however, we learn that wealth and possessions are deeply embedded in social relations. When Luke's Gospel calls for economic distribution, then, it does so in relation to those in need, with the result that the wealthy give without expectation of return and without using their wealth to leverage social advancement. For Jesus to say that the rich ruler should sell what he has and give to the poor, then, is a directive concerned with the rich ruler's proposed, newfound kinship with the poor and not about the evils of wealth per se. Similarly, Levi enacts conversion by extending hospitality to others, and his leaving everything is realized in his placing what he has in the service of Jesus's mission. It is not too much to say that Luke thus identifies this "leaving everything" with "converting."

4. Gathering at the table, seen here, is often associated with conversion—as in the father's insistence that the recovery of his son required a celebrative feast (15:22–32) or in the meal at the Philippian jailer's house (Acts 16:30–34). Eating is a creaturely necessity, of course, but *eating together* is a social event that extends boundaries and cultivates solidarity. Not surprisingly, then, one of the characteristic features of the community of those who convert, are baptized, and receive the gift of the Holy Spirit is that they share food in each other's homes (Acts 2:46). Since meals in Roman antiquity encoded messages about hierarchy and inclusion/exclusion (e.g., Luke 14:7–14), it is telling that Levi throws a banquet that throws cautionary words about proper social and religious boundaries to the wind. Jesus's presence at the table with the socio-religious fringe publicly interprets the good news. Therefore, the hospitality Luke portrays here is the gospel performed, conversion enacted.

5. The nature of this table gathering raises questions: Why does Jesus eat with tax collectors and sinners? Why are Jesus's disciples noted for their customary habits of eating and drinking? Tax collectors and sinners may be celebrating, but Pharisees, their legal experts, and some other unnamed people raise their voices in protest, and this clears the path for Jesus's teaching at the table, his table talk. His response turns on three interrelated claims: his mission is to call sinners back to God, the converted include motley folk being formed into a community centered on Jesus, and all of this is rooted in God's ancient purpose (5:30–39). Note that each of the questions raised against Jesus has to do with boundaries and boundary maintenance: Who belongs to this group, and why? What are the practices by which this group is identified? The answer to the question of who belongs is repentant sinners, even when they come from outside the ranks of those with solid social and religious credentials. Why them? This is actually the nature of Jesus's mission,

which is tied to the ancient ways of God. The answer to the question of what are their characteristic practices is celebrating in the presence of the Messiah with feasts at which there is no room for old hostilities, outdated hierarchies, or former judgments. In this way we see that the conversionary practice of gathering at the table is christologically oriented and theologically grounded.

LUKE 15:1–32

Turning to the second of our three texts, we should note, first, the lack of any clear break between chaps. 14 and 15. This is important for three reasons. First, the focus of 14:1–24 on welcoming into one's homes those who eke out their lives on society's margins continues, though now we shift from "the poor, the crippled, the lame, and the blind" and from those found in "the highways and back alleys" to "tax collectors and sinners" (14:13, 23; 15:1–2). Up, down, in, out: where people stand in relation to others, "us" versus "them"—such interests spill over from Luke 14 into Luke 15.

Second, Luke 14 ends with a series of remarks on the conditions of discipleship. These are cast especially in terms of kinship relations and possessions, both of which can impede patterns of life appropriate to the journey Jesus has now rejoined (14:25–35).

Third, Jesus's final words are these: "Whoever has ears to hear must hear!" This rather colorless translation draws attention to the repetition of the term ἀκούω (akouō, "to hear") in Jesus's concluding instruction, a repetition that makes the opening of chap. 15 all the more interesting. Tax collectors were gathering around Jesus precisely for this reason: "to hear [ἀκούω, akouō] him." It is hard not to hear echoes from Jesus's parable of the soils in Luke 8:5–15. There we find the identical directive, "Whoever has ears to hear must hear!" And there we learn that fruitfulness depends on good hearing: "The seed that fell on good soil are good-hearted people of integrity who hear the word, embrace it, and produce fruit through their steadfastness" (8:15). Hearing well is thematic for Luke-Acts, where it is descriptive of Jesus's true family (8:21), characteristic of those who build their homes on good foundations (6:49), a quality of human flourishing (11:28), and so on. Hence, the importance of Luke's singular characterization of tax collectors and sinners is transparent. They come to listen.

"Hearing" can refer to auditory processes alone, of course, but this hardly accounts for the texts we are examining. We find phrases like "ears to hear" or "hearing, really hear," as well as directives like "Let these words sink into your ears" (9:44 NRSV). Sometimes hearing is associated with the "heart," the center of a person's dispositions, as in the reference in 8:15 to "good-hearted people of integrity," or in Luke's report that, as Lydia "listened, the

Lord opened her heart to pay attention to the things Paul was saying" (Acts 16:14).[38] Evidence like this moves us well beyond talk of audiologists or audiometers, or the auditory system, with its ear bones, canals, and cochleae. Instead, bodily, sensory experiences of hearing project to abstract concepts like understanding, character, and obedience.

Hearing well depends on having the categories of thought by which to make sense of what one hears. People trained in psychology use and hear words like "borderline" differently from the general populace, just as neuroscientists have a specialized understanding of "insult," and longtime churchgoers, some of them at least, know what to do when they see the word "doxology." Hearing well entails behavior, too. This is explicit in a text like Luke 11:28, where Jesus correlates hearing God's word and putting it into practice with genuine human flourishing, or in the parable of the soils, in which hearing well is identified with hearing that produces fruit (8:5–15), but implicit more broadly.[39] What parent has not responded to evidence of a child's noncompliance by asking, "Didn't you hear me?" Hearing well, then, is a function of formation within particular communities. Hearing well is realized in the formation of patterns of thinking, feeling, believing, and behaving characteristic of one's community of reference. Hearing in this sense is metaphoric for conversion, since it entails transformation of those conceptual patterns. Do tax collectors and sinners gather around Jesus and thus become converted? Or is it that, having been converted, they gather around Jesus? The only possible answer is, "Yes, both." In Luke 15, tax collectors and sinners compose a community gathered around Jesus, and their (re)formation entails hearing, and hearing well.

LUKE 19:1–10

If Zacchaeus's story is a case study, what might we learn about the nature of the conversionary life? First, we discover Zacchaeus positively identified as someone on a quest; he wanted to see Jesus, and he persisted in spite of the crowd that stood between Jesus and himself and in spite of his having to act in a childish way by scaling a sycamore tree (19:3–4). Later, we find that this narrative account is actually a tale of two quests: Zacchaeus in search of Jesus, Jesus in search of the lost (19:10). These two quests overlap as Jesus comes to the foot of the tree, looks up, and speaks to Zacchaeus. In their initial exchange, Zacchaeus's response to Jesus mirrors Jesus's instructions: "Hurry, come down!" // "Hurrying, he came down."[40] "I must stay at your

---

38. See also, e.g., Luke 2:19, 51; 8:12; 24:25, 32; Acts 2:37; 7:51; 16:14; 28:27.
39. The ethical character of hearing is emphasized in Darr, "'Watch How You Listen!'"
40. Luke 19:5: σπεύσας κατάβηθι (*speusas katabēthi*); 19:6: σπεύσας κατέβη (*speusas katebē*).

home today." // "He joyfully opened his home to him."[41] Jesus's instructions assume that staying with Zacchaeus is grounded in his divine mission, with the result that Zacchaeus's response is one of aiding Jesus in his divine mission. Luke's use of the language of "joy" and "happiness" elsewhere encourages the view that, here at the base of the tree, Zacchaeus's life is lived with reference to God's kingdom, as one who participates in God's gift of salvation in Jesus's coming.[42] Second, as I have already documented, Zacchaeus participates in behaviors becoming a child of Abraham: giving to those in need and making restitution when too much was charged (19:8; cf. 3:10–13). These are not the behaviors marked out by the Pharisees and scribes (cf. 18:11–12) but represent the clear message of John and Jesus regarding economic *koinōnia* and economic justice. (How did Zacchaeus know John's and Jesus's teaching on these matters? We are not told and can only assume that the beginning of the story of Zacchaeus's alignment with God's kingdom lies outside the narrative Luke has given us.) With Zacchaeus, then, conversionary behavior is on display in persistence, joyous hospitality, and faithfulness with regard to wealth. Pressing further, we find that, for Zacchaeus, conversionary behavior is tied to identification with Jesus and his mission and to community with the poor.

Lukan Rhetoric

These three accounts—Levi responds to Jesus's invitation, Jesus responds to protests from the Pharisees and legal experts with parables about celebrating the finding of the lost, and Jesus encounters Zacchaeus—share more than a common set of narrative elements. In different ways, they also bear witness to identifiable motifs that are integral to Luke's understanding of conversion. These accounts share an emphasis on the conversionary character of Jesus's mission, and particularly on the centrality to his mission of bringing people into the fold of God's restored people.

Strangely, perhaps, none of these episodes highlights Jesus's conversionary message. To Levi, he simply calls, "Follow me" (5:27). In 15:1–2, tax collectors and sinners come to Jesus in order to listen, but he addresses himself to the Pharisees and legal experts. To Zacchaeus, Jesus says only, "Hurry, come down! I must stay at your home today" (19:5). In none of these texts is the good news sketched, or even mentioned, though in all three texts we do find an emphasis on an orientation toward Jesus: to obeying him, following him, and extending hospitality to him (Levi); to gathering around him and sharing

---

41. Ὑποδέχομαι (*hypodechomai*) refers to "extending hospitality" (19:6). Cf. 10:38; Acts 17:7.
42. See, e.g., 1:14; 2:10; 6:23; 8:13; 10:17, 20; 15:5, 7, 10, 32. See also Green, "Joy," 449.

meals with him (tax collectors and sinners); and to seeking him, obeying him, and joyfully extending hospitality to him (Zacchaeus).

Again, perhaps strangely, none of these texts explicitly reports that anyone "converted." Levi's leaving everything to follow Jesus, then hosting a banquet for Jesus—this apparently entails conversion, even if we look in vain for Luke's observation "Levi converted" or "Levi repented." Tax collectors and sinners gather around Jesus, presumably because they are already undergoing conversion as they attend to his words. The language of conversion is altogether missing from the story of Zacchaeus, though he plainly testifies to a conversionary life in his naming Jesus as "Lord" and in practices involving his possessions, his work, and his home; he bears in his life the unmistakable fruit of conversion (3:7–14). Nevertheless, the orientation toward Jesus of these tax collectors and sinners is realized in ways that express the embodied nature of conversion—through hearing well, for example, and especially with regard to placing one's home and possessions in the service of Jesus's mission.

Finally, in all three texts we find the spotlight directed toward the way Jesus's mission redraws the boundaries around what is acceptable, especially through emphasizing how people are labeled as insiders or outsiders to God's people. Stated simply, old barometers for determining who is up or down, in or out, have been replaced by a single landmark. When Jesus and the good news (rather than the Pharisees and legal experts, together with their distinguishing judgments and practices [5:23–39; 15:1–2], or the unnamed onlookers [19:7]) compose the landmark by which life's orientation and trajectory are mapped, then Luke portrays these tax collectors and sinners as those who have oriented themselves rightly and are now numbered among those faithfully serving God's eschatological purpose. They are converts.

Conclusion

I began this chapter with a provisional definition of conversion in Luke-Acts:

> *Converts are those who have undergone a redirectional shift and are now on the move with the community of those faithfully serving God's eschatological purpose.*

Referring to this definition as "provisional," I anticipated that further reflection on selected Lukan texts might help to give it further substance. What have we learned?

First, we have found further evidence to support our articulating Luke's understanding of conversion in terms of a *journey*. And second, we have found good reason to underscore the *community* dimension of conversion. If CONVERSION IS A JOURNEY, then it is less a solitary trek and more a cavalcade or caravan.

Third, we recognized that the *redirectional shift* integral to conversion is not only theologically grounded but christologically oriented. Jesus, we might say, exegetes and executes *God's eschatological purpose* in his life and ministry. His mission entails calling others to participate in God's agenda, which he mediates to them. If LIFE IS A JOURNEY, then the path taken is not marked by the widespread socioreligious conventions of Luke's world. Jesus and his message compose the key landmark, the singular point of orientation, for conversionary movement.

For readers of Paul, references to "faith" or "believing" will have been strangely absent from the material we have examined. In fact, the language of faith is altogether lacking from conversionary accounts in Luke's Gospel. People nonetheless practice trust and commitment (e.g., leaving everything to follow Jesus); their "faith," we might say, is realized in their "faithfulness." Even Jesus's "message" is defined less in terms of a particular set of beliefs and more in terms of trust that, in Jesus, God's saving purpose is recognized, actualized, and celebrated.

Fourth, then, we have expanded on the dispositions and practices of this *faithful service*, dispositions and practices that, in fact, enact *conversion*. (With the phrase "enact conversion," I mean to say that these practices should not be understood simply or reductively as "putting on display" someone's inner commitment. This is because "inner" and "outer" refer to the same thing, that is, conversionary patterns of thinking, feeling, believing, and behaving.) Although we would be foolish to imagine that we could sketch a definitive or exhaustive list of these dispositions and practices, some have begun to emerge as nonnegotiable for Luke. These would include faithfulness with regard to possessions, especially by placing all that one has in the service of Jesus's mission, and sharing a common table, including the extension of hospitality to those typically excluded from community at the table.

Fifth, we have found that Luke draws on conversionary metaphors (e.g., seeing and hearing) and on conversionary movement (e.g., from darkness to light) that both emphasize the embodied nature of conversion and identify conversionary rhetoric with somatic markers that positively influence (but do not compel) people down a conversionary path.

Luke's portrait of conversion is not yet complete, however. For example, we have found in these texts hints of an important ambiguity. In some cases (Peter and Levi), we have no evidence that people are on a religious quest that eventuates in their conversion; rather, the initiative apparently rests solely with Jesus. In another instance, Jesus's quest to seek and to save the lost is coordinated with Zacchaeus's quest to see Jesus. To use the language of contemporary, sociological study, is conversion "active" or "passive"? Other important questions remain, too, including the nature of the conversionary community and the possibility of deconversion—questions that we will take up in chap. 5.

5

☀

Community, Agency, and Apostasy

Thus far, we have seen that Luke has a heightened interest in conversion and that he represents conversion less with an interest in technique or pattern and more with an interest in certain relatively stable elements. These include a key concern with directionality (with reference particularly to a trajectory defined in terms of God's restorative purpose and oriented toward Jesus and his message), a pervasive emphasis on the journeyed nature of conversion (and thus on a transformative and transforming way of life), a nonnegotiable interest in practices that are themselves conversionary (such as faithfulness with possessions, the shared table, and participation in Jesus's mission), and a central focus on the community of the converted (a community into which one is invited and initiated, and within which one undergoes further identity formation).

Additionally, we have found that conversion is embodied religious experience, that is, an experience that could never be consigned to the ethereal or the "spiritual." "Spiritual conversion" (as well as its corollary, "spiritual formation") is nothing less than human transformation, understanding "human" in its most integrated sense of personal and communal life.[1] With conversion,

---

1. A corollary of the material surveyed in chap. 2 is the seriousness with which we must take the identification of those capacities uniquely constitutive of the human being as biologically anchored processes. If what makes us singularly human are the properties and capacities that have the complex human brain as their anatomical basis, then there can be no formation or transformation that is not fully embodied. To push further, if the neurobiological systems that

people undergo relational reformation and full-bodied transformation of their most basic patterns of believing, thinking, feeling, and behaving. For Luke, conversion places all of life in fresh perspective, with a concomitant reevaluation of one's past, one's possessions, and one's network of friends and family. Conversion entails autobiographical reconstruction, embracing new belief structures by which to make sense of reality, and incorporation into a new community, including adopting the rituals and behaviors peculiar to or definitive of that new community.

It remains for us to explore more fully the nature of that new *community*. Following this, I will take up two further issues that lie at the intersection of Luke's narrative theology of conversion and contemporary study of religious conversion: the question of *agency* in conversion and the possibility of *deconversion*—understood more widely in religious terms as the possibility of apostasy.

Conversionary Community

As the first of a series of summaries that dot the landscape of the narrative of Acts, Acts 2:42–47 exhibits the communal dimension of the consequences of the outpouring of the Spirit and documents the quality of daily life among those who are baptized in the name of Jesus Christ.[2] Narrative summaries generally link scenes, present what is typical, and provide background information, and this is true in the present case, where Luke characterizes the nature of the community of believers in relatively short compass. Luke's desire to write a précis of the shared life of the community of the baptized is highlighted in the generalizing language he employs. The term "all" or "every" occurs in vv. 43, 44, 45; vv. 42–47 are peppered with present participles and imperfect verbs, denoting ongoing, customary behavior; the verb "to hold diligently" or "to persist" is found twice (vv. 42, 46);[3] and two of Luke's favorite ways of expressing the unity of Christ followers—ὁμοθυμαδόν (*homothymadon*, "with one heart and mind") and ἐπὶ τὸ αὐτό (*epi to auto*, "together")—appear in vv. 44, 46–47.[4] Through the repetition of these last two terms, Luke recalls his

---

shape how we think, feel, believe, and behave are continuously sculpted in the context of our social experiences, then in a profound sense we can speak of personal formation and reformation only in relational terms; that is, our autobiographical selves are formed within a nest of relationships, a community. See Green, "Doing Repentance."

2. See Cadbury, "Summaries in Acts"; Co, "Major Summaries in Acts."

3. Προσκαρτερέω (*proskartereō*, "to continue in, to persist") appears in both vv. 42 and 46 as a present active participle.

4. For ὁμοθυμαδόν (*homothymadon*, "with one heart and mind"), see 1:14; 2:46; 4:24; 5:12; for ἐπὶ τὸ αὐτό (*epi to auto*, "together"), see 1:15; 2:1, 44, 47.

earlier description of the significantly smaller community of Christ followers in 1:14 ("these were all persevering together in prayer") and 1:15 ("a company of some one hundred twenty persons were gathered together"). Clearly, it is important for Luke that an enormous increase in the community's numbers must not be regarded as somehow diluting the quality of its life together.

The significance of the summary in 2:42–47 for our purposes is indicated by its parallels with Luke's account of John the Baptist's ministry in Luke 3:1–18. We can map the highlights as follows:

Luke presents John the Baptist's ministry in relation to Israel's restoration (Luke 3:1–6).	Peter presents Jesus's ministry, death, and exaltation in relation to Israel's restoration (Acts 2:14–36).
The crowds, tax collectors, and soldiers ask, "What should we do?" (Luke 3:10–14).	The crowd asked, "What should we do?" (Acts 2:37).
Luke reports that John the Baptist was "proclaiming a baptism of repentance for the forgiveness of sins" (Luke 3:3). John the Baptist announces that the Messiah "will baptize you with the Holy Spirit and fire" (Luke 3:16).	Peter informs the crowds, "Repent! Be baptized, each of you, in the name of Jesus Christ for the forgiveness of sins, and you will receive the gift of the Holy Spirit" (Acts 2:38).
John the Baptist summarizes the nature of faithful response to God's activity with a series of characteristic practices (Luke 3:7–14).	Luke summarizes the nature of faithful response to God's activity with a series of characteristic practices (Acts 2:42–47).

Three points immediately distinguish between these two accounts: the christological focus of the baptism for which Peter calls ("in the name of Jesus Christ"), the move from promised baptism with the Holy Spirit to present baptism with the Holy Spirit, and the reference to those who responded to Peter's message as "believers." Moreover, the elements in Acts 2 occur in an order different from what we find in Luke 3. Nevertheless, the way Peter's instruction places the two pairs—repentance and baptism, baptism and forgiveness—together is fully consonant with Luke's representation of John's baptism in Luke 3:1–18, as are the emphasis on baptism as a communal act and the consequent focus on community-defining practices. John's baptism was a "repentance-baptism" in which cleansing and moral uprightness are conjoined. Submitting to baptism, the converted exhibit a reorientation of life that radiates "fruits worthy of repentance" (Luke 3:8). Both in Luke 3 and in Acts 2, then, repentance is not for Luke an abstract concept but is concretely realized and exemplified in the everyday lives of those people who have made real their alignment with God's agenda through baptism. Setting these two accounts side by side, then, we find a number of stable elements leading from conversion talk to conversionary behavior.

Speech Interrupted

The larger narrative setting of the summary in Acts 2:42–47 is introduced by Luke's account of the Spirit's outpouring in 2:1–13, together with the confusion it engendered: "What does this mean?" (2:12). We can summarize Peter's response with this claim: The age of salvation has dawned! His progressive argument has three parts: (1) what has been witnessed in Jerusalem is nothing less than the end-time work of the Holy Spirit, poured out in fulfillment of Joel's promise of the restoration of God's people; (2) the spectacular phenomena recounted in 2:1–13 join other forms of "witness" (particularly, the Psalms and Jesus's followers) in demonstrating that Jesus has divine prerogatives so that he is able to dispense the blessings of salvation, the gift of the Spirit being chief among these; and (3) these events mark the onset of "the last days," themselves marked by the universal offer of salvation and threat of judgment. Since the times have changed, life can never be the same and all are called to repentance. Christology, eschatology, and missiology run together inseparably in this speech, as Peter explains the significance of the events of Pentecost and authenticates them within God's plan. "Therefore," Peter proclaims, "let the entire house of Israel know with certainty that God has made him both Lord and Christ, this Jesus whom you crucified" (v. 36).

Having thus reached the climax of his speech, Peter is interrupted by voices from the crowd. "When they heard this they were deeply moved. They said to Peter and the rest of the apostles, 'What shall we do, brothers?'" (2:37). The effect is twofold: to demonstrate the persuasiveness of Peter's message and to provide a transition from Peter's exegetical argument to the now-pressing question of the significance of that argument for his audience. "What shall we do?" recalls the questions asked of John the Baptist in Luke 3:10–14 and of Jesus in 10:25; 18:18, and anticipates the questions of the Philippian jailer in Acts 16:30 and of Paul in 22:10. Clearly, God's restorative work demands response.

Luke leaves no doubt about the genuineness of the crowd's question. First, he identifies these Jerusalemites as "hearers" of the word. Peter had already invited careful hearing in vv. 14, 22, and had encouraged a shift in their thinking in vv. 14, 37. When Peter says, "Listen carefully to my words!" (v. 14) or "Hear these words!" (v. 22), he is doing much more than plying oratorical tricks of the trade. What is at stake is authentic hearing, the kind that leads to embracing the word, persevering in the word, and bearing fruit consistent with the word (Luke 8:1–21). What is at stake is a radical makeover of their patterns of faith and thought. Luke's observation that "they heard this" (Acts 2:37) is thus rich with possibilities for marking the transformation of these

Judeans. Second, Luke describes their affective response: "deeply moved" or "overcome with remorse," sometimes translated as "cut to the heart" (e.g., NRSV). In ancient psychology, the "heart" was the center of emotion and understanding, one's innermost being. Accordingly, Luke's language speaks to the depth and authenticity of their encounter with the word. Third, they refer to Peter and the other apostles as "brothers," echoing Peter's own address to his audience in v. 29 (cf. 1:16). The personal, familial identification for which Peter had aimed in his speech has been reached, with the result that his audience is ready not only to embrace a common understanding of Jesus's identity and role in God's saving purpose but also to respond with solidarity of commitment.

Prototypical Response

"What should we do?" What is the appropriate response to God's word? Throughout his two-part narrative, Luke addresses this question with an arsenal of possibilities—for example, believe, be baptized, turn to God, listen, see, repent, and so on. Here in 2:38, though, he presents what we can regard as the default pattern of expected response: "Repent! Be baptized, each of you, in the name of Jesus Christ for the forgiveness of sins, and you will receive the gift of the Holy Spirit." Accordingly, in the book of Acts, all things being equal, (1) responses to God's word should take this form, (2) when one or another aspect of this response is mentioned in the narrative, the others can be assumed as well, and (3) when Luke recounts a series of events that stands in tension with the pattern we find in 2:38, this is because the circumstances are less than ideal.[5] Peter's words thus serve as an internal framing device that can be represented elsewhere in Acts through the mention of one or more of its components. For example, when Luke records in 2:41 that "those who welcomed his word were baptized," lacking any evidence to the contrary, we may assume that "those who welcomed his word" not only were baptized but also repented and received the gift of the Holy Spirit.

Baptism is a community affair. This is evident already in the relation of baptism to the forgiveness of sins. Inasmuch as forgiveness is the means by which persons who had excluded themselves or been excluded from the community of God's people might (re)gain entry into the community, the promise of forgiveness has an obvious social dimension. Moreover, we should not forget that divine forgiveness was central to the promise of Israel's restoration (as we saw in chap. 3). Additionally, even if Peter's instructions in 2:38

---

5. I have explored these "exceptions" (Acts 8:4–25; 10:44–48; 19:1–7) in Green, "Significance of Baptism."

depict baptism as the appropriate individual response to the gospel ("each of you"), it remains true that, as with John's baptism so with baptism here, one does not baptize oneself. One submits to baptism by another. Hence, the converted may present themselves for baptism but, in baptizing people, the community of God's people embraces the baptizand as one of their own, a member integral to this growing kin group. To be baptized is to belong. Baptism is both response and gift.

Baptism "in the name of Jesus Christ" provides an integrating focus for this community, a focus that is dependent on its members' embracing the new way of construing God's purpose as this is articulated by Peter in his Pentecost address (vv. 14–36). More particularly, this means that the baptized consent to Peter's argument that the "Lord" on whose name people are to call for salvation is none other than Jesus of Nazareth (according to Joel 2:28–32; see Acts 2:21). This community affirms that Jesus is "Lord and Christ," and so it has as its rallying point the claim that Jesus is God's coregent. This means, too, that this community will embody the commitments and dispositions characteristic of discipleship as this is represented in Jesus's ministry and spelled out in his teaching in the third Gospel. Baptism in this sense serves a community-defining role: communicating on the part of the baptized an unswerving loyalty to the Lord and on the part of the community of believers the full incorporation of the baptized into the community. This ritual of initiation constitutes one's identification with this new community, which is marked by a transformed social network and group-sanctioned practices.

Conversion Enacted

Luke's summary description of the burgeoning community of believers provides a series of generalizations by which he amplifies the response urged by Peter in 2:38: "Repent!"[6] Thus:

> They were holding diligently to the apostles' teaching, and to the fellowship, the breaking of bread, and to the prayers. Everyone had a sense of awe, and many wonders and signs were being done through the apostles. All the believers were united and were holding everything in common. They were selling pieces of property and possessions and distributing the proceeds to everyone according to each person's need. Every day, while holding diligently to their unity in the temple, they were breaking bread in each other's homes—happily and humbly

6. For this function of the summary form, see Dupriez, *Dictionary of Literary Devices*, 33. Cf. Horn, *Glaube und Handeln*, 46.

sharing food, praising God and having goodwill toward all the people. And the Lord was adding daily to the community those who were being saved. (2:42–47)

Repentance, or conversion, is realized in a community that can be described in just this way. Within the summary, v. 42 functions as a kind of headline, a summary of the summary, with each of its four parts taken up and expanded in vv. 43–47.[7]

1. The apostles' teaching is immediately correlated with the signs and wonders God was doing through them. At this point, Luke provides no window into the content of the apostles' teaching as such, instead highlighting their central role. The phrase "wonders and signs" is reminiscent of the words of the prophet Joel, cited by Peter in 2:19, but recalls even more the words of Peter's summary of Jesus's ministry: "Jesus of Nazareth was a man accredited to you by God by means of powerful deeds, wonders, and signs that God performed through him among you, as you yourselves know" (2:22). The effect of these echoes is to identify the apostles in continuity with the ministry of Jesus as well as to designate their ministry as one of the referents of Joel's prophecy concerning "the last days." The community of believers is the locus of the divine, eschatological work of Israel's renewal.

2. The notion of "fellowship" (*koinōnia*) in v. 42 is developed in vv. 44–45 in economic terms.[8] This does not mean that fellowship is simply to be identified with or reduced to economic sharing, but rather that economic sharing is a concrete enactment and expression of the believers' unity. Those who repented and were baptized are now "believers," and their shared faith is displayed in shared possessions, in their economic solidarity. The picture Luke allows is not one of a common purse, however, nor of disinvestment as a prior condition of entry into the community.[9] In fact, the focus of his summary statement does not fall on idealizing poverty per se, nor on the evil of material possessions, nor even on total renunciation as a prerequisite for discipleship. Selling what one has is customary within the community Luke depicts, but such giving is voluntary and oriented above all toward addressing the plight of the needy.[10]

Luke's description reverberates with similar practices or ideals among ancient people. (a) In the Greco-Roman world, it was proverbial that "friends

---

7. L. Johnson, *Literary Function*, 185; Peterson, "Worship," 389.

8. Dupont, "Community of Goods," 85–87; Panikulam, *Koinōnia*, 123–24.

9. This point is often misunderstood (e.g., Gordon, *Economic Problem*, 77–81), due in part to the tendency to translate Luke's imperfect verbs—ἐπίπρασκον καὶ διεμέριζον (*epipraskon kai diemerizon*, "they were selling . . . and distributing")—with the English past tense (e.g., NIV: "they sold . . . to give"; NLT: "they sold . . . and shared"). I take these verbs as customary imperfects.

10. See, e.g., Dupont, "Community of Goods," 90–91, 94–95; Kim, *Stewardship and Almsgiving*, 241–42.

hold all things in common"; in this case, "friends" has been replaced in the proverb with "believers." Given Greco-Roman models of friendship, however, Luke's portrait is important for its focus on the ideal, that is, on relationships that are not defined by webs of exchange that turn gifts into a never-ending cycle of debt and repayment. (b) The economic sharing Luke describes might remind us of speculative longing for a utopian golden age, a return to a paradisial Greek past. Read against this backdrop, Luke's summary would mark an idyllic state, a new beginning for humanity. (c) Within the patterns of Palestinian life roughly contemporary with the early Christian community, we find remarkable instances of property sharing, not least among the Essenes and at Qumran.[11] In comparison with these, the voluntary character of the *koinōnia* Luke portrays is underscored. Especially important, though, is the premium placed here on concern and care for the needy, as the larger Greco-Roman world provided little by way of analogy for this.[12] Perhaps even more fundamental is how Luke's portrait identifies this community of believers as an extended kin group. In the ancient world, this would entail, among other things, loyalty and trust, truth telling (see 5:1–11), open homes and shared tables (see 2:46), and a sense of shared destiny.

3. The practice of "breaking bread," mentioned in v. 42, is mirrored in v. 46, where "breaking bread" appears in relation to the believers' presence in the temple. What they were doing in the temple is unspecified, though one can imagine participation in activity typically associated with the temple, including set prayers, as well as teaching and learning in the temple courts. The phrase "holding diligently to their unity in the temple," though, encourages the conclusion that what distinguishes this community of believers would be something other than what would have been typical of other Jews, and the only clue about the shape of that identity here is Luke's reference to "breaking bread in each other's homes." Within the Jewish world of the first century, it would not be unusual to locate worship-related activity in the home; what is remarkable is that such activity is focused not in *one's own home* but in *the homes of various believers* (as if they were a network of close kin). Hospitality thus takes center stage as a cornerstone characteristic of the community

11. The background of this aspect of Luke's portrait is variously assessed, with interpreters sometimes arguing for one possibility to the exclusion of the others. However, all of these would have been present in Luke's discourse situation, so it is difficult to prioritize one at the expense of another. For the interweaving of economic factors with friendship models, see, e.g., Garnsey and Saller, *Roman Empire*, 148–59; Eisenstadt and Roniger, *Patrons, Clients and Friends*; see also Aristotle, *Eth. nic.* 9.8.2; Eden, *Friends*; Dupont, "Community of Goods," 89–91, 102; Kim, *Stewardship and Almsgiving*, 226. For Greek utopianism, see, e.g., Mealand, "Acts 2–4." For Palestinian life, see, e.g., Mealand, "Qumran"; Capper, "Palestinian Cultural Context."

12. See Hamel, *Poverty and Charity*.

of believers, with the sharing of food serving as one form of the economic sharing noted in vv. 44–45.

"Sharing food" is shorthand for a widespread cultural script, including the satiation of hunger (including that of the genuinely needy), of course, but signaling as well the sharing of lives: intimacy and kinship. "Happily" characterizes this meal sharing as integral to the larger experience of salvation, whereas "humbly" speaks to the coherence between the gospel and the practice of sharing food. Just as the gospel is given without reference to religious purity or social status, so meals are shared freely, without expectation of payback, without concern for purity and status. Importantly, the counsel Jesus provided in Luke 14:1–24 regarding invitations to festive meals and seating arrangements (including his rejection of those concerns with status and reciprocity characteristic of meals in Roman antiquity) has apparently found a home in the early community.

4. "The prayers" (v. 42) finds its primary counterpart in the reference in v. 47 to "praising God." This would include the set prayers in the temple (see 3:1), but also prayers in each other's homes (cf. 4:24–31).[13] One innovation in their prayer practices is obvious, namely, offering prayers to the Lord Jesus, since his is the name on which persons are to call for salvation (2:21, 36). Otherwise, prayer, as this is developed in the third Gospel, is the means by which Jesus's identity is manifest, God's plan is disclosed, and people align themselves with those plans.[14]

The outward focus of the early community is evident not only in their praising God but also in their gracious disposition toward "all the people." Although almost universally translated as a reference to the popularity of the community among the people, Luke's phrase in 2:47a has the opposite significance. That is, it is not the case that the community of Christ followers enjoys public support, but that these believers are agents of God's good gifts to the larger community.[15] The effect of the outpouring of the Spirit is realized not only in the interior life of the community of believers but also in their ongoing missionary stance with respect to the world around them.

13. On first-century patterns of Jewish prayer, see Falk, "Jewish Prayer Literature."

14. I have developed these motifs in Green, "'Persevering Together in Prayer.'" More broadly, see Holmås, *Prayer and Vindication*.

15. Luke's phrase, ἔχοντες χάριν πρὸς ὅλον τὸν λαόν (*echontes charin pros holon ton laon*, "having goodwill toward all the people"), is often read as a reference to the public favor enjoyed by the community of believers (e.g., NRSV: "having the goodwill of all the people"; NIV: "enjoying the favor of all the people"). This reading may seem more natural, but it is hard to square with the opposition the community engenders in the subsequent narrative and is hardly required by Luke's syntax. Cf. Andersen, "ΕΧΟΝΤΕΣ ΧΑΡΙΝ ΠΡΟΣ"; Cheetham, "Acts ii.47."

A Formative Community

Luke's summary description of the community of believers in Acts 2:42–47 provides a convenient way to identify the character of the conversionary community. In part, this is because this précis follows on from the baptism of these new believers and so exhibits the nature of conversionary life, which for Luke is enabled through the gift of the Holy Spirit.[16] The introduction of this description of the community of believers immediately following their conversion and reception of the Spirit emphasizes the centrality to conversion of the process of incorporation into a new community, which entails a makeover of previous patterns of faith and life into patterns conforming to those of the new community. It makes sense to refer to this process as resocialization, provided we allow Luke to remind us that more is going on than the (human) cultivation of new social habits and relationships. The conversionary community is at one and the same time divine gift; the venue within which patterns of thinking, feeling, believing, and behaving are transformed; and the concrete, observable expression of that transformation. Precisely because they are conversionary, the practices Luke outlines both cultivate and express conversionary life and community.

Additionally, this textual unit captures many of the identifying features of this community as these are developed elsewhere in the book. For example, given the importance of economic sharing to this textual unit, we should not be surprised to find a parallel summary related to economic sharing in 4:32–35, trailed immediately by the positive example of Barnabas's economic practices (4:36–37) and the negative example of Ananias and Sapphira's (5:1–11). And to these summary statements, we add further reflections on and material related to faith and wealth scattered throughout the book of Acts (cf. 3:6; 6:1–7; 8:18–20; 11:27–30; 16:16–19; 19:13–20; 20:33–35; 24:24–26).[17] Other elements of conversionary life, including witness, prayer, and shared meals and hospitality, are advanced elsewhere in the narrative, too. The point is that Luke initiates here, then develops further, something of the concrete shape of communal life among the converted, the fellowship of those baptized in Jesus's name, the community of believers.

Agency: How Does God "Give" Conversion?

Reflecting on the nature of the community of Christ followers in Acts 2:42–47, we have already encountered the question of agency. Is conversion a matter

16. This is helpfully emphasized in Wenk, *Community-Forming Power*, 259–73.
17. See Walton, "Primitive Communism in Acts?," 109–10.

of human self-correction, or is it the consequence of divine initiative? In fact, this has been a point of controversy in recent study of Luke's theology of conversion. Phrased in this way, the emphasis has typically fallen on the human problem that the call to conversion is meant to address. Jacques Dupont's essay on conversion in Acts set the stage for this discussion by drawing attention to the human situation that makes conversion necessary in Luke's theology. His recognition of Luke's emphasis on salvation as forgiveness of sins leads him to reflect on a person's consciousness of his or her own sinfulness and need for pardon. And this leads Dupont to articulate the nature of conversion in moral terms: "We remain faithful to the spirit of the early preaching when we contemplate the details of Jesus's passion in such a way as to grow increasingly aware of the ugliness of sin and arouse in ourselves that sincere repentance to which the promise of forgiveness is tied."[18] Note, first, that Dupont characterizes the human situation in terms of "the ugliness of sin," rectified through God's forgiveness; and, second, that salvation is marked by self-examination and self-arousal of "that sincere repentance to which the promise of forgiveness is tied." Setting aside the reality that Dupont's language at this point seems more indebted to William James than to Luke (see chap. 1), Dupont clearly emphasizes the human side of the conversionary equation. Protesting against this approach to Luke's theology, Jens-W. Taeger urges instead that the human condition in Lukan thought is not sin needing forgiveness but ignorance needing correction: "People do not need salvation, but correction."[19] Even so, for Taeger's reading of Luke-Acts, the problem of human understanding can and must be addressed by *self*-correction. Other scholars, perhaps most of them, champion the priority of divine initiative, however.[20]

Again, this approach to the question takes as its point of departure the consequences of a particular approach to the human situation: What is the human "problem" that needs to be addressed? A more helpful point of entry takes the phenomenological route of describing how conversion is conceptualized and experienced. Conversion studies emphasizing social-psychological or sociological approaches in the last two or three decades have drawn attention to different aspects of the conversion process on the basis of their attention to *agency*. Accordingly, Brock Kilbourne and James Richardson propose an analytical scheme based on the agency assigned to the convert, whether *passive* or *active*.[21]

18. Dupont, "Conversion in the Acts of the Apostles," 69.

19. Taeger, *Mensch und sein Heil*, 225.

20. Bovon, *L'œuvre de Luc*, 165–79; Kim-Rauchholz, *Umkehr bei Lukas*; Stenschke, *Luke's Portrait of Gentiles*; Wenk, "Conversion and Initiation."

21. Kilbourne and Richardson, "Paradigm Conflict." For a recent, useful appropriation of this analytical model, see Tidball, "Evangelical Conversion."

Conversions in the former case are viewed as largely determined by outside forces, whereas the latter are viewed in terms of life choice. When conversion is understood in passive terms, "the individual is conceptualized as a passive recipient of personality changes and life experiences. Whether psychologically disposed or situationally tempered, individuals' conversions are considered determined, in large part, by impersonal and powerful forces acting upon them, within them, or both." Such conversions are typically sudden and dramatic, as in the case of what is for Kilbourne and Richardson the prototypical passive conversion: Paul's so-called Damascus Road experience. When conversion is understood in active terms, converts are portrayed as "seekers, or individuals who actively make plans, choices, and decisions, and generate many of their life experiences."[22] Such conversions are often understood in terms of "process" rather than "event," with ongoing transformation occurring as the individual learns his or her role as a convert. Converts might experience their conversion in terms of either perspective and could possibly recount their conversion according to the script provided by both approaches. The downside of this way of formulating the experience of conversion is that it might lead us to choose sides when sides ought not to be chosen. Rather than taking seriously the explanatory value of both perspectives, we might imagine that they stand in tension with each other (when, after all, each provides a perspective from which to engage in analysis), as though the one emphasis necessarily excluded the other.

If we were to begin with this analytical scheme, we would focus on the agency of conversion and phrase our question in active versus passive terms. Rather than inquiring into whether conversion is a matter of human self-correction or of divine initiative, we might ask how Luke understands or presents the agency of the convert, whether passive or active. In what ways might we say that Luke conceptualizes conversion in terms of volition and choice? Alternatively, in what ways might we say that Luke conceptualizes conversion as happening to a convert, perhaps in a moment of crisis, quite apart from any apparent involvement of or contribution from the convert's will?

That humans have an active role in conversion seems clear enough in much of the narrative of Luke-Acts, a narrative in which the dramatic, crisis account with which Luke presents Paul's encounter with Jesus on the Damascus Road is actually atypical.[23] Responding to the good news, John the Baptist's, Peter's, and Paul's audiences inquire, "What should we do?" (Luke 3:10, 12, 14; Acts

22. Kilbourne and Richardson, "Paradigm Conflict," 2; cf. Rambo and Farhadian, "Introduction," 7.

23. Luke's account in Acts 9 (and its parallels) has attracted significant discussion around the question of whether Luke actually portrays Paul as a "convert" ("converted" versus "commissioned," e.g.). See the useful discussion of this question in Chester, "Paul."

2:38; 16:30). In the early chapters of Acts, speaking to Jerusalem audiences, Peter twice calls on people to "convert," using an aorist imperative form of the verb μετανοέω (*metanoeō*; 2:38; 3:19), at least implying that these people ought to respond in certain ways. Similarly, Paul proclaims to a non-Jewish audience in Lystra, "Turn to the living God!" (14:15), and at Athens, he announces that "[God] now directs all people everywhere to convert" (17:30). Later, he summarizes his ministry as declaring both to Jews and gentiles "that they should convert and turn to God" (26:20). Perhaps this is only to be expected in a narrative in which Jesus articulates his mission as calling sinners to conversion (Luke 5:32). In addition to repeated calls to conversion, we have already drawn attention to the involvement of Jesus's followers in practices through which they are initiated into and transformed as members of the community of the converted—baptism, for example, as well as common meals, economic sharing, worship, attending to the apostles' teaching, and prayer. However else converts in Luke-Acts might be pictured, on the whole they cannot be portrayed as passive recipients of the life transformation marked by the term "conversion."

Two Lukan texts clash with this way of formulating the role of the convert, however, or at least they seem to do so. We find the first in Peter's address to the Jerusalem Council (Acts 5) and the second in the response of the followers of Jesus in Jerusalem to Peter's narration of his encounter with Cornelius's household (Acts 11):

> God exalted this Jesus to his right hand as Leader and Savior that he might give conversion to Israel, as well as forgiveness of sins. (Acts 5:31)

> They praised God, saying, "So God has given even to the gentiles the conversion that leads to life." (Acts 11:18)

How should these two texts be read? John Calvin (1509–64) finds "the whole substance of the Gospel" in 5:31, for Christ's "reign" is evidenced in his bringing his own people to repentance and reconciling them to God by the forgiveness of sins. "Repentance is indeed a voluntary conversion, but what is the source of this willingness except that God changes our heart, making a heart of flesh out of a heart of stone, one that is pliable out of one that is hard and stiff, and, finally, one that is upright out of one that is crooked?" Indeed, Calvin argues, "If the function of giving repentance belongs to Christ, it follows that it is not something that has been put in the power of man."[24] With regard

24. Calvin, *Acts*, 149.

to 11:18, Calvin allows for two possible explanations—either that God has given to the gentiles "the opportunity of repentance" or that God has actually changed their hearts. Of these two options, Calvin chooses the latter, which "suits better; it is less forced; and is more in agreement with the phraseology of Scripture."[25] Given John Wesley's (1703–91) theological differences with Calvin, it is no surprise that Wesley rejects this reading. Indeed, Wesley may have Calvin in mind when he refers in his *Explanatory Notes upon the New Testament* to what "some infer." He writes: *"To give repentance*—Whereby Jesus is received as a Prince. *And forgiveness of sins*—Whereby he is received as a Saviour. Hence some infer, that repentance and faith are as mere gifts as remission of sins. Not so: for man co-operates in the former, but not in the latter. God alone forgives sins."[26] Apart from such voices as these, though, the history of interpretation seems not to have been much exercised over the question of God's role in "giving conversion." Christological and historical questions have tended to dominate instead.[27]

Contemporary interest in the question raised by these two texts can be traced to the work of Hans Conzelmann (1915–89). In his view, the phrase "to give repentance" ought to be understood in the context of Second Temple Jewish and early Christian literature, where it refers to the gift of "the opportunity for repentance." In his study of Lukan theology, he refers to the following parallel texts:[28]

> Stretch out your hands to heaven and ask forgiveness for your previous deeds and make propitiation for bitter impiety with words of praise; God will grant repentance and will not destroy. He will stop his wrath again if you all practice honorable piety in your hearts. (*Sibylline Oracles* 4.168)[29]

> But judging them little by little you gave them an opportunity to repent, though you were not unaware that their origin was evil and their wickedness inborn, and that their way of thinking would never change. . . . Through such works you have taught your people that the righteous must be kind, and you have filled your children with good hope, because you give repentance for sins. (Wisdom 12:10, 19)

25. Ibid., 326–27.
26. Wesley, *Explanatory Notes*, 412, emphasis original. Wesley provides no further discussion on the matter in his comments on 11:18.
27. See, e.g., Bede, *Acts*; Rackham, *Acts*, 162–63; Pelikan, *Acts*, 90.
28. Conzelmann, *Theology of St. Luke*, 100–101. Later, Conzelmann (228n2) refers to the "old, comprehensive meaning" of "conversion" as though it functioned in Acts 5:31; 11:18 as synecdoche for "the gift of salvation."
29. ET in Collins, "Sibylline Oracles," 388.

We should gaze intently on the blood of Christ and realize how precious it is to his Father; for when it was poured out for our salvation, it brought the gracious gift of repentance to the entire world. (*1 Clement* 7.4)[30]

His word of faith, his call to us through his promise, the commandments of the teaching, he himself prophesying in us and dwelling in us who had served death, opening to us the door of the temple, which is the mouth, and giving repentance to us—thus he brings us into his imperishable temple. (*Barnabas* 16.9)[31]

After the shepherd examined everyone's sticks, he said to me, "I told you that this tree is hardy. Do you see," he said, "how many people have repented and been saved?" "I see, Lord," I said. "This is that you may know," he said, "that the compassion of the Lord is great and glorious and that he has given his spirit to those worthy of repentance." "Why then is it, Lord," I asked, "that everyone does not repent?" He replied, "The Lord has given repentance to those whom he saw were about to become pure in heart and serve him from their whole heart. But he did not give it to those in whom he saw deceit and evil, or those who were about to repent hypocritically, lest they should once again blaspheme his law." (*Shepherd of Hermas, Parables* 8.6.1–2)[32]

Subsequently, in his commentary on Acts, Conzelmann reiterates his view that, by the phrase "to give repentance," "Luke means the *opportunity* for repentance." This time, though, he includes a different roster of parallel texts:

Proceeding with his army in this order, Vespasian reached the frontiers of Galilee. Here he established his camp and restrained the ardour of his soldiers, who were burning for the fray, being content to parade his forces before the enemy, with a view to intimidating them and giving time for reconsideration [i.e., repentance], if they wished, before an engagement, to desert their friends. (Josephus, *J.W.* 3.127)[33]

For [Moses] says that the treasures of evil things were sealed in the day of vengeance, the sacred word thus showing that not even against those who sin will God proceed at once, but gives time for repentance and for the healing and setting of his [*sic*] feet again of him who had slipped. (Philo, *Allegorical Interpretation* 3.106)[34]

Arrived before Thebes, and wishing to give her still a chance to repent of what she had done, he merely demanded the surrender of Phoenix and Prothytes,

30. ET in Ehrman, *Apostolic Fathers*, 1:47.
31. ET in ibid., 2:73.
32. ET in ibid., 2:371, 373.
33. ET in Thackery, *Josephus*, 615.
34. ET in Olson and Whitaker, *Philo*, 373.

and proclaimed an amnesty for those who came over to his side. (Plutarch, *Alexander* 11.4)[35]

Conzelmann concludes: "He does not mean that repentance as such is a gift from God, but that God gives μετάνοια in the sense of an opportunity to repent."[36] In other words, Conzelmann opts for the first reading that Calvin regards as possible, the one Calvin rejects, and on this point Conzelmann's position has attracted a number of followers.[37]

Not everyone is persuaded, however. Most notably, Christoph Stenschke is unconvinced, and he devotes a section of his study of Lukan anthropology to a point-by-point refutation of Conzelmann's case.[38] Stenschke's approach is to examine each of Conzelmann's references to non-Lukan material in order to determine whether they genuinely support the claim that Luke's phrasing could be understood to refer not to God's gift of repentance but to God's provision of an opportunity for repentance. His basic charge is that the texts in Luke lack the language of *opportunity*.[39] He also notes that a single verb, "to give," governs both "conversion" and "forgiveness of sins" in 5:31, so that Conzelmann's reading would require that the one verb be taken in two different ways in the same clause. Finally, he observes that nothing about Luke's account suggests that the divine gift refers to anything other than repentance itself.

Four arguments tell against Stenschke's examination of the evidence. First, Stenschke too easily brushes past Conzelmann's understanding of how a native Greek speaker might have heard Luke's language of "giving conversion." To take only one example, Plutarch reports that Alexander, "having arrived before Thebes, and wanting still to give the city *an opportunity for* repentance of its deeds, required . . ." (*Alexander* 11.4),[40] a report in which the phrase "an opportunity for" simply must be introduced for purposes of clarity.

Second, Stenschke does not take seriously enough the general language Luke uses when he names the indirect object of the gift of conversion: "to Israel" (5:31) and "to the gentiles" (11:18). On both occasions, Luke refers to

35. ET in Perrin, *Plutarch's Lives*, 253.

36. Conzelmann, *Acts*, 42, emphasis original.

37. See, e.g., Wilckens, *Missionsreden*, 181–82n4; Schneider, *Apostelgeschichte*, 1:396n94; Taeger, *Mensch und sein Heil*, 130–32; Barrett, *Acts*, 1:291, 543; Jervell, *Apostelgeschichte*, 208, 306; Pokorný, *Theologie der lukanischen Schriften*, 123; Fitzmyer, *Acts*, 338; Wall, "Acts," 107; Pervo, *Acts*, 146.

38. Stenschke, *Luke's Portrait of Gentiles*, 156–64.

39. E.g., the figurative use of the term τόπος (*topos*, "place," though sometimes referring to "opportunity" or "chance"; cf. Acts 25:16).

40. My translation of the Greek text in Perrin, *Plutarch's Lives*, 7:252: προσμίξας δὲ ταῖς Θήβαις καὶ διδοὺς ἔτι τῶν πεπραγμένων μετάνοιαν ἐξῄτει. . . .

the divine gift of conversion in ways that reach far beyond their immediate cotexts. That is, these statements generalize from a particular in ways that frustrate Stenschke's interpretation. In 5:31, as a consequence of his exaltation to God's right hand, Jesus gives repentance to Israel, but nowhere does this signify within the narrative that *all Israel actually repents*. Similarly, with respect to 11:18, we might say that Cornelius and his household belong to the category of gentile converts, but this is not the same thing as saying that the Jerusalem believers now count *all gentiles* among the converted. It simply makes no sense to take these two texts as referring to God's active changing of the hearts and lives of everyone, both Israel and the gentiles (an interpretation that Stenschke's reading seems to require), though it makes good sense of Luke's theology to say that God has opened the way for everyone, both Israel and the gentiles, to convert (as Conzelmann's reading would have it).

We can illustrate this point with reference to Acts 3:26, where divine agency is emphasized with respect to conversion: "After God raised his servant, he sent him first to you, blessing you by turning[41] each of you from your evil ways." According to Peter's sermon on the occasion of the healing of a man crippled from birth (3:12–26), God's ancient purpose and faithfulness enable, invite, and require the response of repentance on the part of Peter's audience (see v. 19: "Repent, therefore, and turn back so that your sins might be wiped out"). This is because they have misconstrued God's aim, failed to understand the Scriptures, and therefore positioned themselves in conflict with God's work. Repentance, then, comprises a returning to God—a realignment of one's allegiances marked by a turning from "evil ways" (v. 26) back toward God (v. 19). Such conversion has a moral-ethical content, though it would be a mistake to think that this was the sum total of the response for which Peter was calling. Evil ways grow out of dispositions wrongly aligned and a view of God badly in need of revision. Peter is concerned with sins, as v. 19 makes clear, but he is also calling on his Jewish audience to a transformation of their view of God and his work. And he offers three motivations for doing so. (1) The first is the promise of forgiveness—a primary staple in Luke's conception of salvation.[42] As we saw in chap. 3, for Israel, divine forgiveness is an act of covenant renewal marking the restoration of God's people. (2) The second is the connection between repentance and the "seasons of refreshment" that come from the Lord (v. 20). Although "the Lord" in this case is clearly

41. Daniel B. Wallace refers to Luke's construction, ἐν τῷ (*en tō*) + infinitive, as an "infinitive of means," answering the question, "How?" (*Greek Grammar*, 597–98); similarly, MHT 4:146 (instrumental).

42. See Acts 2:38; 5:31; 10:43; 13:38; 15:9; 22:16; 26:18. Forgiveness is used in Acts as a synecdoche for salvation too: 13:26//38; 4:10–12//10:43; 10:43//11:14; 5:31.

Yahweh (who sends the Messiah), the thought is similar to the description of
Jesus as "author of life" in v. 15, since the idea of "refreshment" is typically
introduced in contrast to former times of distress or disease.[43] (3) Whereas
the first two motivations are positive in their outlook, the third is negative. If
they fail to repent, Peter insists, they will find themselves "completely rooted
out of the people" (v. 23). This is because, according to the logic of Luke's
identification of Jesus with the promised, eschatological prophet, not to repent
would be to fail to heed the words of God's agent. (For a similar thought, see
Luke 3:8–9, 17.) To put it differently, participation in the covenantal blessings
associated with Abraham depends on accepting (or heeding) the prophet like
Moses, who is Jesus.[44]

With this reference to Abraham, Peter's speech comes full circle. Having
begun with the God of Abraham's having glorified his servant Jesus (v. 13),
the speech now closes with a reference to God's pouring out the Abrahamic
blessing through his servant Jesus whom he had raised up (vv. 25–26). This
means that the healing of the lame beggar anticipates the blessing of all the
earth's families, and that the divine blessing of "complete health" is available to
Peter's audience—who are now given the opportunity to become beneficiaries
of God's blessing rather than opponents of his purpose.[45] Peter's speech comes
full circle in two other ways. On the one hand, he identified his audience as
"people of Israel" (v. 12), a phrase that he interprets by recognizing them as
"children of the prophets and of the covenant" (v. 25). On the other hand,
just as he emphatically indicted the Jerusalemites for acting in opposition to
God's purpose (vv. 13–15), so now he just as emphatically names them as potential recipients of covenantal blessing.[46] The word "potential" is important,
however, since it is not at all certain that Peter's audience will follow him in
his argument and appeal. They are children of the covenant, to be sure, as
well as children of the prophets, but are they children of the covenant and
the prophets *as these have been interpreted by Peter along christological and
eschatological lines*? Importantly, the scene ends with Luke's report of two
quite different responses: "many of those who heard the word believed and
their number grew to about five thousand," but some of Israel's elite took

43. This would be consistent with the Christology developed thus far in Acts, in which
Yahweh's blessings of salvation are available through the agency of the exalted Jesus. Here is a
reminder that, though he is presently in heaven (1:9–11; 3:21), the Messiah is not for this reason
uninvolved in messianic work.

44. Similar language is used in Zechariah's song (Luke 1:68–79). As both John and Simeon
had predicted, the coming of the Messiah signals a point of crisis, bringing division in Israel
(2:34; 3:17).

45. Brawley, "For Blessing All Families of the Earth," 25–26.

46. Tannehill, "Peter's Mission Speeches," 405.

Peter and John into custody, "incensed because of their teaching the people and proclaiming in Jesus the resurrection of the dead" (4:1–4).

Apparently, "turning each of you from your evil ways" actually refers to calling people to turn, extending them opportunity to turn, and providing them with a basis for turning. Accordingly, the divine gift of conversion cannot be reduced to the actual conversion of people. In fact, somewhat ironically, in 5:27–32 it is before a Jewish council that rejects Jesus's spokespersons, has them flogged, and orders them silenced—in short, it is before a Jerusalem council noticeably *not* characterized by a change of heart and life—that Peter proclaims God's gift of conversion to Israel. Similarly, according to Luke, gentiles are divided in their response to the message of repentance (e.g., 17:30, 32). Observations like this clearly stand in tension with the claim that God "gives conversion" both to Israel and to the gentiles.

Of course, Luke is fully capable of portraying God's more direct agency in conversion accounts. Robert Tannehill puts forward some examples, including divine intervention in the case of Saul (9:1–19), Luke's measuring the progress of the mission in terms of people being "added" to the community of believers (2:41, 47), and Luke's observation that the Lord "opened" Lydia's heart (16:14).[47] Such examples do not take us very far in our understanding of how God gave repentance more generally to both Israel and the gentiles, however.

I promised four objections to Stenschke's claim that Luke emphasizes divine agency over against human agency in his theology of conversion. The third has to do with the way he polarizes the options before us: *Do people need to receive repentance from God or can they repent of their own, once the opportunity is made available?*[48] For Stenschke, we seem to be presented with a hard choice—passive conversion (people receive repentance from God) or active (people repent on their own). Acknowledging that Luke provides evidence for both, he wonders, "How can what is called a gift be commanded at the same time?" His answer is that Luke is no systematician, that perhaps the evangelist did not see or recognize the tension between these formulations.[49] In the context of this study, we cannot overlook that the either-or choice Stenschke's question forces and the tension he tries to explain are rooted in a punctiliar understanding of conversion, as though conversion could be reduced to a moment in time or a single decision.

Consider an analogy. A father meets his two children at the door and asks, "Where have you been?" The one responds, "We went to town." The other

47. Tannehill, "Repentance," 92–93.
48. Stenschke, *Luke's Portrait of Gentiles*, 156, emphasis original.
49. Ibid., 163.

answers, "The car's GPS navigational system broke, we got lost, and ended up on the wrong side of town. It took us hours to find our way back home." In one sense, both children have told the same story, though the one compresses a series of events (and what must have been a frustrating, perhaps even frightening journey) into a single moment ("We went to town"). Dozens of similar expressions come to mind: "I finished school," "We became parents," and so on. In the same way, with the language of *conversion*, an ongoing series of transformations is compressed into a single moment. This provides for efficient communication, but only if we understand that compression ("We went to town") invites and requires automatic decompression ("The car's GPS navigational system broke, we got lost, and ended up on the wrong side of town . . .") in order to account for the reality of progressive but incremental transformation over time.

Fourth, Stenschke himself suggests an alternative way forward with his phrase, "once the opportunity is made available." Both texts, Acts 5:31 and 11:18, occur in the context of affirmations of what God has done that makes conversion possible at all. In the former, Peter explains how God raised up Jesus and honored him as leader and savior. In the latter, Peter reminds his audience of the outpouring of the Spirit at Pentecost, with its reverberations of God's coming to restore Israel, and speaks of the coming of the one who would baptize with the Holy Spirit. In other words, God has made conversion possible by keeping his ancient promises and acting to gather his people and initiate the new age.

To borrow terms from formal logic, then, divine action—particularly, the coming of the Messiah—is the necessary but insufficient condition for conversion, for both Jews and gentiles. Moreover, the Holy Spirit forms a conversionary community and enables conversionary practices, both for Jews and gentiles. This means that, for Luke, conversion could never be reduced to a human endeavor or understood merely in terms of resocialization. People cannot convert "on their own." At the same time, conversion is more than a divine act; it involves a journey with companions and choices as the converted experience an ongoing makeover with respect to their patterns of faith and life.

Apostasy: The Threat of Deconversion

Heinz Streib observes that, today, "a growing number of people choose to convert more than once in their lifetime; multiple conversions are unavoidable in cultures in which religion is no longer a single tradition in a mono-religious environment but plural in a pluralistic environment. Multiple conversions, however, involve deconversion(s) as well as conversions."[50] Streib's reflections on "multiple conversions" are appropriate to much of the contemporary West, particularly given the phenomena of heightened individualism and increasing religious pluralism. Talk of "multiple conversions" would be less relevant to traditional cultures, however, and certainly less applicable to the ancient Mediterranean world. Even so, his remarks on deconversion are important for us to consider, not only because in Luke's religion-saturated world, conversion to "the Way of the Lord" would have involved deconversion from some other (social-religious-political) way of life, but also because Luke's narrative includes accounts of people who deconverted from "the Way." Our particular concern in this section is this last possibility.

Building on prior studies of deconversion, Streib is broadly interested in "loss or deprivation of religious faith," which he analyzes with reference to five elements: loss of specific religious experiences; intellectual doubt, denial, or disagreement with specific beliefs; moral criticism; emotional suffering; and disaffiliation from the community. Deconversion, he writes, can also be understood as "migration" within and out of "the religious field."[51] As we will see momentarily, the utility of this way of understanding deconversion in Luke-Acts is minimal. This is because Streib's categories themselves largely reflect a modern interest in interiority, emotional attachment, and self-reflection. Although these psychological, intellectual, and affective elements could be developed in ways that take human embodiment seriously, this would require a more nuanced discussion, one focused far more on integrated patterns of belief, behavior, thought, and feeling. In any case, Luke's narrative provides us with little access to psychological features like these—as would be expected given the embodied nature of ancient psychology, with its overall lack of interest in what our contemporaries might think of as inner awareness, changing self-consciousness, or deliberate mental representation. The ease with which we segregate feeling from doing, interior from exterior, and so on would be quite foreign to inhabitants of Luke's universe.[52]

Far more interesting for our purposes are the metaphors Streib uses for deconversion: "exit" and "migration." Important, too, is his language of "the religious field." Even if his analysis suggests that religion can be treated as though it did not interpenetrate all of life's nooks and crannies, this language nonetheless tracks well with our earlier observation about movement from

50. Streib, "Deconversion," 271. See Partridge and Reid, *Finding and Losing Faith*.

51. Streib, "Deconversion," 271–72; cf. Streib and Keller, "Variety of Deconversion Experiences." Streib is dependent on Barbour, *Versions of Deconversion*; Glock, "Religious Commitment."

52. See K. Berger, *Identity and Experience*.

one "sphere or field of influence" to another (see chap. 4). Not only do these images relate directly to Luke's portrayal of conversion as a "journey," but they hold together cognition and embodiment, community and practice, and patterns of both faith and life in ways very much at home in Luke's narrative theology. B. J. Oropeza offers a comparable perspective in his description of "apostasy": "the phenomenon that occurs when a religious follower or group of followers turn away from or otherwise repudiate the central beliefs and practices they once embraced in a respective religious community."[53] Again, note the journey metaphor Oropeza introduces: "to turn away."

The parable of the soils and its interpretation (Luke 8:4–15) orient us to what would have been for the evangelist the possibility and causes of deconversion. Exploring this parable puts us in a strategic position to examine three deconversionary accounts: the story of Judas, the story of Ananias and Sapphira, and the story of Simon Magus.

Orientation: Parable of the Soils

The parable of the soils (Luke 8:4–8) is set within a larger narrative unit (8:4–21) centrally concerned with good hearing:[54]

8:8: "Whoever has ears to hear must hear!"

8:10: "so that . . . hearing, they don't understand"

8:12: "those who hear"

8:13: "when they hear it"

8:14: "these are the ones who hear"

8:15: "those who hear the word"

8:18: "Pay attention, then, to how you hear"

8:21: "those who hear and do God's word"

Luke's interest is not "hearing" in general, but a particular kind of hearing—good hearing, authentic hearing, appropriate hearing, the kind of hearing associated with attentiveness (vv. 8, 18), believing (vv. 12–13), and embracing God's word, steadfastness with respect to God's word, and doing God's word (vv. 15, 21).

The parable sequence (8:4–15) has four parts: setting (v. 4), parable (vv. 5–8), an interlude concerned with proper hearing (vv. 9–10), and Jesus's explanation of the parable (vv. 11–15). Significantly, the entire sequence takes place in the

---

53. Oropeza, *Judas and Other Defectors*, 1.
54. I have adapted some of this material from Green, *Luke*, 321–29.

context of a large crowd, which is present both before (v. 4) and after (v. 19) the parable and its explanation. This means that the interchange between Jesus and his disciples concerning proper hearing and understanding (vv. 9–15) is not private teaching at all. The entire pedagogical moment is for everyone, not only for a select few. Even if, beginning with v. 9, Luke's camera focuses more narrowly on the disciples, the crowds are included in this opportunity for ongoing instruction and formation.

In Lukan usage more broadly, the crowds are undifferentiated in terms of status, gender, religious purity, or level of religious commitment. Although their presence is sometimes threatening (e.g., 4:42; 8:42, 45; 12:1), typically they are at least potential followers of Jesus (e.g., 6:17–49). Here, they gather around Jesus, just as they did earlier with John the Baptist (3:7, 10) and just as they will later do with Philip, Barnabas, and Paul (Acts 8:6; 13:45; 14:11, 13, 18–19). As Jesus's parable will demonstrate, though, good soil requires more than "hearing," more than this initial openness to listening to God's word.

As Luke tells the story, then, it is not that disciples and members of the amorphous crowds cannot be differentiated but rather that the line between them is fuzzy and permeable. This is crucial for how we understand Jesus's interpretation of Isa. 6:9–10 in v. 10: "You have been given the capacity to comprehend the hidden secrets of God's kingdom, but these secrets come to others in parables so that when they see they don't see and when they hear they don't understand." In the absence of a clear barrier separating the disciples and crowds, we must allow for the possibility among both disciples and crowds for understanding and failure to understand. As the parable and Jesus's interpretation make clear, the pivotal question is whether one hears well—and, then, whether one produces fruit through steadfastness. We might say that Jesus takes the words of Isa. 6:9–10 as descriptive rather than predictive; they explain *why* some do not respond with genuine hearing, but they do not determine *whether* one will do so.

The parable itself is notable for its commonness. The farmer scatters his seed as he normally would, circumventing whatever hazards he can. He avoids the hardened path ("some fell alongside [παρά, *para*] the path," 8:5), for example. The "birds in the sky" (8:5) are "wild birds," not the domestic variety, so their feeding on his seed is out of his control. The picture is as ordinary as it is realistic in its representation of Palestinian farming practice.[55] The unfolding of the parable draws attention, first, to what happens

55. For background, see Hedrick, *Parables as Poetic Fictions*, 172–73; Snodgrass, *Stories with Intent*, 166–67.

to the seed as it encounters each soil type: it fell *along* the path, *on* the rock, *among* the thorns, and *into* good soil. Only with this last soil type is it clear that the seed actually made its way organically deep into the soil where it could take root and grow. Second, the parable turns its attention to the outcome—not of the scattering of seed per se but of the fruitfulness of each soil type, particularly given the natural threats to growth that Jesus mentions. Note the parable's repeated refrain (this soil, this result), as well as its compression of time, indicating immediately the seed's fate as soon as it is scattered.

In response to his disciples' question, Jesus interprets the parable. "The seed is God's word" (8:11), he says, thus providing the lens by which to read the rest of the story. Of course, "God's word" has a rich history in Israel's story, tied as it is to creation, promise, blessing and judgment, and covenant. God reveals himself and his design through his word, and this is precisely what Jesus has been doing in word and deed: scattering God's word. God's word is not static, though, but enables and invites, one might even say necessitates, response, and this encourages us to reflect carefully on the nature of the obstacles to good response pictured in the parable of the soils.

In Jesus's interpretation of the first three vignettes, different hindrances to growth in the agricultural world—the wild birds, a thin layer of topsoil covering rock, and hardy, spikey weeds—represent not simply different responses to God's word but also different impediments to hearing well. Hearing well, we learn in the fourth vignette, is the consequence of integrity of heart and life, embracing God's word, and producing fruit by means of steadfastness.

Good hearing is faithful hearing enacted through faithful living. What disables this kind of hearing?

1. The first obstacle is the devil, who snatches God's word from the hearts of some who hear, with the result that, failing to believe, they are not saved. This is the devil's aim, to obstruct faith, to hinder people from entrusting themselves to God and his word (see the devil's encounter with Jesus in the wilderness, 4:1–13). This reference to the "heart" is telling since, in ancient psychology, the heart was the center of a person's dispositions, including allegiances, devotion, will, understanding, and longings. With agricultural images abounding in this parable sequence, it is hard to miss the picture Jesus paints of a faith that must organically penetrate the whole of a person—or, in this instance, a person's incapacity to cultivate such a faith on account of diabolic intervention. This vignette prepares for Jesus's emphasis on "good-hearted people of integrity" whose hearing is authentic (v. 15).

2. The second impairment to good hearing is likened to shallow topsoil covering rock, shallow enough to impede the growth of roots capable of supporting a flourishing crop. Jesus's vignette documents some growth, but only hardy plants can survive obstructions to growth like too much heat and too little water, and hardy plants depend on deep roots. The difficulties Jesus mentions parade under the heading of "temptation" (πειρασμός, *peirasmos*), which in Luke-Acts refers to occasions to sin typically associated with the devil (e.g., 4:1–13), including duress, betrayal, and persecution.[56] This second vignette prepares for Jesus's emphasis on the faithful steadfastness characteristic of authentic hearing (v. 15).

3. The third barrier to hearing well comprises the triumvirate of anxieties (cf. 12:22–34; 21:34), wealth, and life's immoral pleasures[57]—all of which represent for Luke attempts to achieve security and prestige, and to thrive, apart from God and without concern for one's neighbor.[58] By comparison, those who hear well are not overcome with worry and do not hold tightly to their possessions, nor are their behaviors guided by lust; instead, they grasp God's word and persevere in practices grounded in God's word (v. 15).

What Luke has given us, then, is a catalog of explanations of the failure of some who fail to hear well and to produce the fruit of God's word. Alternatively, perhaps better, he provides a series of warnings to his audience to attend well to their hearing of God's word. The journey frame is signaled in the second and third vignettes—in the language of "turning away" (v. 13),[59] and, less directly, in the imagery of "choking" (v. 14), which raises questions about what people attempt to carry with them on the conversionary journey. In the first three vignettes, people hear God's word, even if we can trace a crescendo in the level of their reception of God's word. Even in the first, though, God's word has found its way into people's hearts, as this is the site of the devil's banditry. In the second, people receive and believe God's word. In the third, people actually produce fruit, even though it never reaches maturity. In the first two, the devil is implicated. In the second, duress, betrayal, persecution, and other forms of temptation are named. In the third, anxieties, wealth, and life's immoral

---

56. Luke 11:4; 22:28, 39–46; Acts 20:19. That persecution should be included here, see the discussion in Cunningham, "*Through Many Tribulations*," 76–78.

57. In moral discourse, ἡδονή (*hēdonē*) typically refers to lust or illicit desire. See Weiser, "ἡδονή, ῆς, ἡ."

58. See Green, "Good News to the Poor."

59. Ἀφίστημι (*aphistēmi*): "to cause someone to move from a reference point," a metaphor for "altering allegiance," to "go away" (BDAG 157–58).

pleasures violently counter conversionary hearing. With this orientation in view, we are in a position to examine stories of deconversion in the Lukan narrative.

The Tragic Story of Judas

As a barometer of Judas's infamy, we can do no better than to observe how he is known prospectively and retrospectively for one thing, betraying Jesus. First mentioned in Luke 6:16, he is the last of the Twelve to be named, and Luke attaches to his name the scandalous modifier "who became a betrayer." The final time he appears in Luke's narrative, the now-deceased Judas is about to be replaced by Matthias, who was chosen "to take the place of this service and apostleship from which Judas turned aside to go to his own place" (Acts 1:25). Note the travel language:[60] Judas goes from one "place" to another, in this case from the place chosen for him by God to a place of his own choosing (hell?);[61] in so doing, he "turned aside," an echo of the beginning of Luke's passion account, when Judas "departed" Jesus and his followers to negotiate Jesus's betrayal with the chief priests and officers of the temple guard (Luke 22:4). Rather than produce fruit through steadfast faithfulness to God's word (Luke 8:15), Judas "turned aside to go to his own place." Rather than God's way, the way of service, he chose to go his own way.[62] Having turned aside, Judas finds himself no longer in partnership with Jesus and the circle of disciples, and thus no longer in partnership with God; rather, partnered with the Jerusalem elite, he is an agent of the power of darkness, Satan (cf. Luke 22:1–6, 47–53).

Acts 1:15–26 weaves together two stories, the one concerning Judas, the other the stimulus for his being replaced and the process by which this was accomplished. A series of common elements draw these stories together and help to indicate the nature of Judas's embeddedness within Jesus's inner circle and, thus, the tragic nature of his defection:

Acts 1:17	Acts 1:20	Acts 1:25–26
"numbered"		"added"
"among us"		"with the Eleven"

60. Similarly, one of the qualifications of Judas's replacement is journeying with Jesus throughout his career (v. 21). Luke's phrase, "coming and going," borrows an idiom from Israel's Scriptures for "one's way of life" (e.g., Num. 27:17; Deut. 31:2; Josh. 14:11; 2 Sam. 3:25; Ps. 121:8). Jervell's attempt to oppose "walking" and behavior (*Apostelgeschichte*, 126–27) overlooks the idiomatic understanding of "walking" as "way of life."

61. A number of commentators understand "his own place" as a euphemism for "hell" (e.g., Barrett, *Acts*, 1:103; Roloff, *Apostelgeschichte*, 34; Haenchen, *Acts*, 162). Outside of this textual unit, one may find justification for this reading in Luke 16:28: "place of torment." L. Johnson (*Acts*, 37) draws attention to the notion of a "final destiny" in Tob. 3:6; 1 *Clement* 5.4; Ignatius, *Magnesians* 5.1.

62. Ἴδιος (*idios*, "one's own") is in the final, emphatic position.

Acts 1:17	Acts 1:20	Acts 1:25–26
"allotted his share (lot)"		"cast lots . . . the lot"
"this service"		"this service"
	deserted home	deserted place
	position as leader	place of apostleship

Additionally, the portrayal of Judas in Acts 1 is cast in ways reminiscent of Luke's Gospel: Judas is "the traitor" (Luke 6:16), who "turned aside" (Luke 22:4; Acts 1:25) and led a posse to arrest Jesus (Luke 22:47; Acts 1:16), even though he was "one of us" or "one of the Twelve" (Luke 22:3, 21, 47; Acts 1:17), and so received his "wicked payment" (Acts 1:18; cf. Luke 16:9, 11; 22:5). Luke's phrase "he was allotted a share in this service" (Acts 1:17) hints at what we already know, namely, that Judas's selection as an apostle was not arbitrary but was a disclosure of the divine will; indeed, he was chosen "through the Holy Spirit" (v. 2) after a night of prayer (Luke 6:12–16). Note the thinly veiled play on the description of the practice of casting lots in Acts 1:17, where we find language used in a more literal fashion in v. 26 to describe the actual casting of lots. In this instance, "casting lots" is used figuratively to denote Jesus's choice of Judas as an obvious expression of divine volition.[63]

These data drive home the place of Judas as a follower of Jesus and participant in his ministry. He was, after all, "one of the Twelve" (Luke 22:3), a table intimate (22:21). They also show that, even if God's purpose is decisive, God calls for human partnership, and faithful partnership cannot be guaranteed, since God's purpose can be opposed. Evidence of divine foreknowledge and choreography pervades Luke's account, but the story of Judas nonetheless casts a dark shadow of warning. Just as Zechariah's response to Gabriel (Luke 1:18–20) signaled the possibility of less-than-wholehearted response to God's redemptive visitation, even among God's own people, so the Judas cycle heralds the possibility of rejecting God's aim, a turning aside and going one's own way rather than embracing God's Way.[64]

For Luke, then, Judas exemplifies deconversion. He is a case study in what the parable of the soils might look like when acted out on the stage of human relationships and cosmic forces, with diabolic intervention (Luke 8:12–13) and wealth (8:14) providing the impetus for his turning away. In 22:3–6, we find that Satan entered into Judas and that a deal with the chief priests and officers of the temple guard was sealed with the promise of money. In Acts 1:18, his perversity is tied even more explicitly to the problem of wealth. He

63. This usage was already known in the OT and among the Dead Sea Scrolls; see Beardslee, "Casting of Lots"; see also Acts 8:21.
64. Vogler, *Judas Iskarioth*, 75–92; S. Brown, *Apostasy and Perseverance*, 82–109.

receives a "wicked payment,"[65] and this aligns Judas with the "children of this age" who deal shrewdly with wealth (Luke 16:8–9). Ironically, disciples give up everything they have to follow Jesus (cf. Luke 5:27–28; 9:57–58; 18:28; Acts 20:33–35), but this disciple, Judas, takes money to betray Jesus. Ironically, Judas goes to his *own* place (τὸν ἴδιον, *ton idion*, "one's own"), but the disciples left their *own* possessions (τὰ ἴδια, *ta idia*, "own things") to follow Jesus. Ironically, we learn from Luke's parable of using wealth to make friends (16:1–9), echoed here, that wealth properly used on behalf of the needy buys an eternal home, but Judas gains wealth by betraying his close friend Jesus to the Jerusalem authorities and then buys for himself a burial ground. Ironically, whereas Judas buys a field, the faithful sell their property to provide for the community's needy (Acts 2:44–45; 4:32–37; cf. Luke 18:22; 19:1–10). Judas's use of his "wicked payment" is thus a sign of his apostasy.

The Horrific Tale of Ananias and Sapphira

The infamous story of Ananias and Sapphira (Acts 5:1–11) is part of a larger narrative segment concerned with how the community of believers embodied (or, in their case, failed to embody) the resurrection message (4:32–5:11). This segment follows immediately on the heels of the community's prayer that the Lord might enable signs and wonders to be performed in Jesus's name and after they were all filled with the Holy Spirit (4:30–31). This shows that the economic sharing Luke goes on to sketch is both the result of the Spirit's work and is characteristic of the Spirit-endowed community of Christ followers. The structure of this section of Acts is as follows:

> 4:32: Heading: Unity of heart, mind, and possessions
> > 4:33–35: Summary: Resurrection message enacted in care
> > for the needy
> > 4:36–37: Barnabas, a positive exemplar
> > 5:1–11: Ananias and Sapphira, negative exemplars

The whole is held together by a common pattern of activity: they had land, they sold land, and they placed the proceeds at the apostles' feet (4:34b–35, 37; 5:1–2). Of course, in the case of Ananias and Sapphira, the pattern is

---

65. Luke's phrase ἐκ μισθοῦ τῆς ἀδικίας (*ek misthou tēs adikias*) could be read as an objective genitive ("reward for his wicked act," popular among English translations: e.g., NRSV, CEB, NAB, NET, NIV), but this phrase recalls the parallel phrase in Luke 16:9: ἐκ τοῦ μαμωνᾶ τῆς ἀδικίας (cf. 16:11: τῷ ἀδίκῳ μαμωνᾷ; and the similar form in 18:6: ὁ κριτὴς τῆς ἀδικίας). An adjectival reading, "wicked payment," therefore seems preferable (cf. S. Brown, *Apostasy and Perseverance*, 85–86).

broken: they keep part of the proceeds for themselves and place only part of the proceeds at the apostles' feet.

Acts 4:32–35 is remarkable for the way it associates bearing witness to the resurrection with care for the needy. Hospitality and food show up together with being "raised up" elsewhere in the Lukan narrative (e.g., Luke 4:38–39; 8:49–56; 15:11–32; 24:13–35; Acts 10:41), just as elsewhere Luke ties care for the needy to the resurrection (e.g., Luke 14:13–15; 16:19–31). Since in Israel's Scriptures, the promise of resurrection is a promise of Israel's restoration (e.g., Hosea 6:1–3; Ezek. 37:1–14),[66] we should also acknowledge that Luke portrays the economic sharing of the early church with language borrowed from the formation of God's people after the exodus: "There was no needy person among them" (Acts 4:34; see Deut. 15:4). Apparently, care for the needy is characteristic of the new-exodus community, the community whose resurrection witness is made plain in part through its care for the needy.

Luke's summary draws deeply on the nature of economics in traditional societies, where economic sharing is enmeshed in social relations (and vice versa).[67] People of the same kin group—whether understood, for example, as a clan in traditional societies or, in some Greco-Roman philosophy, as ideal friends—share everything, including possessions and truth. As Luke puts it, they were sharing "one heart and mind" and holding "all things in common" (4:32). Luke's summary also emphasizes apostolic authority, since the formula "to place x at the feet of y" is a gesture of submission (e.g., 1 Sam. 25:24, 41; 2 Sam. 22:39). The presence of an emphasis on authority in this context is not coincidental, since the robust intermingling of economic and social realities brings with it a concomitant emphasis on maintaining group boundaries and therefore on discipline.[68]

If Barnabas precisely recapitulates in his behavior what is characteristic of the community of the faithful, we might say that Ananias and Sapphira provide a negative image of that faithfulness. They hold back money, they lie, and they only pretend to submit to the authority of the apostles. Cast initially as insiders, part of this community of believers,[69] in this anecdote they immediately distance themselves from the faithful through their economic

66. See Anderson, *"But God Raised Him,"* 48–91.

67. See Sahlins, *Stone Age Economics.*

68. David R. McCabe examines the range of potential backgrounds for economic sharing in Luke's world, concluding that the community-of-goods discourse has two primary features: the laudatory esteem in which such communities are held as examples of a utopian ideal and the severe judgment practiced in cases of transgressing that ideal. See McCabe, *How to Kill Things with Words,* 56–123.

69. On the analogy of the two-stage process of membership at Qumran, Capper ("Palestinian Cultural Context," 337–41) urges that Ananias and Sapphira were only prospective members

practices. When their actions are read against the backdrop of the parable of
the soils (Luke 8:4–15), it is easy to find in their story mirror reflections of the
first and third soil types. With the first soil type, the devil steals God's word
from people's hearts so they cannot believe and be saved (Luke 8:12). In Acts 5,
Peter recognizes in their behavior that Satan has "filled" Ananias's "heart"
(5:3), and this explains how this deceitful deed came to reside in Ananias's
"heart" (5:4). Luke draws a devastating contrast. On the one hand, we have a
people who were filled with the Spirit (4:31), a fellowship comprising "those
who exercise faith" (4:32). On the other hand, we have Ananias, whose heart
Satan filled, and we recall from the parable of the soils that Satan's aim is to
short-circuit the growth of faith. The community of believers were of "one
heart and mind," but Satan's work ensured that Ananias no longer shared
with them "one heart and mind." As Daniel Marguerat puts it, "Satan has
taken over the territory that should be the Spirit's: the heart of the believer."[70]
The proof of this is that Ananias no longer holds all possessions in common
with them. With the third soil type, growth is interrupted by anxieties, wealth,
and immoral pleasures. Unsurprisingly, then, economic language is scattered
throughout Acts 5:1–11: the selling of property, the value of the property and
proceeds from the sale, property ownership and sale, and so on. Accordingly,
Ananias and Sapphira exit the community of believers under the influence of
Satan, choked by money.

The rhetoric of Luke's account requires that we take seriously that the
whole of this section, 4:32–5:11, has 4:32 as its heading and 4:33–34 as its
summary; this means that the whole of 4:32–5:11 describes what is internal
to the fellowship of Christ followers. Hence, what Luke relates in Acts 5:1–11,
too, describes the community of believers. This means that we must take with
equal seriousness how Ananias and Sapphira's collective behavior enacts their
deconversion, their failure to produce fruit with a good heart and through
steadfastness (Luke 8:15). And this helps us to understand better why "the
whole church" was horrified when they heard about Ananias and Sapphira
(Acts 5:11; cf. 5:5). Can Satan's influence and wealth's allure waylay even those
who have begun the conversionary journey? Apparently so!

A Tale of Conversion Interrupted: Simon Magus

In the NT, Simon Magus is known to us only in Acts 8:5–25, in the first
of two scenes demonstrating the character of Philip's ministerial leadership

---

of the community of Christ followers. Cf., however, Walton, "Primitive Communism in Acts?,"
106–8.

70. Marguerat, *First Christian Historian*, 170.

(cf. 6:1–7). This material is crucial to the narrative Luke writes but is also anomalous in two ways. It is crucial because of Philip's move into a Samaritan city (8:5). Inhabitants of Samaria traced their ancestry back to Abraham but rejected the view that God's purpose for his people centered on Jerusalem and its temple.[71] We read earlier of the antipathy between Jews and Samaritans in Luke 9:52–56; 10:33–35; 17:11–19—narrative accounts that emphasize the inhospitality between the two groups and, from a Jewish perspective, the Samaritans' status as "foreigners" (17:18). These texts also anticipate the inclusion of Samaritans within God's redemptive plan, a divine aim unmistakably documented in Jesus's commission to his followers in Acts 1:8: "You will be my witnesses in Jerusalem, in all Judea and Samaria, and to the end of the earth." Given our interest in Luke's understanding of conversion, we should reflect on how this commission extends the boundaries of God's saving grace but also on what conversion would require of the Samaritans. I refer to their need to reformulate their understanding of salvation history in ways that make room for Philip's reconceptualization of Yahweh's purpose and the nature of Yahweh's promises to Abraham. The histories they told and the self-understanding they formulated would require reevaluation in light of the fresh understanding of God's purpose resident in Jesus's crucifixion and exaltation. Conversion in this sense undoes taken-for-granted belief structures in order to reconstruct them—and this is implied in Philip's ministry of "proclaiming the good news of God's word" (Acts 8:4), "proclaiming the Messiah" (8:5), and "proclaiming the good news about God's kingdom and the name of Jesus Christ" (8:12). Importantly, then, the persuasiveness of his conversionary rhetoric is clear: they were united in their hearing of Philip's message (8:4), "they believed . . . and were being baptized, both men and women" (8:12), and they "received God's word" (8:14).

The first anomaly Luke presents in his recounting of what happened in Samaria resides in the separation of water baptism from Spirit baptism. In a clear departure from the expectations set up in the Pentecost address, which closely associates baptism in the name of Jesus Christ and reception of the gift of the Holy Spirit (2:38), here Luke notes in a narrative aside that "the Holy Spirit hadn't yet fallen on any of them, but they had only been baptized in the name of the Lord Jesus" (8:16). How do we explain this apparent inconsistency? Was Philip's ministry deficient? This is difficult to argue, since Luke otherwise allows no censure of Philip's work, his message parallels Jesus's own message and that of other witnesses in Acts, and, like theirs, his ministry is accompanied by signs, healings, and exorcisms (8:6–7). Moreover,

71. For background, see Williamson and Kartveit, "Samaritans."

Philip's mission actualizes the commission Jesus gives his followers in Acts 1:8. Perhaps, then, the Samaritans' faith was inadequate.[72] This reading decisively falters in light of Luke's report that the Samaritans believed and had been baptized "in the name of the Lord Jesus" (8:16). Another possibility is that Luke has Peter and John bestow the Holy Spirit on the Samaritans in order to identify the Jerusalem church as a kind of headquarters, as though, from Luke's perspective, the Holy Spirit could not be poured out except through authorized representatives of the Jerusalem community.[73] But Luke otherwise gives no indication that the Spirit could be withheld or given by human beings (irrespective of their status), emphasizing instead the Spirit's autonomy (cf. 10:1–11:18!). This view also gives Jerusalem greater prestige than it actually possesses for Luke. Another, more helpful way to make sense of this puzzle is to focus on the apostles who for the first time journey from Jerusalem to Samaria—in spite of the clear mandate in 1:8 to witness to Jesus "in all Judea and Samaria, and to the end of the earth," as well as Luke's testimony that Stephen's execution resulted in the scattering of the church throughout Judea and Samaria (8:1). From this vantage point, the apparent delay in the outpouring of the Spirit in Samaria serves to assist in the ongoing conversion of Peter and John, so that they finally engage in a ministry among the Samaritans (8:25), and to prepare for the Jerusalem Council, where those gathered come to recognize that the chasm between Jews and gentiles (and thus also between Jews and Samaritans) is bridged ultimately by God (15:8–9).

The second anomaly is the way Luke's account follows the response of the inhabitants of this Samaritan city in general but introduces as a subplot the story of Simon Magus. A powerful magician, Simon dazzled (ἐξίστημι, existēmi) the Samaritans with his magic (8:11). Along with them, though, he believed and was baptized, after which he was dazzled (ἐξίστημι, existēmi) by the signs and miracles accompanying Philip's ministry (8:13). Luke sets up two series of parallels:

Simon Magus	Philip	Simon Magus	The Samaritans
Practiced magic (8:9–11)	Performed miracles (8:6, 13)	Believed (8:13)	Believed (8:12)
Attracts crowds (8:9–11)	Attracts crowds (8:6)	Baptized (8:13)	Baptized (8:12)
They paid attention to him (8:10–11)	They paid attention to him (8:6)		

72. Thus, Dunn, *Baptism*, 55–72; note the critical remarks in, e.g., Turner, *Power from on High*, 362–67.

73. Thus, e.g., O'Toole, "Christian Baptism in Luke," 861–62; Shepherd, *Holy Spirit*, 181–82; Hartman, *Baptism*, 136–37.

Simon Magus	Philip	Simon Magus	The Samaritans
Simon is "the great power" (8:10)	Performs "great powers" (8:13)		

Setting these two sets of parallels side by side, we see how Luke presents Simon Magus and Philip in a kind of power encounter, in competition for the crowds, and how Luke traces Simon's movement from his being distinguished from the inhabitants of this city by his elevated status as "the power of God called Great" (8:10) to his solidarity with the crowds who believed and were baptized in the name of the Lord Jesus. Luke gives us no reason to doubt that, when "they received the Holy Spirit" (8:13), Simon was included among them.

Only after Peter and John arrive on the scene does Luke again differentiate Simon from the rest of the Samaritan believers. We may find a hint of what is to come in Luke's observation that Simon was especially attentive to the signs and great miracles accompanying Philip's ministry (8:13). In other words, he may have transferred his allegiance to the Lord Jesus, but he seems still to think like a magician. In any case, as much as he was bedazzled by Philip's ministry, he was apparently even more impressed when Peter and John laid their hands on the Samaritans so that they received the Holy Spirit.[74] This is the point at which the story takes a wrong turn.

> When Simon saw that the Spirit was given through the laying on of the apostles' hands, he offered them money, saying, "Give me this authority too, so that anyone on whom I lay hands can receive the Holy Spirit." Peter replied, "May you and your money be damned, since you imagined that you could buy God's gift with money! You have no part or share in God's word, for your heart isn't right [or isn't straight] with God. Turn from your wickedness! Plead with the Lord in the hope that he might forgive your heart's intent, for I see that you are full of bitterness and in wicked chains." Simon responded, "Plead to the Lord on my behalf, all of you, that nothing you have said may happen to me." (8:18–24)

The picture is wrong in so many ways. Why does Simon have money, when, as we have seen, conversion is enacted through placing all that one has in service to Jesus? Why does Simon have money of his own, to spend as he desires, when believers hold all things in common? Is he really trying to use his resources to purchase the authority to bestow the Spirit, when believers are those who sell what they have to care for the needy? Why does Simon suppose that he needs to use his silver (ἀργύριον, *argyrion*; 8:20) to bargain for authority

---

74. A major gap occurs at this point in Luke's narration: What was it that Simon witnessed? Did glossolalia (or some other related phenomena) accompany the gift of the Spirit, as in 2:1–13; 10:46; 19:6?

over the Spirit, when these same two apostles, Peter and John, are agents of healing even though they have no "silver [ἀργύριον, *argyrion*] or gold" (3:6)? Does Simon really imagine that the Holy Spirit—who is, after all, *the Father's* promise (1:4; 2:33) and *God's* gift (8:20)—is under human authority? Does he really suppose that the Holy Spirit can be given to people through the laying on of hands quite apart from their repentance, faith, and baptism?

This closing scene echoes what we have found thus far in our ruminations about deconversion. When his actions are read against the backdrop of the parable of the soils (Luke 8:4–15), we find Simon's conversion obstructed by wealth. And, far from having a heart of integrity and persevering through faith, Simon's heart is crooked; his heart's intent and his behavior set him in opposition to God's ways. Peter goes on to characterize Simon with unflattering language dependent on Israel's Scriptures: "full of bitterness" is an expression reminiscent of Deut. 29:18, which describes those who have turned away from the Lord and toward idolatry; and "in wicked chains" is a phrase that recalls Isa. 58:6, which suggests that Simon has yet to be released fully from the vile web of his former life. We can also read Simon's story against the background of the stories of Judas and of Ananias and Sapphira. Judas forfeited his "share in this service" (1:17), just as Simon has "no part or share in God's word." Judas used his "wicked payment" (1:18) to purchase a field, whereas Simon remains in "wicked chains." Satan filled Ananias's "heart" (Acts 5:3), and deceit found a home there (5:4); similarly, Simon's heart is not right with God, and his heartfelt resolve opposes God's ways. Of course, the motif of money runs like a red thread through all of this material.[75]

Beginning with the early church's reception of Acts, many interpreters have regarded Simon Magus's faith as insincere and his baptism as hypocritical. Stories developed as a result, pitting him against Peter or pitting the movement Simon allegedly founded against the true faith. The Venerable Bede summarizes:

> It was either that he too was overcome by the power of the blessed Philip's words so that he truly believed in the Lord, or, as is more believable, that he pretended that he believed until he could receive baptism. For he was so eager for praise that he wished to be believed to be the Christ, as histories tell, and he

---

75. Missing from these parallels is any reference to the devil or Satan in the Simon material. A connection to the devil is inferred by some interpreters (e.g., Garrett, *Demise of the Devil*, 65–78; she thinks Simon is under Satan's mastery). Given the other points of contact with the parable of the soils and with Luke's presentation of Judas and of Ananias and Sapphira, the lack of any explicit mention of Satan, the devil, or demons must be significant. It may well be tied to another glaring difference: the devil snatches faith from people's hearts (keeping them from being saved), Satan enters into Judas (who dies condemned), and Satan fills Ananias's heart (who dies condemned), but Simon is told to turn from his wicked ways and to pray in the hope that he will be forgiven.

hoped to learn from him the arts by which he worked miracles. His followers were also taught to do this. *Trained in the evil arts of their founder to enter the church by any sort of deception* they were accustomed to steal baptism.[76]

Actually, though, this is not Luke's portrait. Presumably, this interpretation gained traction among those who read 8:18–23 back into 8:13, and from the erroneous assumption that belief and baptism occasion an immediate and thoroughgoing transformation of one's patterns of thinking, believing, feeling, and behaving. Simply put, Simon's story shows us that conversion is not easy; with Simon's story, as with Peter's (see chap. 4), the conversionary journey may include its stops and starts, its detours. Conversion is a process of reformation. Accordingly, it is no surprise that, perhaps after the passing of only a few days since his baptism, Simon remains within the grip of his former habits of heart and life. Seeing what he takes to be the authority wielded by Peter and John, he reverts to his old dispositions. "His precarious faith has the potential to become stable," Hans-Josef Klauck observes, "but for the moment it remains at risk."[77]

Simon's conversion, we might say, is interrupted, and it is not clear whether he will continue down a conversionary path. Having traversed life's path and enjoyed public notoriety as a magician "for a long time" (8:11), Simon would not find it a simple matter to jump from one set of well-traveled tracks to another, fresh set of tracks. Will his hearing turn out to be authentic? Or will his hearing falter in the face of temptation, choked by anxiety, wealth, and illicit desire? As with a handful of other stories Luke relates, Simon's is open-ended (e.g., Luke 15:11–32; 18:18–23). We do not learn from Luke's narrative whether Simon in fact turns from his wickedness, as Peter demands, though it is surely suggestive that the Simon introduced to us as the great power at the beginning of the story appears at the end of the story as powerless, able only to beg others to pray on his behalf.

Lukan Rhetoric

Clearly, Luke knows the phenomenon of deconversion, the migration of people away from the fellowship of Christ followers. Jesus's parable of the

---

76. Bede, *Acts*, 79, emphasis original. See, e.g., Casey, "Simon Magus"; Martin, *Acts*, 93–95; Chung-Kim and Hains, *Acts*, 106–9.

77. Klauck, *Magic and Paganism*, 18. Similarly, Rudolf Pesch (*Apostelgeschichte*, 275) denies that Simon engages in hypocrisy while at the same time noting that "he remains caught up in thinking like a magician." (Der Text unterstellt ihm dabei keine Heuchelei. . . . Daß Simon in magischem Denken begangen bleibt, kommt freilich in der Begegnung mit den Aposteln Petrus und Johannes heraus.) A number of contemporary commentators now see Simon as a "Christian" (e.g., Barrett, *Acts*, 1:409; L. Johnson, *Acts*, 152; Fitzmyer, *Acts*, 405).

soils sets out the patterns of this potential migration, as well as, by way of contrast, the kind of authentic hearing of God's word that leads to persistence along the path leading to a bountiful harvest of conversionary fruit. Luke interweaves elements of the parable of the soils with the deconversionary tales of Judas, of Ananias and Sapphira, and of Simon Magus. Chief among these elements are emphases on Satanic influence, a person's core dispositions (that is, his or her "heart"), and the allure of wealth.

The first emphasis is integral to Luke's theology of God's kingdom, which stands in opposition to all other realms, since all other kingdoms are really under the devil's control (e.g., Luke 4:5–6). Accordingly, conversion entails nothing less than movement from the sphere of Satan's authority to the sphere of God's (e.g., Acts 26:17–18). Although numbered as "one of the Twelve" (Judas) or with the community of believers (Ananias and Sapphira), these three underwent deconversion as they migrated into enemy territory.

The second emphasis draws its significance from ancient psychology, for which the "heart" was the organ of volition, insight and understanding, feeling—or what I have repeatedly referred to as patterns of thinking, feeling, believing, and behaving. In this ancient sense, "heart" figures prominently in two of our stories: Satan filled Ananias's heart so that his heart devised a deceitful plan, and Simon's heart was "crooked" before God and his heart's intention was set against God's ways. Luke makes no reference to the condition of Judas's heart, though Luke 22:3 does have it that Satan "entered into" Judas.

The third emphasis participates in and supports the central significance Luke's narrative theology allocates to issues of wealth and possessions. It is not too much to say that, for Luke, the disposition of one's wealth is the public face of the disposition of one's heart. Fascinatingly, this third emphasis provides the single constant across these three examples of deconversion. Moving from Luke's agricultural images in the parable of the soils, where spiny weeds choke out the wanted plants, to a wrestling image, it is as if Luke pictures wealth as potentially having a choke hold on Christ followers. As countermoves, Luke offers such conversionary practices as submission of all that one has in service to Jesus, placing wealth in the service of friendship with the poor, and the sort of economic sharing signified by Luke's vision of the community of goods. When we examine these three stories of deconversion, it is difficult not to imagine possessions and wealth as nearly godlike powers aligned against God's agenda, and thus we hear with an added sense of urgency Jesus's uncompromising words: "You can't serve God and Wealth" (Luke 16:13).

Why does Luke include this material in his narrative? Undoubtedly, these accounts serve multiple purposes. Among them would be the following:

1. To draw attention (through negative examples) to the nature of genuine conversion, which requires a deep-seated and fully embodied transformation of heart and life, ongoing allegiance to the Lord, and persistence along the path.
2. To pinpoint the dangerous mistake of imagining that the way of conversion could be reduced to a momentary decision.
3. To explain why some, like Judas, begin well but turn away from the Way.
4. To warn Christ followers of impediments to conversionary life and, indeed, of the possibility of deconversion.

Conclusion

Conversionary community, agency, and deconversion—how has exploration of these three issues contributed to our understanding of Luke's theology of conversion? Importantly, our work with representative texts has demonstrated the usefulness of the insights generated by our exploration of conversion in chaps. 3–4. In particular, we have found reason to affirm, and affirm again, such conversionary motifs as directionality (life's trajectory determined with reference to God's restorative purpose, oriented toward Jesus and his message), the journeyed nature of conversion (and so a transformative and transforming way of life), the practices that both enact and exhibit conversion (such as baptism, faithfulness with possessions, witness, prayer, and the shared table), and the formative nature of the community of believers. From beginning to end, too, we find a dual emphasis on conversion as divine gift that also must be appropriated—and continuously appropriated—through proper human response. Although conversion is God's act, it entails more than God's activity; it involves an ongoing journey with companions, choices, and practices as the converted experience an ongoing transformation of their patterns of faith and life. Deconversion, then, would signal not a divine failure but a human one, as people who have received God's word fail to move deeper and deeper into the sphere of God's salvation through ongoing faithfulness but, instead, migrate into the territory controlled by the darkness, with its dispositions, allegiances, and practices set in opposition to God's way.

Epilogue

For many, "conversion" is a quintessentially religious term associated especially with the early Christian movement and the subsequent history of the church and its mission. This is true in spite of the twin realities that this concept had a history already in Israel's Scriptures and is evidenced more broadly in Greco-Roman antiquity, and that, early in the twenty-first century, the experience of religious conversion is hardly unique to the church. The expansion of the religious marketplace in our increasingly globalized world has as its consequences not only the increased frequency of conversions within and among the major world religions but also an increased interest in conversion as a topic of study, especially within the social and personality sciences. Accompanying this increased attention has been the pressing need for greater clarity about the nature of conversion—how to define it, what motivates it, what it entails, and so on. Although this increased attention has brought with it the danger, from a Christian perspective, of reducing conversion to a psychosocial phenomenon, it has helpfully drawn back the curtain on the ease with which modern definitions have been read back into ancient texts and emphasized the need for a fresh assessment of what the scriptural texts contribute to the discussion.

Among the NT writings, none is more concerned with conversion than Luke-Acts. This is widely acknowledged. What conversion entails for Luke-Acts has attracted less agreement, however. My approach has been exegetical, to be sure, but an exegesis informed by the cognitive sciences and thus by the assumption that we might hear Luke's voice better if we first minimize the voice of René Descartes—whose volume is hardly noticeable today since our hearing long ago habituated to it. Like urbanites whose ears have adjusted to

161

traffic sounds or country dwellers who no longer hear the frogs and crickets at night, modern folk generally take for granted Descartes's fundamental distinction between body and mind, between interior and exterior. Following Descartes, then, they prioritize the interior, the mind. A cognitive approach undermines this one, first, by drawing attention to its taken-for-granted status and exposing it for the problematic constellation of assumptions it is. Second, a cognitive approach posits the critical importance of somatic, or bodily, existence as the basis and means of human experience, including religious experience. Simply put, if what makes us human are the properties and capacities that have the human brain and body as their anatomical basis, then there can be no transformation that is not fully embodied. Moreover, if the neurobiological systems that shape how we think, feel, believe, and behave are continuously molded in the context of our social experiences, then personal formation and reformation are unavoidably relational. Who we are—and, therefore, what it means to undergo conversion—is inescapably tied to our bodies and to the community (or communities) we inhabit. Here, then, is the wager I made as this examination developed: Could it be that a cognitive (as opposed to a Cartesian) approach to the evidence Luke provides helps us to see that evidence in a new light and, in fact, to reflect more faithfully on the story Luke has told? This study supports an affirmative answer to this question.

Initial inquiry into Luke's theology of conversion led to a provisional definition:

> *Converts are those who have undergone a redirectional shift and are now on the move with the community of those faithfully serving God's eschatological purpose.*

Accordingly, we discerned four emphases: (1) Embedded in the notion of conversion as a journey is a prominent emphasis on directionality. Conversion is less acquiescence to a particular set of faith claims and more participation in the unfolding of a particular story. (2) Conversion entails an orientation toward God's eschatological purpose. This means that conversion is deeply embedded in the ancient story of God's dealings with Israel, so that it is to this God that life is directed. Moreover, this life is eschatologically focused, since it is the eschatological coming of God to restore Israel that marks the turn of the ages, places before people the word of repentance, and enables conversion. (3) Conversion is basic to Luke's presentation of God's restoration of God's people. Conversion can be understood in personal terms but not in individualistic ones. (4) Conversion is inseparable from participation in the practices constitutive of the remnant comprising God's restored people.

Further interpretive work thickened and extended this definition in key ways. In terms of thickening this definition, an examination of representative texts underscored especially the journeyed nature of conversion—including the need for persistence along the Way—and the significance of a conversionary community, together with those practices that enact and exhibit ongoing conversion. Luke's inclusion of deconversionary episodes in his narrative served only to highlight even more such motifs as these, particularly as these episodes demonstrated the tight grip exercised by one's prior patterns of faith and life—and, thus, the need for integrity of heart and persistence along the Way. In terms of extending this definition, we found reason (5) to underscore the christological lens through which we are to understand God's eschatological purpose and (6) to account for both human and divine agency in conversion. Jesus and his mission compose the key landmark, the singular point of orientation, for conversionary movement, so that belonging (inside or outside), status (up or down), and movement toward or away from the center are determined by the character of his mission. Since Luke grounds conversion in the grand narrative of God's ancient and ongoing purpose, the first and initiating act is God's; however, God's saving initiative calls for (just as it enables) response. Conversion is therefore both gracious gift and response. Adjusting our provisional definition somewhat, then, we can affirm the following from our reading of Luke's theology:

> *Converts are those who, enabled by God, have undergone a redirectional shift and now persist along the Way with the community of those faithfully serving God's eschatological purpose as this is evident in the life, death, and exaltation of the Lord Jesus Christ, and whose lives are continually being formed through the Spirit at work in and through practices constitutive of this community.*

Bibliography

Adams, Dwayne H. *The Sinner in Luke*. ETSMS. Eugene, OR: Pickwick, 2008.

Ananthaswamy, Anil. "Bodily Minds: How We Think outside the Brain." *New Scientist* 205, no. 2753 (2010): 8–9.

Andersen, T. David. "The Meaning of ΕΧΟΝΤΕΣ ΧΑΡΙΝ ΠΡΟΣ in Acts 2.47." *NTS* 34 (1988): 604–10.

Anderson, Kevin L. *"But God Raised Him from the Dead": The Theology of Jesus' Resurrection in Luke-Acts*. PBM. Carlisle, UK: Paternoster, 2006.

Anderson, Steven W., et al. "Impairment of Social and Moral Behavior Related to Early Damage in Human Prefrontal Cortex." *Nature Neuroscience* 2, no. 11 (1999): 1032–37.

Arzy, Shahar, et al. "Neural Basis of Embodiment: Distinct Contributions of Temporoparietal Junction and Extrastriate Body Area." *Journal of Neuroscience* 26, no. 31 (2006): 8074–81.

"Ashland Church Can Brew Hallucinogenic Tea for Services, Judge Rules." *The Oregonian*, March 20, 2009. http://www.oregonlive.com/news/index.ssf/2009/03/ashland_church_can_brew_halluc.html. Accessed March 23, 2009.

Augustine (Saint). *On Christian Teaching*. Translated by R. P. C. Green. Oxford World's Classics. Oxford: Oxford University Press, 1997.

Babuts, Nicholae. *Memory, Metaphors, and Meaning: Reading Literary Texts*. New Brunswick, NJ: Transaction, 2009.

Badian, E. *Publicans and Sinners: Private Enterprise in the Service of the Roman Republic*. Ithaca, NY: Cornell University Press, 1983.

Bailey, Kenneth E. *Poet and Peasant*. Grand Rapids: Eerdmans, 1976.

Baird, William. "Visions, Revelation, and Ministry: Reflections on 2 Cor. 12:1–5 and Gal. 1:11–17." *JBL* 104 (1985): 651–62.

Banks, Robert. "'Walking' as a Metaphor of the Christian Life: The Origins of a Significant Pauline Usage." Pages 303–13 in *Perspectives on Language and Text: Essays and Poems in Honor of Francis I. Andersen's Sixtieth Birthday July 29,*

1985. Edited by Edgar W. Conrad and Edward G. Newing. Winona Lake, IN: Eisenbrauns, 1987.

Barbour, John D. *Versions of Deconversion: Autobiography and the Loss of Faith*. Charlottesville: University Press of Virginia, 1994.

Barrett, C. K. *A Critical and Exegetical Commentary on the Acts of the Apostles*. 2 vols. ICC. Edinburgh: T&T Clark, 1994–98.

Barth, Gerhard. *Die Taufe in frühchristlicher Zeit*. BThSt 4. Neukirchen-Vluyn: Neukirchener Verlag, 1981.

Barton, Stephen C. "New Testament Interpretation as Performance." *SJT* 52 (1999): 179–208.

Bayer, Hans F. "The Preaching of Peter in Acts." Pages 257–74 in *Witness to the Gospel: The Theology of Acts*. Edited by I. Howard Marshall and David Peterson. Grand Rapids: Eerdmans, 1998.

Beardslee, William A. "The Casting of Lots at Qumran and in the Book of Acts." *NovT* 4 (1960): 245–52.

Beauregard, Mario, and Vincent Paquette. "Neural Correlates of a Mystical Experience in Carmelite Nuns." *Neuroscience Letters* 405 (2006): 186–90.

Bechara, Antoine. "The Role of Emotion in Decision-Making: Evidence from Neurological Patients with Orbitofrontal Damage." *Brain and Cognition* 55 (2004): 30–40.

Bechara, Antoine, Antonio R. Damasio, Hanna Damasio, and Steven W. Anderson. "Insensitivity to Future Consequences Following Damage to Human Prefrontal Cortex." *Cognition* 50 (1994): 7–15.

Bede, the Venerable. *Commentary on the Acts of the Apostles*. Translated, with an introduction and notes, by Lawrence T. Martin. Cistercian Studies Series 117. Kalamazoo, MI: Cistercian, 1989.

Berger, Klaus. *Identity and Experience in the New Testament*. Minneapolis: Fortress, 2003.

Berger, Peter L. *A Far Glory: The Quest for Faith in an Age of Credulity*. New York: Doubleday, 1992.

———. *The Sacred Canopy: Elements of a Sociological Theory of Religion*. Garden City, NY: Doubleday, 1967.

Berger, Peter L., and Thomas Luckmann. *The Social Construction of Reality: A Treatise in the Sociology of Knowledge*. Garden City, NY: Doubleday, 1966.

Bird, Michael F. "The Unity of Luke-Acts in Recent Discussion." *JSNT* 29 (2007): 425–48.

Black, Robert Allen. "The Conversion Stories in the Acts of the Apostles." PhD diss., Emory University, 1985.

Blair, R. J. R. "The Roles of Orbital Frontal Cortex in the Modulation of Antisocial Behavior." *Brain and Cognition* 55 (2004): 198–208.

Blanke, Olaf, Theodor Landis, Laurent Spinelli, and Margitta Seeck. "Out-of-Body Experience and Autoscopy of Neurological Origin." *Brain* 127 (2004): 243–58.

Blanke, Olaf, Christine Mohr, Christoph M. Michel, Alvaro Pascual-Leone, Peter Brugger, Margitta Seeck, Theodor Landis, and Gregor Thut. "Linking Out-of-Body

Experience and Self Processing to Mental Own-Body Imagery at the Temporoparietal Junction." *Journal of Neuroscience* 25, no. 3 (2005): 550–57.

Blanke, Olaf, Stéphanie Ortigue, Theodor Landis, and Margitta Seeck. "Stimulating Illusory Own-Body Perceptions." *Nature* 419 (2002): 269–70.

Bläser, Peter. "ἀπειθέω." *EDNT* 1:118–19.

Boda, Mark J. *A Severe Mercy: Sin and Its Remedy in the Old Testament.* Siphrut: Literature and Theology of the Hebrew Scriptures 1. Winona Lake, IN: Eisenbrauns, 2009.

Böhlemann, Peter. *Jesus und der Täufer: Schlüssel zur Theologie und Ethik des Lukas.* SNTSMS 99. Cambridge: Cambridge University Press, 1997.

Borg, Marcus. *Conflict, Holiness and Politics in the Teachings of Jesus.* Lewiston, NY: Edwin Mellen, 1984.

Bourdieu, Pierre. *The Logic of Practice.* Stanford, CA: Stanford University Press, 1990.

Bourdieu, Pierre, and Loïc J. D. Wacquant. *An Invitation to Reflexive Sociology.* Chicago: University of Chicago Press, 1992.

Bovon, François. *Luke 1: A Commentary on the Gospel of Luke 1:1–9:50.* Hermeneia. Minneapolis: Fortress, 2002.

———. *L'œuvre de Luc: Études d'exégèse et de théologie.* Paris: Cerf, 1987.

Bowen, Clayton Raymond. "The Meaning of Συναλιζόμενος in Acts 1,4." *ZNW* 13 (1912): 247–59.

Braithwaite, Jason J., and Kevin Dent. "New Perspectives on Perspective-Taking Mechanisms and the Out-of-Body Experience." *Cortex* 47 (2011): 628–32.

Braithwaite, Jason J., D. Samson, I. Apperly, E. Broglia, and J. Hulleman. "Cognitive Correlates of the Spontaneous Out-of-Body Experience (OBE) in the Psychologically Normal Population: Evidence for an Increased Role of Temporal-Lobe Instability, Body-Distortion Processing, and Impairments in Own-Body Transformations." *Cortex* 47, no. 7 (2011): 839–53.

Brawley, Robert L. "For Blessing All Families of the Earth: Covenant Traditions in Luke-Acts." *CTM* 22 (1995): 18–26.

Brown, Colin. "What Was John the Baptist Doing?" *BBR* 7 (1997): 37–50.

Brown, Raymond E. *The Birth of the Messiah: A Commentary on the Infancy Narratives in the Gospels of Matthew and Luke.* Rev. ed. ABRL. New York: Doubleday, 1993.

Brown, Schuyler. *Apostasy and Perseverance in the Theology of Luke.* AnBib 36. Rome: Pontifical, 1969.

Brown, Warren S., and Brad D. Strawn. "Self-Organizing Personhood: Complex Emergent Developmental Linguistic Relational Neurophysiologicalism." Pages 91–101 in *Ashgate Research Companion to Theological Anthropology.* Edited by Joshua R. Farris and Charles Taliaferro. Burlington, VT: Ashgate, 2015.

Bruce, F. F. *The Acts of the Apostles: Greek Text with Introduction and Commentary.* 3rd ed. Grand Rapids: Eerdmans, 1990.

Bulkeley, Kelly. "Religious Conversion and Cognitive Neuroscience." Pages 240–55 in *The Oxford Handbook of Religious Conversion*. Edited by Lewis R. Rambo and Charles E. Farhadian. Oxford: Oxford University Press, 2014.

Cadbury, Henry J. *The Making of Luke-Acts*. With a new introduction by Paul N. Anderson. 2nd ed. Peabody, MA: Hendrickson, 1999 (1958; 1st ed., 1927).

————. "The Summaries in Acts." Pages 382–402 in *The Acts of the Apostles*, vol. 5, *Additional Notes to the Commentary*. Edited by F. J. Foakes Jackson and Kirsopp Lake. BC 1. London: Macmillan, 1933.

Calvin, John. *The Acts of the Apostles 1–13*. Calvin's Commentaries. Edited by David W. Torrance and Thomas F. Torrance. Grand Rapids: Eerdmans, 1965.

Capper, Brian J. "The Palestinian Cultural Context of Earliest Christian Community of Goods." Pages 323–64 in *The Book of Acts in Its Palestinian Setting*. Edited by Richard Bauckham. BAFCS 4. Grand Rapids: Eerdmans, 1995.

Casey, Robert P. "Simon Magus." Pages 151–63 in *The Acts of the Apostles*, vol. 5, *Additional Notes to the Commentary*. Edited by F. J. Foakes Jackson and Kirsopp Lake. BC 1. London: Macmillan, 1933.

Cheetham, F. P. "Acts ii.47: ἔχοντες χάριν πρὸς ὅλον τὸν λαόν." *ExpTim* 74 (1962–63): 214–15.

Chester, Stephen J. "Paul: Archetypal Convert and Disputed Convert." Pages 123–49 in *Finding and Losing Faith: Studies in Conversion*. Edited by Christopher Partridge and Helen Reid. Studies in Religion and Culture Series. Milton Keynes, UK: Paternoster, 2006.

Cheyne, J. Allan, and Todd A. Girard. "The Unbound Body: Vestibular-Motor Hallucinations and Out-of-Body Experiences." *Cortex* 45 (2009): 201–15.

Childs, Brevard S. *Isaiah*. OTL. Louisville: Westminster John Knox, 2001.

Chung-Kim, Esther, and Todd R. Hains, eds. *Acts*. RCS: New Testament 6. Downers Grove, IL: InterVarsity, 2014.

Co, Maria Anicia. "The Major Summaries in Acts: Acts 2,42–47; 4,32–35; 5,12–16; Linguistic and Literary Relationship." *ETL* 68 (1992): 49–85.

Colijn, Brenda B. *Images of Salvation in the New Testament*. Downers Grove, IL: InterVarsity, 2010.

Collins, John J. "Sibylline Oracles: A New Translation and Introduction." *OTP* 1:317–472.

Conzelmann, Hans. *A Commentary on the Acts of the Apostles*. Hermeneia. Philadelphia: Fortress, 1987.

————. *The Theology of St. Luke*. London: SCM, 1960.

Craig-Snell, Shannon. "Command Performance: Rethinking Performance Interpretation in the Context of Divine Discourse." *ModT* 16 (2000): 475–94.

Cranefield, Paul F. "A Seventeenth Century View of Mental Deficiency and Schizophrenia: Thomas Willis on 'Stupidity or Foolishness.'" *Bulletin of the History of Medicine* 35 (1961): 291–316.

Croft, William, and D. Alan Cruse. *Cognitive Linguistics*. CTL. Cambridge: Cambridge University Press, 2004.

Crook, Zeba A. *Reconceptualising Conversion: Patronage, Loyalty, and Conversion in the Religions of the Ancient Mediterranean.* BZNW 130. Berlin: de Gruyter, 2004.

Culianu, Ioan Petru. *Psychanodia I: A Survey of the Evidence concerning the Ascension of the Soul and Its Relevance.* Leiden: Brill, 1983.

Cunningham, Scott. *"Through Many Tribulations": The Theology of Persecution in Luke-Acts.* JSNTSup 142. Sheffield: Sheffield Academic Press, 1997.

Damasio, Antonio R. *Descartes' Error: Emotion, Reason, and the Human Brain.* New York: Avon, 1994.

———. "Thinking about Belief: Concluding Remarks." Pages 325–33 in *Memory, Brain, and Belief.* Edited by Daniel L. Schacter and Elaine Scarry. Cambridge, MA: Harvard University Press, 2000.

d'Aquili, Eugene, and Andrew B. Newberg. *The Mystical Mind: Probing the Biology of Religious Experience.* TSc. Minneapolis: Fortress, 1999.

Darr, John A. "'Watch How You Listen!' (Luke 8.18): Jesus and the Rhetoric of Perception in Luke-Acts." Pages 87–107 in *The New Literary Criticism and the New Testament.* Edited by Elizabeth Struthers Malbon and Edgar V. McKnight. JSNTSup 109. Sheffield: Sheffield Academic Press, 1994.

Davis, Carl Judson. *The Name and Way of the Lord: Old Testament Themes, New Testament Christology.* JSNTSup 129. Sheffield: Sheffield Academic Press, 1996.

Dean, Cornelia. "Science of the Soul? 'I Think, Therefore I Am' Is Losing Force." *New York Times,* June 26, 2007. http://www.nytimes.com/2007/06/26/science/26soul.html. Accessed February 7, 2011.

Dean-Otting, Mary. *Heavenly Journeys: A Study of the Motif in Hellenistic Jewish Literature.* Judentum und Umwelt 8. Frankfurt am Main: Peter Lang, 1984.

De Ridder, Dirk, et al. "Visualizing Out-of-Body Experience in the Brain." *New England Journal of Medicine* 357, no. 18 (2007): 1829–33.

Dibelius, Martin. "The Speeches in Acts and Ancient Historiography." Pages 138–85 in *Studies in the Acts of the Apostles.* Edited by Heinrich Greeven. London: SCM, 1956. Reprint, Mufflintown, PA: Sigler, 1999.

Di Vito, Robert A. "Here One Need Not Be One's Self: The Concept of 'Self' in the Old Testament." Pages 49–88 in *The Whole and Divided Self: The Bible and Theological Anthropology.* Edited by David E. Aune and John McCarthy. New York: Crossroad, 1997.

———. "Old Testament Anthropology and the Construction of Personal Identity." *CBQ* 61 (1999): 217–38.

Donahue, John R. "Tax Collectors and Sinners." *CBQ* 33 (1971): 39–61.

Dunn, James D. G. *Baptism in the Holy Spirit: A Re-examination of the New Testament Teaching on the Gift of the Spirit in Relation to Pentecostalism Today.* London: SCM, 1970.

———. "Pharisees, Sinners, and Jesus." Pages 264–89 in *The Social World of Formative Christianity and Judaism: Essays in Tribute to Howard Clark Kee.* Edited by Jacob Neusner et al. Philadelphia: Fortress, 1988.

Dupont, Jacques. "Community of Goods in the Early Church." Pages 85–102 in *The Salvation of the Gentiles: Studies in the Acts of the Apostles.* New York: Paulist, 1979.

———. "Conversion in the Acts of the Apostles." Pages 61–84 in *The Salvation of the Gentiles: Studies in the Acts of the Apostles*. New York: Paulist, 1979. ET of "La conversion dans les Actes des Apôtres," *LumVie* 47 (1960): 47–70.

Dupriez, Bernard. *A Dictionary of Literary Devices*. New York: Harvester Wheatsheaf, 1991.

Eco, Umberto. "A Portrait of the Elder as a Young Pliny." Pages 122–36 in *The Limits of Interpretation*. Advances in Semiotics. Bloomington: Indiana University Press, 1990.

———. *The Role of the Reader: Explorations in the Semiotics of Texts*. Advances in Semiotics. Bloomington: Indiana University Press, 1979.

Eden, Kathy. *Friends Hold All Things in Common: Tradition, Intellectual Property, and the Adages of Erasmus*. New Haven: Yale University Press, 2001.

Egolf, D. B., and L. E. Corder. "Height Differences of Low and High Job Status, Female and Male Corporate Employees." *Sex Roles* 24 (1991): 365–73.

Ehrman, Bart D. *The Apostolic Fathers*. 2 vols. LCL. Cambridge, MA: Harvard University Press, 2003.

Ehrsson, H. Henrik. "The Experimental Induction of Out-of-Body Experiences." *Science* 317 (2007): 1048.

Eisenstadt, S. N., and L. Roniger. *Patrons, Clients and Friends: Interpersonal Relations and the Structure of Trust in Society*. TSS. Cambridge: Cambridge University Press, 1984.

Evans, Vyvyan, and Melanie Green. *Cognitive Linguistics: An Introduction*. Edinburgh: Edinburgh University Press, 2006.

Falk, Daniel K. "Jewish Prayer Literature and the Jerusalem Church in Acts." Pages 267–301 in *The Book of Acts in Its Palestinian Setting*. Edited by Richard Bauckham. BAFCS 4. Grand Rapids: Eerdmans, 1995.

Fauconnier, Gilles, and Mark Turner. *The Way We Think: Conceptual Blending and the Mind's Hidden Complexities*. New York: Basic Books, 2002.

Feinberg, Todd E. *Altered Egos: How the Brain Creates the Self*. Oxford: Oxford University Press, 2001.

Feldman, Jerome A. *From Molecule to Metaphor: A Neural Theory of Language*. Cambridge, MA: MIT Press, 2006.

Ferguson, Everett. *Baptism in the Early Church: History, Theology, and Liturgy in the First Five Centuries*. Grand Rapids: Eerdmans, 2009.

Fillmore, Charles. "Frame Semantics." Pages 111–37 in *Linguistics in the Morning Calm*. Edited by Linguistic Society of Korea. Seoul: Hanshin, 1982.

Finger, Stanley. *Origins of Neuroscience: A History of Explorations into Brain Function*. Oxford: Oxford University Press, 1994.

Finn, Thomas M. *From Death to Rebirth: Ritual and Conversion in Antiquity*. New York: Paulist, 1997.

Fitzgerald, John T. "Greco-Roman Philosophical Schools." Pages 135–48 in *The World of the New Testament: Cultural, Social, and Historical Contexts*. Edited by Joel B. Green and Lee Martin McDonald. Grand Rapids: Baker Academic, 2013.

Fitzmyer, Joseph A. *The Acts of the Apostles*. AB 31. New York: Doubleday, 1998.

————. *The Gospel according to Luke.* 2 vols. AB 28–28a. Garden City, NY: Doubleday, 1981–85.

Flanagan, Owen. *The Problem of the Soul: Two Visions of Mind and How to Reconcile Them.* New York: Basic Books, 2002.

Forbes, Christopher. "Comparison, Self-Praise, and Irony: Paul's Boasting and the Conventions of Hellenistic Rhetoric." *NTS* 32 (1986): 1–30.

————. *Prophecy and Inspired Speech in Early Christianity and Its Hellenistic Environment.* WUNT 2/75. Tübingen: Mohr Siebeck, 1995. Reprint, Peabody, MA: Hendrickson, 1997.

Fretheim, Terence E. "Theological Reflections on the Wrath of God in the Old Testament." *HBT* 24 (2002): 1–26.

Fuller, Michael E. *The Restoration of Israel: Israel's Re-gathering and the Fate of the Nations in Early Jewish Literature and Luke-Acts.* BZNW 138. Berlin: de Gruyter, 2006.

Furnish, Victor Paul. *II Corinthians.* AB 32A. Garden City, NY: Doubleday, 1984.

Garnsey, Peter, and Richard Saller. *The Roman Empire: Economy, Society and Culture.* Berkeley: University of California Press, 1987.

Garrett, Susan B. *The Demise of the Devil: Magic and the Demonic in Luke's Writings.* Minneapolis: Fortress, 1989.

Gaventa, Beverly Roberts. *From Darkness to Light: Aspects of Conversion in the New Testament.* OBT 20. Philadelphia: Fortress, 1986.

Gibbs, Raymond W., Jr. *Embodiment and Cognitive Science.* Cambridge: Cambridge University Press, 2006.

Giessner, S. R., and T. W. Schubert. "High in the Hierarchy: How Vertical Location and Judgments of Leaders' Power Are Interrelated." *Organizational Behavior and Human Decision Processes* 104 (2007): 30–44.

Glock, Charles Y. "On the Study of Religious Commitment." Pages 98–110 in *Kirche und Gesellschaft: Einführung in die Religionssoziologie.* Edited by Joachim Matthes. Reinbek: Rowohlt, 1969.

Godet, F. *A Commentary on the Gospel of Luke.* 5th ed. 2 vols. Edinburgh: T&T Clark, 1870.

Goldberg, Elkhonon. *The Executive Brain: Frontal Lobes and the Civilized Mind.* Oxford: Oxford University Press, 2001.

Goldenberg, Georg. "Disorders of Bodily Perception." Pages 289–96 in *Behavioral Neurology and Neuropsychology.* Edited by Todd E. Feinberg and Martha J. Farah. New York: McGraw Hill, 1997.

Goldingay, John. *Old Testament Theology.* Vol. 2, *Israel's Faith.* Downers Grove, IL: InterVarsity, 2006.

Gordon, Barry. *The Economic Problem in Biblical and Patristic Thought.* VCSup 9. Leiden: Brill, 1989.

Goulder, Michael. "Vision and Knowledge." *JSNT* 56 (1994): 53–71.

Grant, Deena. "Wrath of God." *NIDB* 5:932–37.

Graupner, M., and Heinz-Josef Fabry. "שׁוּב." *TDOT* 14:461–522.

Green, Joel B. *Body, Soul, and Human Life: The Nature of Humanity in the Bible.* STI. Grand Rapids: Baker Academic; Carlisle, UK: Paternoster, 2008.

————. "Doing Repentance: The Formation of Disciples in the Acts of the Apostles." *ExAud* 18 (2003): 1–23.

————. "From 'John's Baptism' to 'Baptism in the Name of the Lord Jesus': The Significance of Baptism in Luke-Acts." Pages 157–72 in *Baptism, the New Testament and the Church: Historical and Contemporary Studies in Honour of R. E. O. White.* Edited by Stanley E. Porter and Anthony R. Cross. JSNTSup 171. Sheffield: Sheffield Academic Press, 1999.

————. "Good News to the Poor: A Lukan Leitmotif." *RevExp* 111, no. 2 (2014): 173–79.

————. *The Gospel of Luke.* NICNT. Grand Rapids: Eerdmans, 1997.

————. "Hospitality for Kids: A Lukan Perspective on Children and God's Agenda." Pages 25–39 in *Exploring and Engaging Spirituality for Today's Children.* Edited by La Verne Tolbert. Eugene, OR: Wipf & Stock, 2014.

————. "Joy." *DJG*² 448–50.

————. "Luke-Acts, or Luke and Acts? A Reaffirmation of Narrative Unity." Pages 101–19 in *Reading Acts Today: Essays in Honor of Loveday C. A. Alexander.* Edited by Steve Walton et al. LNTS 427. London: T&T Clark, 2011.

————. "The Nature of Conversion in the Acts of the Apostles." Pages 327–34 in *San Luca evangelista testimone della fede che unisce: Atti del congresso internazionale (Padova, 16–21 ottobre 2000),* vol. 1, *L'unita letteraria e teologica dell'opera di Luca.* Edited by Giovanni Leonardi and Francesco G. B. Trolese. Padova: Istituto per la storia ecclesiastica padovana, 2002.

————. "'Persevering Together in Prayer' (Acts 1:14): The Significance of Prayer in the Acts of the Apostles." Pages 183–202 in *Into God's Presence: Prayer in the New Testament.* Edited by Richard N. Longenecker. MNTS 5. Grand Rapids: Eerdmans, 2001.

————. "Science, Religion, and the Mind-Brain Problem: The Case of Thomas Willis (1621–1675)." *S&CB* 15 (2003): 165–85.

————. "'They Made a Calf': Idolatry and Temple in Acts 7." In *The Golden Calf in Biblical Traditions.* Edited by Alec J. Lucas, Edmondo Lupieri, and Eric F. Mason. Themes in Biblical Narratives. Leiden: Brill, forthcoming.

————. "What about . . . ? Three Exegetical Forays into the Body-Soul Discussion." *CTR,* n.s., 7 (2010): 3–18.

Grigsby, Jim, and David Stevens. *Neurodynamics of Personality.* New York: Guilford, 2000.

Haenchen, Ernst. *The Acts of the Apostles: A Commentary.* Oxford: Blackwell, 1971.

Hamel, Gildas. *Poverty and Charity in Roman Palestine, First Three Centuries C.E.* UCPNES 23. Berkeley: University of California Press, 1990.

Hamm, Dennis. "Luke 19:8 Once Again: Does Zacchaeus Defend or Resolve?" *JBL* 107 (1988): 431–37.

————. "Sight to the Blind: Vision as Metaphor in Luke." *Bib* 67 (1986): 457–77.

Harris, Murray J. *The Second Epistle to the Corinthians.* NIGTC. Grand Rapids: Eerdmans, 2005.

Hartman, Lars. *"Into the Name of the Lord Jesus": Baptism in the Early Church*. SNTW. Edinburgh: T&T Clark, 1997.

Hays, Richard B. "Reading Scripture in Light of the Resurrection." Pages 216–38 in *The Art of Reading Scripture*. Edited by Ellen F. Davis and Richard B. Hays. Grand Rapids: Eerdmans, 2003.

Hedrick, Charles W. *Parables as Poetic Fictions: The Creative Voice of Jesus*. Peabody, MA: Hendrickson, 1994.

Hefner, Philip. *The Human Factor: Evolution, Culture, and Religion*. TSc. Minneapolis: Fortress, 1993.

Helfmeyer, F. J. "הלך." *TDOT* 3:388–403.

Herrenbrück, Fritz. *Jesus und die Zöllner: Historische und neutestamentlich-exegetische Untersuchungen*. WUNT 2/41. Tübingen: Mohr Siebeck, 1990.

Hiebert, Paul G. "The Category of Christian in the Mission Task." Pages 107–36 in *Anthropological Reflections on Missiological Issues*. Grand Rapids: Baker, 1994.

Himmelfarb, Martha. *Ascent to Heaven in Jewish and Christian Apocalypses*. Oxford: Oxford University Press, 1993.

Holladay, William L. *The Root Šûbh in the Old Testament: With Particular Reference to Its Usages in Covenantal Contexts*. Leiden: Brill, 1958.

Holmås, Geir Otto. *Prayer and Vindication in Luke-Acts: The Theme of Prayer within the Context of the Legitimating and Edifying Objective of the Lukan Narrative*. LNTS 433. London: T&T Clark, 2011.

Hölzel, Britta K., et al. "Mindfulness Practice Leads to Increases in Regional Brain Gray Matter Density." *Psychiatric Research: Neuroimaging* 191, no. 1 (2011): 36–43.

Horn, Friedrich Wilhelm. *Glaube und Handeln in der Theologie des Lukas*. 2nd ed. GTA 26. Göttingen: Vandenhoeck & Ruprecht, 1986.

Huttenlocher, Peter R. *Neural Plasticity: The Effects of Environment on the Development of the Cerebral Cortex*. Perspectives in Cognitive Neuroscience. Cambridge, MA: Harvard University Press, 2002.

Immanuel, Babu. *Repent and Turn to God: Recounting Acts*. Perth: HIM International Ministries, 2004.

James, William. *The Varieties of Religious Experience: A Study in Human Nature, Being the Gifford Lectures on Natural Religion Delivered at Edinburgh in 1901–1902*. London: Longmans, Green, 1902.

Jeremias, Joachim. "Proselytentaufe und Neues Testament." *TZ* 5 (1949): 418–28.

———. *Die Sprache des Lukasevangeliums: Redaktion und Tradition im Nicht-Markusstoff des dritten Evangeliums*. KEKS. Göttingen: Vandenhoeck & Ruprecht, 1980.

———. "Der Ursprung der Johannestaufe." *ZNW* 29 (1929): 312–20.

Jervell, Jacob. *Die Apostelgeschichte*. KEK 3. Göttingen: Vandenhoeck & Ruprecht, 1998.

———. "The Church of Jews and Godfearers." Pages 11–20 in *Luke-Acts and the Jewish People: Eight Critical Perspectives*. Edited by Joseph B. Tyson. Minneapolis: Augsburg, 1988.

———. *The Theology of the Acts of the Apostles*. New Testament Theology. Cambridge: Cambridge University Press, 1996.

Johnson, Luke Timothy. *The Acts of the Apostles*. SP 5. Collegeville, MN: Liturgical Press, 1992.

————. *The Literary Function of Possessions in Luke-Acts*. SBLDS 39. Missoula, MT: Scholars Press, 1977.

Johnson, Mark. *The Body in the Mind: The Bodily Basis of Meaning, Imagination, and Reason*. Chicago: University of Chicago Press, 1987.

Judge, T. A., and D. M. Cable. "The Effect of Physical Height on Workplace Success and Income: Preliminary Test of a Theoretical Model." *Basic and Applied Social Psychology* 89 (2004): 428–41.

Keil, C. F., and F. Delitzsch. *Commentary on the Old Testament*. Grand Rapids: Eerdmans, n.d.

Kilbourne, Brock, and James T. Richardson. "Paradigm Conflict, Types of Conversion, and Conversion Theories." *Sociological Analysis* 50, no. 1 (1988): 1–21.

Kim, Kyoung-Jin. *Stewardship and Almsgiving in Luke's Theology*. JSNTSup 155. Sheffield: Sheffield Academic Press, 1998.

Kim-Rauchholz, Mihamm. *Umkehr bei Lukas: Zu Wesen und Bedeutung der Metanoia in der Theologie des dritten Evangelisten*. Neukirchen-Vluyn: Neukirchener Verlag, 2008.

Kinzler, Katherine D., et al. "Accent Trumps Race in Guiding Children's Social Preferences." *Social Cognition* 27, no. 4 (2009): 623–34.

Klassen, William. "'A Child of Peace' (Luke 10.6) in First Century Context." *NTS* 27 (1980–81): 488–506.

Klauck, Hans-Josef. *Magic and Paganism in Early Christianity: The World of the Acts of the Apostles*. Edinburgh: T&T Clark, 2000.

Klein, Hans. *Das Lukasevangelium*. KEK. Göttingen: Vandenhoeck & Ruprecht, 2006.

Koenigs, Michael, et al. "Damage to the Prefrontal Cortex Increases Utilitarian Moral Judgements." *Nature* 446 (2007): 908–11.

Kumari, Veena. "Do Psychotherapies Produce Neurobiological Effects?" *Acta Neuropsychiatrica* 18 (2006): 61–70.

Lakoff, George, and Mark Johnson. *Philosophy in the Flesh: The Embodied Mind and Its Challenge to Western Thought*. New York: Basic Books, 1999.

Lakoff, George, and Mark Turner. *More Than Cool Reason: A Field Guide to Poetic Metaphor*. Chicago: University of Chicago Press, 1989.

Larsson, Göran. *Bound for Freedom: The Book of Exodus in Jewish and Christian Traditions*. Peabody, MA: Hendrickson, 1999.

Lawrence, Louise J. *Reading with Anthropology: Exhibiting Aspects of New Testament Religion*. Milton Keynes, UK: Paternoster, 2005.

Laytham, D. Brent. "Interpretation on the Way to Emmaus: Jesus Performs His Story." *JTI* 1 (2007): 101–15.

Lee, Spike W. S., and Norberto Schwarz. "Dirty Hands and Dirty Mouths: Embodiment of the Moral-Purity Metaphor Is Specific to the Motor Modality Involved in Moral Transgression." *Psychological Science* 21, no. 10 (2010): 1423–25.

————. "Washing away Postdecisional Dissonance." *Science* 328 (2010): 709.

———. "Wiping the Slate Clean: Psychological Consequences of Physical Cleansing." *Current Directions in Psychological Science* 20, no. 5 (2011): 307–11.

Lenggenhager, Bigna, et al. "Video Ergo Sum: Manipulating Bodily Self-Consciousness." *Science* 317 (2007): 1096–99.

Levison, John R. *The Spirit in First Century Judaism.* AGJU 29. Leiden: Brill, 1997.

Libet, Benjamin, et al., eds. *The Volitional Brain: Towards a Neuroscience of Free Will.* Thorverton: Imprint Academic, 1999.

Lietaert Peerbolte, Bert Jan. "Paul's Rapture: 2 Corinthians 12:2–4 and the Language of the Mystics." Pages 159–76 in *Experientia*, vol. 1, *Inquiry into Religious Experience in Early Judaism and Early Christianity.* Edited by Frances Flannery et al. SBLSymS 40. Atlanta: Society of Biblical Literature, 2008.

Liljenquist, Katie, Chen-Bo Zhong, and Adam D. Galinsky. "The Smell of Virtue: Clean Scents Promote Reciprocity and Charity." *Psychological Science* 21, no. 3 (2010): 381–83.

Lincoln, Andrew T. *Paradise Now and Not Yet: Studies in the Role of the Heavenly Dimension in Paul's Thought with Special Reference to His Eschatology.* SNTSMS 43. Cambridge: Cambridge University Press, 1981.

Lindstromberg, Seth. *English Prepositions Explained.* Rev. ed. Amsterdam: John Benjamins, 2010.

Loetscher, Tobias, et al. "Eye Position Predicts What Number You Have in Mind." *Current Biology* 20, no. 6 (2010): 264–65.

Lohfink, Gerhard. *Die Himmelfahrt Jesu: Untersuchungen zu den Himmelfahrts- und Erhöhungstexten bei Lukas.* SANT 26. Munich: Kösel, 1971.

Luders, Eileen, et al. "The Underlying Anatomical Correlates of Long-Term Meditation: Larger Hippocampal and Frontal Volumes of Gray Matter." *NeuroImage* 45, no. 3 (2009): 672–78.

Lund, Øystein. *Way Metaphors and Way Topics in Isaiah 40–55.* FAT 2/28. Tübingen: Mohr Siebeck, 2007.

Lunde, Jonathan M. "Repentance." *DJG* 669–73.

Macmillan, Malcolm. "Restoring Phineas Gage: A 150th Retrospective." *Journal of the History of the Neurosciences* 9 (2000): 46–66.

Maddox, Robert. *The Purpose of Luke-Acts.* SNTW. Edinburgh: T&T Clark, 1982.

Maguire, Eleanor A., David G. Gadian, Ingrid S. Johnsrude, Catriona D. Good, John Ashburner, Richard S. J. Frackowiak, and Christopher D. Frith. "Navigation-Related Structural Change in the Hippocampi of Taxi Drivers." *Proceedings of the National Academy of Sciences* 97 (2000): 4398–403.

Maguire, Eleanor A., Hugo J. Spiers, Catriona D. Good, Tom Hartley, Richard S. J. Frackowiak, and Neil Burgess. "Navigation Expertise and the Human Hippocampus: A Structural Brain Imaging Analysis." *Hippocampus* 13, no. 2 (2003): 250–59.

Maguire, Eleanor A., Katherine Woollett, and Hugo J. Spiers. "London Taxi Drivers and Bus Drivers: A Structural MRI and Neuropsychological Analysis." *Hippocampus* 16, no. 12 (2006): 1091–101.

Manna, Antonietta. "Neural Correlates of Focused Attention and Cognitive Monitoring in Meditation." *Brain Research Bulletin* 82 (2010): 46–56.

Marguerat, Daniel. *The First Christian Historian: Writing the "Acts of the Apostles."* SNTSMS 121. Cambridge: Cambridge University Press, 2002.

Marsh, Michael N. *Out-of-Body and Near-Death Experiences: Brain-State Phenomena or Glimpse of Immortality?* OTM. Oxford: Oxford University Press, 2010.

Marshall, I. Howard. *The Gospel of Luke: A Commentary on the Greek Text.* NIGTC. Grand Rapids: Eerdmans, 1978.

Martin, Francis, ed. *Acts.* ACCS: New Testament 5. Downers Grove, IL: InterVarsity, 2006.

Matson, David Lertis. *Household Conversion Narratives in Acts: Pattern and Interpretation.* JSNTSup 123. Sheffield: Sheffield Academic Press, 1996.

Mauser, Ulrich W. *Christ in the Wilderness: The Wilderness Theme in the Second Gospel and Its Basis in the Biblical Tradition.* SBT 39. London: SCM, 1963.

McCabe, David R. *How to Kill Things with Words: Ananias and Sapphira under the Prophetic Speech-Act of Divine Judgment (Acts 4.32–5.11).* LNTS 454. London: T&T Clark, 2011.

McIntire, C. T. "Transcending Dichotomies in History and Religion." *History and Theory* 45 (2006): 80–92.

McKnight, Scot. *A Light among the Nations: Jewish Missionary Activity in the Second Temple Period.* Minneapolis: Fortress, 1991.

Mealand, David. "Community of Goods and Utopian Allusions in Acts 2–4." *JTS* 28 (1977): 96–99.

———. "Community of Goods at Qumran." *TZ* 31 (1975): 129–39.

Meeks, Wayne A. *The Origins of Christian Morality: The First Two Centuries.* New Haven: Yale University Press, 1993.

Méndez-Moratalla, Fernando. *The Paradigm of Conversion in Luke.* JSNTSup 252. London: T&T Clark, 2004.

Merrill, Eugene H. "הלך." *NIDOTTE* 1:1032–35.

Metzinger, Thomas. *Being No One: The Self-Model Theory of Subjectivity.* Cambridge, MA: MIT Press, 2003.

Michel, Otto. "τελώνης." *TDNT* 8:88–105.

Middleton, J. Richard, and Michael J. Gorman. "Salvation." *NIDB* 5:45–61.

Miller, John B. F. *Convinced That God Had Called Us: Dreams, Visions, and the Perception of God's Will in Luke-Acts.* BibIntS 85. Leiden: Brill, 2007.

———. "Dreams/Visions and the Experience of God in Luke-Acts." Pages 177–92 in *Experientia*, vol. 1, *Inquiry into Religious Experience in Early Judaism and Early Christianity.* Edited by Frances Flannery et al. SBLSymS 40. Atlanta: Society of Biblical Literature, 2008.

Mills, Watson E., ed. *Speaking in Tongues: A Guide to Research on Glossolalia.* Grand Rapids: Eerdmans, 1986.

Mobbs, Dean, and Caroline Watt. "There Is Nothing Paranormal about Near-Death Experiences: How Neuroscience Can Explain Seeing Bright Lights, Meeting the Dead, or Being Convinced You Are One of Them." *Trends in Cognitive Science* 15, no. 10 (2011): 447–49.

Morlan, David S. *Conversion in Luke and Paul: An Exegetical and Theological Exploration*. LNTS 464. London: Bloomsbury, 2013.

Motyer, J. Alec. *Isaiah: An Introduction and Commentary*. TOTC 18. Downers Grove, IL: InterVarsity, 1999.

Murphy, Nancey. *Bodies and Souls, or Spirited Bodies?* CIT. Cambridge: Cambridge University Press, 2006.

Murphy, Nancey, and Warren S. Brown. *Did My Neurons Make Me Do It? Philosophical and Neurobiological Perspectives on Moral Responsibility and Free Will*. Oxford: Oxford University Press, 2007.

Najman, Hindy. "Towards a Study of the Uses of the Concept of Wilderness in Ancient Judaism." *DSD* 13 (2006): 99–113.

Nave, Guy D., Jr. "Conversion." *NIDB* 1:728–29.

———. *The Role and Function of Repentance in Luke-Acts*. AcBib 4. Atlanta: Society of Biblical Literature, 2002.

Neale, David A. *None but the Sinners: Religious Categories in the Gospel of Luke*. JSNTSup 58. Sheffield: Sheffield Academic Press, 1991.

Newberg, Andrew B., Abass Alavi, Michael Baime, Michael Pourdehnad, Jill Santanna, and Eugene d'Aquili. "The Measurement of Regional Cerebral Blood Flow during the Complex Cognitive Task of Meditation: A Preliminary SPECT Study." *Psychiatry Research: Neuroimaging* 106 (2001): 113–22.

Newberg, Andrew B., Michael Pourdehnad, Abass Alavi, and Eugene d'Aquili. "Cerebral Blood Flow during Meditative Prayer: Preliminary Findings and Methodological Issues." *Perceptual and Motor Skills* 97 (2003): 625–30.

Newberg, Andrew B., and Mark R. Waldman. *Why We Believe What We Believe: Uncovering Our Biological Need for Meaning, Spirituality, and Truth*. New York: Free, 2006.

Newberg, Andrew B., Nancy A. Wintering, Donna Morgan, and Mark R. Waldman. "The Measurement of Regional Cerebral Blood Flow during Glossolalia: A Preliminary SPECT Study." *Psychiatry Research: Neuroimaging* 148, no. 1 (2006): 67–71.

Nock, Arthur Darby. *Conversion: The Old and the New in Religion from Alexander the Great to Augustine of Hippo*. Oxford: Clarendon, 1933.

Nolland, John. *Luke*. 3 vols. WBC 35A–C. Dallas: Word, 1989–93.

Olson, F. H., and G. H. Whitaker, trans. *Philo*. Vol. 1. LCL. Cambridge, MA: Harvard University Press, 1929.

Oropeza, B. J. *In the Footsteps of Judas and Other Defectors: The Gospels, Acts, and Johannine Letters*. Apostasy in the New Testament Communities 1. Eugene, OR: Cascade, 2011.

O'Toole, Robert F. "Christian Baptism in Luke." *RevRel* 39 (1980): 855–66.

———. *The Unity of Luke's Theology: An Analysis of Luke-Acts*. GNS 9. Wilmington, DE: Michael Glazier, 1984.

Panikulam, George. *Koinōnia in the New Testament: A Dynamic Expression of Christian Life*. AnBib 85. Rome: Biblical Institute Press, 1979.

Pao, David W. *Acts and the Isaianic New Exodus*. WUNT 2/130. Tübingen: Mohr Siebeck, 2000.

Parsons, Mikeal C. *Body and Character in Luke and Acts*. Grand Rapids: Baker Academic, 2006.

Parsons, Mikeal C., and Richard I. Pervo. *Rethinking the Unity of Luke and Acts*. Minneapolis: Fortress, 1993.

Partridge, Christopher, and Helen Reid, eds. *Finding and Losing Faith: Studies in Conversion*. Studies in Religion and Culture. Carlisle, UK: Paternoster, 2006.

Peace, Richard V. *Conversion in the New Testament: Paul and the Twelve*. Grand Rapids: Eerdmans, 1999.

Pelikan, Jaroslav. *Acts*. Brazos Theological Commentary on the Bible. Grand Rapids: Brazos, 2005.

Perrin, Bernadotte, trans. *Plutarch's Lives*. Vol. 7. LCL. Cambridge, MA: Harvard University Press, 1919.

Pervo, Richard I. *Acts: A Commentary*. Hermeneia. Minneapolis: Fortress, 2009.

Pesch, Rudolf. *Die Apostelgeschichte*. Vol. 1. EKKNT 5.1. Zürich: Benziger; Neukirchen-Vluyn: Neukirchener Verlag, 1986.

Peterson, David. "The Worship of the New Community." Pages 373–95 in *Witness to the Gospel: The Theology of Acts*. Edited by I. Howard Marshall and David Peterson. Grand Rapids: Eerdmans, 1998.

Plunkett, Mark A. "Ethnocentricity and Salvation History in the Cornelius Episode (Acts 10:1–11:18)." *SBLSP* (1985): 465–79.

Pokorný, Petr. *Theologie der lukanischen Schriften*. FRLANT 174. Göttingen: Vandenhoeck & Ruprecht, 1998.

Posner, Michael J., and Marcus E. Raichle. *Images of Mind*. New York: Freeman, 1997.

Powell, Mark Allan. *What Do They Hear? Bridging the Gap between Pulpit and Pew*. Nashville: Abingdon, 2007.

Preuss, Horst Dietrich. *Old Testament Theology*. Vol. 2. OTL. Louisville: Westminster John Knox, 1996.

Pusey, Karen. "Jewish Proselyte Baptism." *ExpTim* 95 (1984): 141–45.

Rackham, Richard Belward. *The Acts of the Apostles: An Exposition*. London: Methuen, 1906.

Ramachandran, V. S. *A Brief Tour of Human Consciousness*. New York: Pi, 2004.

Rambo, Lewis R. "Current Research on Religious Conversion." *RSR* 8 (1982): 145–59.

———. *Understanding Religious Conversion*. New Haven: Yale University Press, 1993.

Rambo, Lewis R., and Charles E. Farhadian. "Introduction." Pages 1–22 in *The Oxford Handbook of Religious Conversion*. Edited by Lewis R. Rambo and Charles E. Farhadian. Oxford: Oxford University Press, 2014.

Ravens, David. *Luke and the Restoration of Israel*. JSNTSup 119. Sheffield: Sheffield Academic Press, 1995.

Riese, Walther. *A History of Neurology*. New York: MD Publications, 1959.

Robertson, A. T. *A Grammar of the Greek New Testament in the Light of Historical Research*. 4th ed. New York: Hodder & Stoughton, 1923.

Roloff, Jürgen. *Die Apostelgeschichte: Übersetzt und erklärt.* NTD 5. Göttingen: Vandenhoeck & Ruprecht, 1981.

Roukema, Riemer. "Paul's Rapture to Paradise in Early Christian Literature." Pages 267–83 in *The Wisdom of Egypt: Jewish, Early Christian, and Gnostic Essays in Honour of Gerard P. Luttikhuizen.* Edited by Anthony Hilhorst and George H. Van Kooten. AGJU 59. Leiden: Brill, 2005.

Rousseau, Philip. "Conversion." *OCD* 386–87.

Rowe, C. Kavin. *Early Narrative Christology: The Lord in the Gospel of Luke.* BZNW 139. Berlin: de Gruyter, 2006.

———. "The Grammar of Life: The Areopagus Speech and Pagan Tradition." *NTS* 57 (2011): 31–50.

———. *World Upside Down: Reading Acts in the Graeco-Roman Age.* Oxford: Oxford University Press, 2009.

Runehow, Anne L. C. *Sacred or Neural? The Potential of Neuroscience to Explain Religious Experience.* Religion, Theologie und Naturwissenschaft 9. Göttingen: Vandenhoeck & Ruprecht, 2007.

Sacks, Oliver. *The Man Who Mistook His Wife for a Hat and Other Clinical Tales.* New York: Touchstone, 1985.

Sahlins, Marshall. *Stone Age Economics.* London: Routledge, 1972.

Sanders, E. P. *Jesus and Judaism.* London: SCM, 1985.

———. "Testament of Abraham: A New Translation and Introduction." *OTP* 1:871–902.

Schnall, Simone, Jennifer Benton, and Sophie Harvey. "With a Clean Conscience: Cleanliness Reduces the Severity of Moral Judgments." *Psychological Science* 19, no. 12 (2008): 1219–22.

Schnall, Simone, Jonathan Haida, Gerald L. Clore, and Alexander H. Jordan. "Disgust as Embodied Moral Judgment." *Personality and Social Psychology Bulletin* 34, no. 8 (2008): 1096–1109.

Schneider, Gerhard. *Die Apostelgeschichte.* 2 vols. HTKNT 5. Freiburg: Herder, 1980–82.

Schofield, Alison. "Wilderness." *EDEJ* 1337–38.

Schubert, T. W. "Your Highness: Vertical Positions as Perceptual Symbols of Power." *Journal of Personality and Social Psychology* 89 (2005): 1–21.

Schürer, Emil. *The History of the Jewish People in the Age of Jesus Christ.* Revised and edited by Geza Vermes, Fergus Millar, and Matthew Black. Vol. 2. Edinburgh: T&T Clark, 1979.

Schürmann, Heinz. *Das Lukasevangelium.* 2 vols. HTKNT 3. Freiburg: Herder, 1984–94.

Schwartz, Jeffrey M., and Sharon Begley. *The Mind and the Brain: Neuroplasticity and the Power of Mental Force.* New York: HarperCollins, 2002.

Schweizer, Eduard. *The Good News according to Luke.* Atlanta: John Knox, 1984.

Sebanz, Natalie, and Wolfgang Prinz, eds. *Disorders of Volition.* Cambridge, MA: MIT Press, 2006.

Segal, Alan F. "The Afterlife as Mirror of the Self." Pages 19–40 in *Experientia*, vol. 1, *Inquiry into Religious Experience in Early Judaism and Early Christianity*. Edited by Frances Flannery et al. SBLSymS 40. Atlanta: Society of Biblical Literature, 2008.

———. "Heavenly Ascent in Hellenistic Judaism, Early Christianity and Their Environment." *ANRW* 23.2:1333–94. Part 2, *Principat*, 23.2. Edited by H. Temporini and W. Haase. New York: de Gruyter, 1980.

———. "Paul and the Beginning of Jewish Mysticism." Pages 93–120 in *Death, Ecstasy, and Other Worldly Journeys*. Edited by John Collins and Michael Fishbane. Albany: State University of New York Press, 1995.

———. *Paul the Convert: The Apostolate and Apostasy of Saul the Pharisee*. New Haven: Yale University Press, 1990.

Shantz, Colleen. *Paul in Ecstasy: The Neurobiology of the Apostle's Life and Thought*. Cambridge: Cambridge University Press, 2009.

Shepherd, William H., Jr. *The Narrative Function of the Holy Spirit as a Character in Luke-Acts*. SBLDS 147. Atlanta: Scholars Press, 1993.

Shumate, Nancy. *Crisis and Conversion in Apuleius'* Metamorphoses. Ann Arbor: University of Michigan Press, 1996.

Siegel, Daniel J. *The Mindful Brain: Reflection and Attunement in the Cultivation of Well-Being*. New York: Norton, 2007.

Slingerland, Edward G. "Conceptual Blending, Somatic Marking, and Normativity: A Case Example from Ancient Chinese." *Cognitive Linguistics* 16 (2005): 557–84.

———. "Conceptual Metaphor Theory as Methodology for Comparative Religion." *JAAR* 72, no. 1 (2004): 1–31.

Smith, Derwood C. "Jewish Proselyte Baptism and the Baptism of John." *ResQ* 25 (1982): 13–32.

Snodgrass, Klyne R. *Stories with Intent: A Comprehensive Guide to the Parables of Jesus*. Grand Rapids: Eerdmans, 2008.

———. "Streams of Tradition Emerging from Isaiah 40:1–5 and Their Adaptation in the New Testament." *JSNT* 8 (1980): 24–45.

Snow, David A., and R. Machalek. "The Convert as a Social Type." Pages 259–89 in *Sociological Theory 1983*. Edited by R. Collins. San Francisco: Jossey-Bass, 1983.

Soja, Edward W. *Postmodern Geographies: The Reassertion of Space in Critical Social Theory*. London: Verso, 1989.

———. *Thirdspace: Journeys to Los Angeles and Other Real-and-Imagined Places*. Malden, MA: Blackwell, 1996.

Spencer, Patrick E. "The Unity of Luke-Acts: A Four-Bolted Hermeneutical Hinge." *CBR* 5 (2007): 341–66.

Starbuck, Edwin Diller. *Psychology of Religion: An Empirical Study of the Growth of Religious Consciousness*. London: Walter Scott, 1899.

Steck, Odil Hannes. *Israel und das gewaltsame Geschick der Propheten*. WMANT 23. Neukirchen-Vluyn: Neukirchener Verlag, 1967.

Stendahl, Krister. "Paul and the Introspective Conscience of the West." *HTR* 56 (1963): 199–215.

Stenschke, Christoph W. *Luke's Portrait of Gentiles prior to Their Coming to Faith.* WUNT 2/108. Tübingen: Mohr Siebeck, 1999.

Steyn, Gert J. "Soteriological Perspectives in Luke's Gospel." Pages 67–99 in *Salvation in the New Testament: Perspectives on Soteriology.* Edited by Jan G. van der Watt. NovTSup 121. Atlanta: Society of Biblical Literature, 2005.

Stone, James L. "Transcranial Brain Injuries Caused by Metal Rods or Pipes over the Past 150 Years." *Journal of the History of the Neurosciences* 8 (1999): 227–34.

Strahan, Joshua Marshall. *The Limits of a Text: Luke 23:34a as a Case Study in Theological Interpretation.* JTISup 5. Winona Lake, IN: Eisenbrauns, 2012.

Streib, Heinz. "Deconversion." Pages 271–96 in *The Oxford Handbook of Religious Conversion.* Edited by Lewis R. Rambo and Charles E. Farhadian. Oxford: Oxford University Press, 2014.

Streib, Heinz, and Barbara Keller. "The Variety of Deconversion Experiences: Contours of a Concept in Respect to Empirical Research." *Archive for the Psychology of Religion / Archiv für Religionssoziologie* 26, no. 1 (2014): 181–200.

Susa, Kyle J., et al. "Modeling the Role of Social-Cognitive Processes in the Recognition of Own- and Other-Race Faces." *Social Cognition* 28, no. 4 (2010): 523–37.

Tabor, James D. *Things Unutterable: Paul's Ascent to Paradise in Its Greco-Roman, Judaic, and Early Christian Contexts.* Studies in Judaism. Lanham, MD: University Press of America, 1986.

Taeger, Jens-Wilhelm. *Der Mensch und sein Heil: Studien zum Bild des Menschen und zur Sicht der Bekehrung bei Lukas.* SNT 14. Gütersloh: Gerd Mohn, 1982.

Talbert, Charles H. "Conversion in the Acts of the Apostles: Ancient Auditors' Perceptions." Pages 141–53 in *Literary Studies in Luke-Acts: Essays in Honor of Joseph B. Tyson.* Edited by Richard P. Thompson and Thomas E. Phillips. Macon, GA: Mercer University Press, 1998. Reprint, pages 135–48 in *Reading Luke-Acts in Its Mediterranean Milieu.* NovTSup 107. Leiden: Brill, 2003. References are to the later publication.

Talmon, Shemaryahu. "The 'Desert Motif' in the Bible and in Qumran Literature." Pages 31–63 in *Biblical Motifs: Origins and Transformation.* Edited by Alexander Altman. Cambridge, MA: Harvard University Press, 1966.

Tannehill, Robert C. "The Functions of Peter's Mission Speeches in the Narrative of Acts." *NTS* 37 (1991): 400–414.

———. "Repentance in the Context of Lukan Soteriology." Pages 84–101 in *The Shape of Luke's Story: Essays on Luke-Acts.* Eugene, OR: Wipf & Stock, 2005.

Tannen, Deborah. "What's in a Frame? Surface Evidence for Underlying Expectations." Pages 14–56 in *Framing in Discourse.* Edited by Deborah Tannen. New York: Oxford University Press, 1993.

Taylor, Charles. *Sources of the Self: The Making of the Modern Identity.* Cambridge, MA: Harvard University Press, 1989.

———. *Varieties of Religion Today: William James Revisited.* Cambridge, MA: Harvard University Press, 2002.

Taylor, Joan E. *The Immerser: John the Baptist within Second Temple Judaism.* Grand Rapids: Eerdmans, 1997.

Taylor, Nicholas H. "The Social Nature of Conversion in the Early Christian World." Pages 128–36 in *Modelling Early Christianity: Social-Scientific Studies of the New Testament in Its Context*. Edited by Philip F. Esler. London: Routledge, 1995.

Thackery, H. St. J., trans. *Josephus*. Vol. 2. LCL. Cambridge, MA: Harvard University Press, 1927.

Thompson, J. A., and Elmer A. Martens. "שׁוּב." *NIDOTTE* 4:55–59.

Tidball, Derek T. "The Social Construction of Evangelical Conversion: A Sideways Glance." Pages 81–102 in *Finding and Losing Faith: Studies in Conversion*. Edited by Christopher Partridge and Helen Reid. Studies in Religion and Culture Series. Milton Keynes, UK: Paternoster, 2006.

Transport for London. "Test Your Awareness: Do the Test." http://www.dothetest .co.uk/basketball.html. Accessed February 9, 2011. On YouTube: https://www .youtube.com/watch?v=Ahg6qcgoay4. Accessed April 14, 2015.

Turner, Max. *Power from on High: The Spirit in Israel's Restoration and Witness in Luke-Acts*. JPTSup 9. Sheffield: Sheffield Academic Press, 1996.

VanderKam, James C. "The Judean Desert and the Community of the Dead Sea Scrolls." Pages 159–71 in *Antikes Judentum und Frühes Christentum: Festschrift für Hartmut Stegemann zum 65. Geburtstag*. Edited by Bernd Kollmann et al. BZNW 97. Berlin: de Gruyter, 1998.

van der Watt, Jan G., ed. *Salvation in the New Testament: Perspectives on Soteriology*. NovTSup 121. Atlanta: Society of Biblical Literature, 2005.

van Gennep, Arnold. *The Rites of Passage*. Chicago: University of Chicago Press, 1961 (1909).

Vermes, Geza. *The Complete Dead Sea Scrolls in English*. New York: Penguin, 1997.

Vizioli, Luca, et al. "Neural Repetition Suppression to Identity Is Abolished by Other-Race Faces." *Proceedings of the National Academy of Sciences* 107, no. 46 (2010): 20081–86.

Vogler, Werner. *Judas Iskarioth: Untersuchungen zu Tradition und Redaktion von Texten des Neuen Testaments und außerkanonischer Schriften*. Berlin: Evangelische, 1983.

Wall, Robert W. "The Acts of the Apostles: Introduction, Commentary, and Reflections." *NIB* 10:1–368.

Wallace, Daniel B. *Greek Grammar beyond the Basics: An Exegetical Syntax of the New Testament*. Grand Rapids: Zondervan, 1996.

Walls, Andrew F. "Converts or Proselytes? The Crisis over Conversion in the Early Church." *IBMR* 29 (2004): 2–6.

Walton, Steve. "Primitive Communism in Acts? Does Acts Present the Community of Goods (2:33–34; 4:32–35) as Mistaken?" *EvQ* 80, no. 2 (2008): 99–111.

Watts, John D. W. *Isaiah 34–66*. WBC 25. Waco: Word, 1987.

Watts, Rikki E. "Consolation or Confrontation? Isaiah 40–55 and the Delay of the New Exodus." *TynBul* 41 (1990): 31–59.

———. "Exodus." *NDBT* 478–87.

Webb, Robert L. *John the Baptizer and Prophet: A Socio-Historical Study*. JSNTSup 62. Sheffield: Sheffield Academic Press, 1991.

Weiser, Alfons. "ἡδονή, ῆς, ἡ." *EDNT* 2:114.

Wenk, Matthias. *Community-Forming Power: The Socio-Ethical Role of the Spirit in Luke-Acts*. JPTSup 19. Sheffield: Sheffield Academic Press, 2000.

———. "Conversion and Initiation: A Pentecostal View of Biblical and Patristic Perspectives." *JPT* 17 (2000): 56–80.

Werline, Rodney A. "The Experience of Prayer and Resistance to Demonic Powers in the Gospel of Mark." Pages 59–71 in *Experientia*, vol. 1, *Inquiry into Religious Experience in Early Judaism and Early Christianity*. Edited by Frances Flannery et al. SBLSymS 40. Atlanta: Society of Biblical Literature, 2008.

Wesley, John. *Explanatory Notes upon the New Testament*. London: Epworth, 1754.

Wilckens, Ulrich. *Die Missionsreden der Apostelgeschichte: Form- und traditionsgeschichtliche Untersuchungen*. 3rd ed. WMANT 5. Neukirchen-Vluyn: Neukirchener Verlag, 1974.

Williamson, H. G. M., and M. Kartveit. "Samaritans." *DJG*² 833–36.

Willis, Thomas. *The Anatomy of the Brain and Nerves*. Translated by Samuel Pordage. Edited by William Feindel. CML. Birmingham: McGill-Queens University Press, 1978 (1681).

Witherup, Ronald D. *Conversion in the New Testament*. ZS: NT. Collegeville, MN: Liturgical Press, 1994.

Wolter, Michael. *Das Lukasevangelium*. HNT 5. Tübingen: Mohr Siebeck, 2008.

Woollett, Katherine, Janice Glensman, and Eleanor A. Maguire. "Non-spatial Expertise and Hippocampal Gray Matter Volume in Humans." *Hippocampus* 18, no. 10 (2008): 981–84.

Woollett, Katherine, and Eleanor A. Maguire. "Acquiring 'the Knowledge' of London's Layout Drives Structural Brain Changes." *Current Biology* 21, no. 24 (2011): 2109–14.

Wright, Christopher J. H. "Implications of Conversion in the Old Testament and the New." *IBMR* 28 (2004): 14–19.

Wright, N. T. *Jesus and the Victory of God*. Christian Origins and the Question of God 2. Minneapolis: Fortress, 1996.

Wuellner, Wilhelm H. *The Meaning of "Fishers of Men."* Philadelphia: Westminster, 1967.

Yamazaki-Ransom, Kazuhiko. *The Roman Empire in Luke's Narrative*. LNTS 404. London: T&T Clark, 2010.

Yang, Yaling, et al. "Prefrontal White Matter in Pathological Liars." *British Journal of Psychiatry* 187 (2005): 320–25.

Yu, Ning. "Metaphor from Body and Culture." Pages 247–61 in *The Cambridge Handbook of Metaphor and Thought*. Edited by Raymond W. Gibbs Jr. Cambridge: Cambridge University Press, 2010.

Zhong, Chen-Bo, and Katie Liljenquist. "Washing away Your Sins: Threatened Morality and Physical Cleansing." *Science* 313 (2006): 1451–52.

Zimmer, Carl. *Soul Made Flesh: The Discovery of the Brain—and How It Changed the World*. New York: Free, 2004.

Index of Scripture
and Other Ancient Sources

Index of Modern Authors

Index of Subjects